Praise

del Rosso navigates the sense of the split between our veneer of wholeness and completion that people see compared to the internal sense of fragmentedness that we so often feel.

—William Christopher Brown, Ph.D., Professor of English and Technical Writing, Dept. Co-Chair of English and Language Arts, Midland College.

At the turn of the first millennium in Heian Period Japan, Sei Shōnagon wrote *The Pillow Book*, a hybrid collection of musings, lists, anecdotes, poems and descriptions, connected only by the authentic and lyric dailyness of their observations; Lisa del Rosso's *You Are All a Part of Me* is a pillow book for the next millennium. Consisting of dramatic interludes, emails, found text, fair itineraries, travelogues, and canny essays, this book is connected by the absurd tragedy of quotidian city life. The author's voice is at turns wry, romantic, urbane, grieving, and very much shaped by the modern sensibility of someone who has had to live with an ex- to save money on rent and persevere to make art. Her list of difficult men include a father, Jimmie the Jeweler, and King Lear; and through her keen eyes, we see a Confederate cemetery in Fredericksburg, Virginia, Edward Albee auditioning actresses for "Who's Afraid of Virginia Woolf" and Nora Ephron being conjured in the sleeveless sheath of a grey dress. Evoking those larger lights, Lisa del Rosso casts her own beam over the peaks and valleys of her past, illuminating vivid moments of awe and agony that resonate with remembrance.

—Ravi Shankar, Pushcart Prize winning author of 15 books, including the forthcoming memoir *Correctional*

If you read this book--and you really should!--you will encounter characters worthy of a classic film, mordant wit, insightful observations about the beauty and absurdity of life, all wrapped up in del Rosso's generous and thoughtful prose.

—Stephen Policoff, author of *Come Away* (Dzanc Books 2014)

del Rosso rarely fails to deliver a nugget of wisdom or a wisecrack that resonates in the essays on the myriad ways friends become family, often entirely by chance, say a shared flat, a stray cat, or a newspaper ad answered at a subway stop. Other relationships seem to spring from life decisions that seem defy all logic (Imagine how best friends might include both a man you decided never to date and a man you divorced but never stopped loving.) These stories combine strong character sketches with well-told anecdotes and offer insights that are often both laugh-out-loud funny and poignant.

The Difficult Men section is not, as a reader might expect, about boyfriends, but about difficult men who del Rosso has come to know through blood, through friendship and through random chance – like, for example, the Vietnam vet who lives in a treehouse with his arsenal and his cache of jewels in Provincetown, Mass, and hands her a folder full of stories with no punctuation and no real spelling. In the finale, she explores heartbreak when after her parents divorced, her father "moved his heart away from me." These stories are her real gems.

—Lise Olsen, Senior Writer and Editor at *The Texas Observer*

What a delight to be inside the head of Lisa del Rosso in this open-hearted exploration of her life, her ideas, her travels. Beginning with formative childhood experiences in some accidental address, running through developmental incidents and Hugely Important Decisions, it's a breeze to read—serious and funny at the same time, like a gangster cleaning his fingernails with the blade that may or may not wind up between your ribs. It's one of those hard-to-categorize hybrids that probably fits best under the memoir-in-essays banner. Stylistically and structurally, there's nothing she doesn't try. Poetry, eulogy, text messages, veritable transcripts of group therapy sessions. "All the sounds of the earth are like music" unfolds like a tale out of Dickens. "Jimmie the Jeweler" begins on Commercial Street, Provincetown, MA, then takes a left turn off a left turn and suddenly you're in Yusef Komunyakaa/Vietnam veteran purgatory (in verse). The exhilarating freedom in the structures gets you moving with increasing velocity and you don't even notice there's no longer any ground beneath your feet until you're well off the cliff. The thing is, del Rosso is with you, providing indelible description, crackling dialogue, and hard-won wisdom tempered with heart. Her thematic range is encompassing: family, love, loss, death, friendship, gratitude, renewal. By book's end, she is a part of you.

—Tim Tomlinson, author of *Requiem for the Tree Fort I Set on Fire* (poetry) and *This Is Not Happening to You* (short fiction). He is a co-founder of New York Writers Workshop and a professor in NYU's Global Liberal Studies.

Lisa del Rosso's memoir-in-essays, *You Are All a Part of Me*, meanders with intelligence and verve from family and friends to lovers and troubles, on journeys undertaken both around the globe and into the personal interior. Reading these essays is like sitting down with a wise, funny friend who has great stories to tell, "bracing, like a dip in the Atlantic in March." This book is delicious and full of surprises, like "potent homemade wine" from Sardinia, served in tiny plastic cups on the Feast of St. Anthony. Enjoy.

—Moira Egan, author of *Synæsthesium*

YOU ARE ALL
A PART OF ME

by Lisa del Rosso

SERVING
HOUSE
BOOKS

You Are All a Part of Me

Copyright 2021 © Lisa del Rosso

All Rights Reserved

Published by Serving House Books

Copenhagen, Denmark and South Orange, NJ

www.servinghousebooks.com

ISBN: 978-1-947175-45-7

Library of Congress Control Number: 2020949122

Member of The Independent Book Publishers Association

First Serving House Books Edition 2021

Cover Painting: Evelyn Lucas

Author Photograph: Marzia Candelora

Serving House Books Logo: Barry Lereng Wilmont

For Maria Philomena & Achilles Nicoletti

Foreword

IN JANUARY 2020 I ATTENDED A WRITERS' IMMERSION WORKSHOP in Sardinia, Italy. I had won a scholarship to be there, so I was thrilled. I met some terrific people; one of them, Very Tall David, also teaches writing at NYU. Why had I not run into him in eleven years? Because he teaches at NYU Shanghai. He is married to an Asian woman and has a young daughter. He is from the Midwest, where his mother still lives. So on a long coach trip, we were talking about our respective pasts, traveling and moving and the concept of home. I said, "Because I chose to move to London at eighteen, I deliberately blew up my sense of home. Never mind it was for college. I didn't have to go. I wanted to go, for reasons other than college. I loved living in London, and stayed there for ten years. Now I love living in New York City. But when I travel, I don't miss it. When I was away from London, I didn't miss that city, either. When the plane comes in to land at JFK, I don't get excited. I don't look forward to being back. This happens wherever I have lived. I only miss people. My people. If I could take them all with me, that would be ideal. Deeply impractical, as they are all over the map, but ideal."

Very Tall David said, "A part of me misses the Midwest. Having space. Quiet. A yard."

"A yard is a good thing for a child."

I am really happy Very Tall David did not think I was a weirdo after that conversation.

This collection of essays, most of them already published elsewhere, are about people. My people. Compiling this in the midst of a pandemic, my people are at the forefront of my mind — my people, and time. There are friends who come under the heading of Family, who live in Europe and I have no idea when I will be allowed to see them again. There are dear friends in far-flung countries, friends on the Left Coast, and I long for their company. There is a biological relation who I will never see again. There are mentors who literally changed my life, unsung heroes who deserve a mention and students whose impact never left. There are New Yorkers and Floridians, and there is immeasurable loss.

What you get to take with you when you leave this earth is the following: what you did, how you lived, who you loved, who loved you. All the people that made you — for better or worse — who you are. People matter. To me. People matter, and time: the finite time you have with your people, and the finite time they have with you.

LdR

You Are All a Part of Me

EMILY:
In a loud voice to the stage manager.
I can't. I can't go on. It goes so fast. We don't have time to look at one another.
She breaks down sobbing.
The lights dim on the left half of the stage. MRS. WEBB disappears.
I didn't realize. So all that was going on and we never noticed. Take me back—up the hill—to my grave. But first: Wait! One more look.
Good-by, Good-by, world. Good-by, Grover's Corners ...
Mama and Papa. Good-by to clocks ticking ... and Mama's sunflowers.
And food and coffee. And new-ironed dresses
and hot baths ... and sleeping and waking up. Oh, earth,
you're too wonderful for anybody to realize you.

She looks toward the stage manager and asks abruptly,
through her tears:

Do any human beings ever realize life while they live it?—
every, every minute?

STAGE MANAGER:
No.
Pause.
The saints and poets, maybe—they do some.

from *Our Town,* by Thornton Wilder

Table of Contents

Blood

Family

Students & Teachers

Floridians

New Yorkers

Difficult Men

BLOOD

The more you read, the more inter-related the people in these essays are. There are family members connected to me by blood and those who are not blood that I consider family. Some of my people are living and some are dead. Death ends the life, not the relationship. The relationship continues.

Bicycle

MY MOTHER CAME INTO MY BEDROOM and sat down on my bed. That didn't happen very often and it made me really nervous. I started picking up clothes off of the floor, which should have made my mother nervous, but did not.

"Something wrong, Mom?"

"No," she answered, "everything's fine. I want to ask you something."

I got even more nervous. "What?" I said, scratching my shoulder.

"Well, he has asked me to marry him, and I wondered if you'd mind." I knew she meant the smoker.

I hate being asked questions I don't know how to answer.

"Lisa?" she said.

"No, Mom, I don't mind."

"Good," she said, slapping herself on the knees, "that's settled then."

And she stood up and gave me a big hug, as if I approved, and left my room. I sat down on my bed, winded, like I'd just finished running all those sprints I hate for soccer practice. I couldn't tell her the truth. I just couldn't. I had no facts, only feelings. I didn't like him, but couldn't explain why.

They hadn't been seeing each other that long, but that didn't seem to bother my mother. He had never done anything to me, except maybe tried to get me fat with all that ice cream and hot fudge he brought in from Friendly's. And for the first time in a long time, my mother seemed happy. She dressed nicer, and finally started wearing some of the perfume that sat in dust-covered bottles on her bureau; the ones that stood right next to a portrait of Elvis Presley, with the words to "Love Me Tender" printed next to his face. So who was I to tell her not to marry him?

I didn't go to the wedding at the Protestant church. I wasn't invited and my mother didn't tell me why. Maybe it was just for adults. I had never been in a Protestant church, actually. In the photos, she looked really nice; she was wearing a pale green dress and a floppy hat that I thought covered too much of her face. I was secretly glad I got to spend the weekend at my best friend Val's house; she had a sleepover party just for me. We had a blast but every now and then I'd catch her mom looking at me funny. I would have felt like a hypocrite at the wedding. I would have had to have stood around and put a big smile on my face and acted happy. They all looked happy in the pictures: my mother, the smoker, my aunt and uncle. I wouldn't have, and then everyone would have wondered why.

I didn't like the smoker from the get-go, when he started hanging around last summer. I knew all that Friendly's ice cream and hot fudge was a bribe! She didn't, though. My mother didn't know. Maybe it was because there hadn't been any guy at all around to be nice to her since my Dad left. But my Dad wasn't too nice to anybody even when he was around, and I hadn't seen much of him since he moved out of our house.

The smoker liked food a lot, I think; he took her out to dinner every Friday night, and they'd go to some club to hear oldies music, the kind she likes to listen to on the car radio that makes me fall asleep. And he liked her. That was obvious. She kept seeing him and he kept coming over and eventually they went away to Cape Cod for a weekend and I… just watched. I watched from the sidelines, like some of my soccer team-mates did when I played and they wanted to play but they didn't play and couldn't do anything about it.

A month later, it was my first birthday with the smoker permanently in the house. I wondered what he would give me. More Friendly's ice cream, I bet. But I had stopped eating that stuff because it made me feel sick to my stomach. I didn't matter, anyway; I knew what I was getting from my mother, and that's what counted. So when I looked at the tag on my new bike, I was surprised that it read, "Happy Birthday Lisa, with love from Mom and the smoker." I tried not to let his signature bother me too much. I had wanted that bike for a long time. It was a three-speed, with a purple frame and silver handlebars, and purple and silver stream-ers spurting from their ends. There was a white stripe on either side. He probably didn't even pay for any of it, so couldn't he give me his own gift, and let the bike be just from her? Last year, when she and I celebrated my eleventh birthday, we opened presents and went out to dinner, just the two of us. This year, we had cake and dinner at home. I thanked them both. I kissed my mother, but I didn't want to go near him, partly because he had lit up one of his horrible-smelling cigarettes. I waved to him instead. Then I brought my bike up to the churchyard.

The churchyard I rode in was circular, and right up the hill from my house. It's still there, as well as the church: Immaculate Conception Catholic Church. It was built in the 1960's, my mother told me, after the old church burned down. It didn't look like the other churches in my town or the ones that were in Boston: those all looked the same, like big, plain, white boxes. My church was a funny shape, like a chocolate one-layer cake with a pointy spire stretched up from the middle. Inside, it was minimal: two-foot long, rectangular panes of glass, each a washed-out, beach glass color dotted all the way around the top of the enormous circular structure. The rest was plain wood, except for the grey marble altar, and an enormous gold Christ suspended from the ceiling. Christ looked like he was departing from his crucifix, his arms raised, his garments billowing out behind him, ascending. All of my Italian, Roman-Catholic life, I had been surrounded by crucifixes: bleeding from wounds, face contorted in pain, head bowed with thorny crown. But this one I had never understood. This Christ looked elated.

In the churchyard, there were speed bumps so I had to be really careful; I had to concentrate because I couldn't always see them. That day, there were leaves everywhere, dried brown mixed with new green leaves, and the faster I went, the higher they flew up, like odd-colored tumbling gymnasts. It wasn't dark yet, but the way the sun hit the glass on the church, I knew my mother would be calling me soon. I didn't have much time. I knew I'd feel something. I just had to keep going, and go faster.

I thought I'd feel different once I hit twelve, but I didn't. I thought I'd know the answers to all my questions. But maybe I couldn't do it by myself; maybe I needed help I could only get in proximity to the church. My church.

Except, we didn't go to my church anymore. After my parents divorced when I was ten, the Catholic Church ex-communicated both of them, and my mother, raised in parochial schools and all her life a devout Catholic, was so hurt she never went back. However, she insisted that I still go through Confirmation, fearing that I would otherwise not be saved if I did not complete this sacrament. I wasn't very happy about this, because I didn't understand why I needed to be saved, or what from. But for the first time, on the day of my twelfth birthday, the word "saved" meant something to me.

I wanted to go faster to get where I needed to go. Faster, faster, faster, couldn't this bike go any faster? I was racing now, racing the sun to get around the church before it set, racing to gather speed, hoping to feel something inside me instead of just the wind on my face and in my hair. The leaves were spinning up in the air, and the sun glinted off of the glass panes into my eyes and at the exact moment I hit the speed bump, I lifted my hands off of the handlebars, hoping to fly, like the elated gold Christ leaving the cross. Couldn't He, who could do anything, take me with Him? Couldn't He save me? Take me away from here and smoke and my mother's happiness?

Earthbound, I landed flat on my back, and my bike crashed a few feet in front of me. He left me behind, I thought, as a lump began sprouting on the back of my head. He hadn't heard me. I ignored the blood that ran down my arm. He didn't care. My bike seemed okay. I picked it up, and apologized profusely to my bike on the walk home, promising never to do that again. When I got in, my mother was still sitting next to the smoker at the kitchen table, and he was still in his cut-off denim shorts, but now they were laughing together about something, something private. She looked at me, her face changing to alarm, and said, "Lisa, what happened?" I walked to her, sat down in her lap and sobbed into her warm neck, as if I were a baby.

I said, "I was going as fast as I could and I couldn't feel anything, I can't feel anything, inside of me I can't feel anything!"

And though I was telling her the truth, and though she rubbed my back in sympathy, I knew that she didn't understand. And I wasn't sure if I would ever be able to explain it to her.

Achilles

My MOTHER CALLED ON JUNE 9TH, my twenty-seventh birthday, as she normally would on any birthday, except this time instead of saying, Happy Birthday, what she said was, "Your grandfather died today." Even with the time difference between the U.S. and my home in London, Achilles Nicoletti had died on my birthday.

"I'm sorry," she said.

"Don't be," I said.

It was fitting, really. He was the only decent male role model I had growing up and the proximity was fortunate in that he lived right next door in our lower middle class, south of Boston neighborhood. In fact, our yards adjoined because that's what immigrant Italians did: you bought the land next door, so your children could live in the house that you built them and that way, the family was kept close. At least, that's what my grandfather told me. Every Sunday after church, we went for dinner at his and my Nana's (Maria Philomena's) house, which entailed walking through the backyard. There were yards of sloping green lawn, and at the bottom, right in front of the high fence that blocked out the creek, was a swing set; to the left was my father's tool shed that resembled a dark, cobwebby, scary, miniature haunted house. To the right, everything belonged to my grandfather. There was his peach tree, which, though it was stranded in New England, yielded fruit I am sure because he willed it so. Next to that was his enormous garden, which he took great pride in. It was he who taught me how to water his garden at exactly the right time of day, pick the tomatoes and zucchini when ready to burst, pick the Swiss Chard that Nana would eventually sauté with garlic, olive oil, and cannellini beans.

Beyond the garden was his tool shed, which was not only twice the size of my father's, but also bright, neat and clean inside; then a massive old oak tree, then his ranch house that he designed. I still have the blueprints, rolled neatly at the bottom of his armoire that now sits in my bedroom. Up a small incline was my grandmother's clothesline and a little further, a shrubby-looking grapevine where my grandfather harvested the fruit for his home-made wine that was only consumed during dinner. Beginning early, I was given the wine when I was a child, but it was very bitter, so after he poured me a small amount out of a large, green glass jug, he would grudgingly cut it with orangeade. He was not a warm and fuzzy person, but he cared. Once, I had a terrible flu and my mother brought me with her to his house. He said, "What're you, sick?" I said, "Yes, I'm sick. I feel awful." I was about fourteen or so. He said, "Wait a minute." He got up from the table and went to his special closet, where he kept his wine. He brought out a much slimmer green bottle and took a shot glass from the cabinet. He poured the brown liquid to the top and said, "Drink it."

I took a sip. "Oh my god, disgusting!"

"Drink the whiskey! Drink it in one. Don't sip it. It'll make you feel better!"

I did and it did but I hated it at the time. Now, whisky is a staple kept on my kitchen windowsill.

It was my grandfather who I brought my report card to and he would take off his thick, black glasses, study it, smile, nod, tell me I did well, and then give me a dollar or two. I wanted to please him by being smart. He had the Junior Classics Encyclopedias at his house and I used to sit in his parlor on the green velvet couch and pore over them, each volume in a different color, with gold lettering, spelling out "Myths and Legends," and "Stories of Wonder and Magic." I loved the Brothers Grimm, Greek and Roman mythology, and read the volumes over and over again. "The Three Billy Goats Gruff" was my favorite. Grimm tales did not all end happily: toes were cut off, blood spurted out, and animals were killed by mean people. Occasionally, there was a rescue by a hero.

It's family folklore now. Like a Grimm tale. I had to have been six or seven, perhaps younger. I'd done something naughty that made my father absolutely livid. Expecting a beating, I ran. And he chased me around the house. But I was faster, and I got to the door and ran outside, screaming. My father came after me. I remember feeling like I was running for my life, hoping that one of my shoes would not come off. I ran into the backyard. It was March, so the trees were still bare, and I could see clear across the fence past the creek to the vacant lot, and the neighbor's house. My grandfather must have been turning soil in his garden earlier in the day, because there were tools lying all around. My father picked up one of the tools and continued to chase me. Well, that day, the neighbor, who was a family friend, happened to look out his window to see a red-faced man chasing a little girl with a pitchfork, and he called my grandfather, who came storming out of the house like I'd never seen. He tackled my father, then grabbed him by the shirt. "What are ya, crazy? The *whole neighborhood* can see you! Running after your daughter with this? And what did you think you were going to do once you caught her, eh? Eh?" He was livid. My father just looked at the ground, his chest heaving, ashamed. Then Grampy took me into his house, sat me down and gave me a glass of water.

Not a Grimm ending, a happy one. I was saved from an angry father, not by a prince on a white horse, but by an angrier grandfather. That time.

✳

My grandfather came from Anversa degli Abruzzo, Italy, via Canada in 1926 when he was thirteen. Like most of that generation, he could not tell my mother and my aunt that he loved them in words, but they knew that he did. He was more demonstrative in the love he bestowed on his grandchildren. On me. Or perhaps I forced him, because when I came flying into his house breathless with laughter, clutching a report card and then threw myself into his arms, what choice did he have but to hug me?

I have written about Achilles before. He was an autodidact: taught himself everything there was to know about cars, about building houses, and his profession was rolling tar on the highways of New England with his crew. Whenever my mother happened to drive by their site with me and my two sisters in the car, she'd slow down and he'd take off his hard hat and wave, then he'd make all the other guys in his crew take off their hard hats and wave to us, too.

What I omitted was this: My grandfather worked for thirty-three years rolling tar, without a day missed. I remember looking at the engraved plaque he was given when he retired. He got that, and a watch. He had big plans for his retirement, and he and my grandmother were going to travel. They had already done a fair bit of traveling, judging by the souvenirs all over their house, including the Canary Islands, Bermuda, Jamaica, Grenada. But, the best laid plans.

Instead, he elected to take early retirement. My Nana began to lose her memory when I was fourteen, receding back into her past, into her girlhood, until the day I walked over for a visit and found all of the doors open and her gone. Everyone who was available fanned out all over the neighborhood, until someone found her wandering about a mile away, looking for her childhood home.

We were told she had Alzheimer's Disease, which was uncommon at the time. We were also told it was degenerative and there was no cure.

I remember talking to my grandfather about planning her care, about what to do. He said, "I'm going to look after her."

I said, "I think that's a wonderful sentiment, but you have no patience! How are you going to manage? You can't do it all."

He said, "She looked after me for forty years. Now it's my turn."

There was nothing I could say to that.

He did his best for two years, but his health began to deteriorate. He had smoked since he was fifteen. Every single photograph I have of him, with the exception of his wedding portrait, he was holding a cigarette. He quit for many years, then started again when Nana got sick. He had issues with his veins, hardening of the arteries. He suffered a series of strokes. Eventually, Nana went into a nursing home where she got very good care. He visited her every day. She lay prone in a bed, unable to speak, being fed by fantastic nurses and turned from time to time so she would not get bed sores. I think she knew he was there. I say that because from her diagnosis, she lived for another thirteen years. Perhaps I am just hoping against hope that she sensed his presence. But consider this: my grandfather died in June. My grandmother followed him exactly six months later.

✳

He was the only one happy for me on the day I left for London, the only one who whispered in my ear, when I hugged him goodbye, "You do it now, when you're young. You do it now." We were the only two who did not cry.

I flew home for the funeral on June 10th. Everything happened so fast and I was in such a rush that I had no time to contact any friends. My mother had asked me to write something for the service at Immaculate Conception Catholic Church, where I was baptized, confirmed and had neither love nor respect for when I was finally allowed to choose what I believed.

There was a wake first, which was typically dreadful. My grandfather had wanted a closed casket and for some reason, once we got into the funeral parlor, my mother and Aunt Jan began hemming and hawing: "Maybe we should have it open for all of his friends who haven't seen him," "Maybe we should have it open because of his cousins who..." This I could not bear. In a voice much too loud for a funeral parlor, I said, "NO. IT STAYS CLOSED BECAUSE THAT'S WHAT HE WANTED. THE FRIENDS AND COUSINS WHO DIDN'T COME TO VISIT HIM? FUCK THEM. THEY SHOULD HAVE DONE THAT WHILE HE WAS ALIVE."

The casket remained closed.

The next day was the funeral. A limo picked us up, which was totally unnecessary as Immaculate Conception was literally across the street and up a set of stairs from my childhood home. I was extremely nervous. I knew there would be a ton of picky Italian relatives in the pews, not all of them a fan of my grandfather, who, to be fair, was tough if you crossed him. He was not a warm, fuzzy person.

I joined my two younger sisters, Kris and Jen, in the back of limo while holding one of my mother's heavy crystal glasses, filled to the brim with vodka and orange juice, not because the drink was suitable for 8 AM, but because that was the only liquor I could find in the house. My mother was in the front seat. She turned around and looked at me, looked at the drink. She said, "Oh, you don't need that. You're a natural performer. A natural. I always knew ever since you were three years old and danced at the front of the class in kindergarten when none of the other children would, I knew. The teacher taught the class a routine and you were the only one who could do it. I was allowed to observe behind a glass, probably because I was so upset that I had to leave you. It was the first day of class. You were the only one who did the dance. I cried. I knew you would be fine. A natural performer."

By this point, I had stopped drinking, stunned, my sisters were looking at me wide-eyed and I was thinking that the reason I had only found the vodka was because my mother had imbibed everything else in the liquor cabinet.

We got into the church and the service began. It felt like the alcohol had had zero effect on me. I wondered why I wore heels and figured that I'd probably slip on the marble altar for comic relief. But I slowly made it to the pulpit. I put the pages down and looked out into the crowd. I had the letter almost memorized. I had written to my mother a month before, when her father's death was imminent and she was naturally distraught. I said that the only thing that would get her through was the power of memory: She had gone from her father's house to the house he built for her next door, so she had spent over fifty years seeing him on a daily basis. That is astonishing to me now, a way of life I know nothing about. But for her, it was a gift. He raised her and she took care of him at the end. She had years and years of goodness: of a terrible Christmas after the divorce when my father emptied the bank account and took both cars. She had been humiliated at the checkout line in Zayre's Department Store when it came to pay for Christmas presents, because my father had also canceled the credit cards without telling her. Three hundred dollars that she could not afford. My mother came home empty-handed, sat down and cried at the kitchen table when my grandfather walked in and asked what was wrong. She told him. He took a roll of bills out of his pocket, put three hundred dollars on the table and said, "Go buy your daughters Christmas presents." That was my grandfather.

I once asked him who was the best president he had lived under. He said, "FDR." I was surprised, because I thought he would say JFK.

I said, "Why?"

You Are All a Part of Me

He said, "Because he gave a shit about people." I did not use those words in the church. But my grandfather gave a shit about people: about my mother, about my aunt, about me and my sisters, about his wife. He had been there for me growing up, he had cared, in his gruff way. He was the man who had been my savior, my guide, my grandfather.

Phil and Claire

A FEW DAYS AGO, I found out that my Uncle Phil, my godfather and my father's eldest brother, died at the age of eighty-seven on March 10th 2020. The last time I saw him was perhaps eight or nine years ago, when I went back to Boston from New York City for a rare visit. I had heard that he and his wife, my Aunt Claire, were living in South Weymouth, so I borrowed a friend's car and drove myself to their house. I did not call first. I decided to do the "pop in." I know this annoys a lot of people. But at that time, I had not seen them in years and I was nervous. I wasn't sure they would be as eager to see me. So, I risked the pop in.

I rang their doorbell, sweating on their steps in a hot pink dress I had chosen knowing my Aunt Claire would approve. She came to the door first. Then he did. She said, "My God!" Then she turned to Phil and said, "It's Lisa. Your goddaughter." For a moment, I thought I might have changed so much that he did not recognize me. But as Claire opened the screen door and he said, "Hey! Hey, Lisa!" I put that thought out of my mind. Their expressions were ones of shocked delight. They welcomed me into their home, as they had always done, and we walked through to the kitchen, the beating heart of most Italian homes. Even at eighty, sitting at his kitchen table with Claire, Phil's hair was still black and curly, a bit of grey visible only in his mustache. He was always in good shape, and that had not changed. Only his skin tone was a bit lighter, from deep olive to pale. Claire had lost some of her plumpness, her once-long black hair was now streaked with grey and cut short. But apart from the grey, neither looked as if they had aged much.

Claire made coffee and brought out homemade pastries, which I declined, no gluten for me. Then she asked if I wanted to try her meatballs. How could I refuse? She heated them up with a bit of sauce, and her kitchen began to smell like it did in the Braintree house, the party house of my childhood.

You Are All a Part of Me

When I was a little girl, my father took me to every party my Aunt and Uncle threw: every birthday, anniversary, first Holy Communion, Baptism, Confirmation, graduation — and in addition to my father, there were three more aunts, one uncle and countless cousins, so there were many parties. Phil and Claire's house in Braintree became the party house of choice: it had a sprawling sitting room where usually a football game, a baseball game or a show deemed wholesome entertainment, like The Waltons or Little House on the Prairie was always playing on the enormous television set.

There was however, an exception: the first time I saw The Godfather Parts 1 & 2 also was in Phil and Claire's house. All of the men in the Del Rosso family loved that film. My father in particular got a kick out of the fact that Michael Corleone turned out to be, as he said, "worse than the father." So after watching the film, I was baffled as to how it had gotten by the alleged "wholesome censor," though this was yet another adult contradiction that I knew not to question.

Claire's large kitchen regularly smelled of her red sauce, her manicotti stuffed shells, her ricotta pie, the latter of which I still make today using her recipe. In their rumpus room, the older cousins hung out around a pool table and occasionally snuck a beer inside the pocket of a leather jacket. The parlor was elegant, looked as if Marie Antionette had decorated it and then decided to throw a plastic covering over the sofa and *no one, especially the children*, was allowed in that room. Part of the land their house sat on was woods (now I think this would be called conservation land), but another part had been transformed into an epic in-ground pool where, when it was very hot, everyone else would stay indoors enjoying the air conditioning and watching through the huge bay window as my uncle, fit and trim in a very small bathing suit, reclined on a lounge chair beside the pool and baked his already dark olive body in the sun. "I swear he's part Arab," Aunt Claire said once, shaking her head. Phil did indeed love the sun, loved getting as deeply tanned as possible and in fact, resembled Omar Sharif.

I loved those parties. I don't think I have ever felt so connected to family, so clearly understood what "La Famiglia e Tutto" meant, and learned about banter and gossip and brotherly love — and how incredibly frustrating it was that the adults spoke in Italian when they didn't want the children to understand what they were saying — envy and loyalty, all accompanied by my Aunt's amazing food.

When my parents divorced, my father continued to take me and my two younger sisters to Phil and Claire's. After his second marriage, nothing changed. But after he managed to get the marriage to my mother annulled and got remarried again in the Catholic Church, suddenly the parties at Claire's stopped. I was about thirteen or so at the time, and when I questioned my father as to why, he said that she and Phil didn't want to see us anymore. It was a result of the divorce, he said, and he blamed my mother.

Years later, when I was home for Thanksgiving from studying abroad in London, I borrowed a car and popped by Claire's house, the party house in Braintree that they were still living in. I was nineteen or twenty. She and Phil welcomed me into their home. In the past, I had never had many conversations with Phil: I had more admired him as a bronzed, smiling god who bantered back and forth with Claire, though Claire usually won. Phil returned to his chair in the sitting room, and Claire made coffee for us. She sat down across from me at the kitchen table and asked about what I was doing in London. Her daughter, my cousin Diana, who was twelve or thirteen at the time, came out from her bedroom and sat down next to Claire to examine me, a cousin she had not seen in years. Diana asked what London was like, and my Aunt said, "It's foggy, not a lot of sun, but there's a lot of moisture in the air and that's why the women have such beautiful skin." She smiled at me.

We talked a bit more and finally I asked, "Claire, why did you stop inviting us to your house for parties?"

She said, "Lisa, I never did."

I said, "My father stopped taking us. He said you didn't want to see us anymore."

Claire said, slowly, "Lisa. Your father told us that you didn't want to come here anymore."

I said, weakly, "You could have called?" But I knew that would not have been possible.

She said, "Lisa. You know I couldn't have called your mother's house; your father hated her with a passion. Then I'd be fighting with my husband's brother. You see?"

I did see. But all I wanted to do was break down and cry. How could I have been so stupid to believe my father? How could I have taken him at his word? *Why didn't I call?*

My Aunt Claire had unusual eyes: black, like her hair that she always piled on top of her head in a messy bun back then, so black that you could barely see the pupils. Usually, they were upturned at the sides because she was always smiling, always laughing or making a joke. At that moment, though, I saw the realization of all those lost years, lost time, that betrayal, and the black eyes I stared into smoldered like she could kill someone.

I said, "That fucking son-of-a-bitch."

Shaking her head, she said, "You got that right."

We did stay in touch after that. I don't think she was particularly happy that I chose to study in London, or eventually chose to live there - "Why not travel around your own country instead?" - because that meant I was far from family. I did not tell her that was part of the reason I stayed in London, though we both knew we wanted each other in our respective lives.

How could I explain to Clare that I was haunted by a past I could not shake? That her house was an oasis of lush life while mine had only ever compressed me within its walls? How could I say that the house I grew up in was chaotic once my parents' marriage went south, full of angry voices and fighting, and that I remembered my father's rage more than his laughter? That I had learned how to behave to avoid getting hit? By the time I was seven, my father had chosen another target, my younger sister, who got far worse than I ever did.

On another visit to Aunt Claire's from London, I asked, "Why wasn't it me?" Who got beaten the most, I meant. Now, Claire's house was not perfect, and Phil, the disciplinarian, also believed in corporal punishment. I had witnessed that myself, with one of his sons. But never with his daughter. She knew what I was asking.

Claire said, "Lisa. You were such a strong-willed little girl. You would have run away."

I guess by going to London — even to study singing, even though I had earned that opportunity by audition — it was also a form of running away. I just didn't know it at the time.

After Claire had poured me another cup of coffee post-delicious meatballs, she sat down and said, "Phil is going blind."

"Oh no!" I said, shocked because I had not noticed.

Claire said, "There's nothing they can do, it's degenerative."

Phil said, "I memorized the layout of the house, so I can get around pretty good. I can see shapes and outlines. Sit close to me, so I can see your face." Now I understood why Claire had told him who I was at the door. He couldn't see me.

Claire functioned as his eyes, leading him through the rooms to sit down, going down to the basement if he wanted, reading to him, and this seemed to work. Their ease together was pretty amazing. All told, they were married for over sixty years. During the explaining of all this, Phil, the eternal optimist, never sounded defeated. A lot of that had to do with Claire.

They asked about New York City, where I had resettled after ten years in London, then carefully about my personal life. "Now… are you still… married?" We got onto the rest of the family, so many stories I could not keep straight. Then my Uncle said, "Your father calls me a few times a week from the mountain in Vermont. He's lonely. He says he misses his family."

"Oh," I said. I had neither seen nor heard from him in about ten years.

"Yeah," said Phil, "He misses being close to his family. I think he's going to move down here soon."

I said, "Oh, really?"

Phil said, "Yeah. I almost got him convinced."

I said, "What about his wife?"

Phil said, "She got no choice."

I said, "Well, I hope you're right."

Phil said, "He'll do it. He'll move. I tell you, he's lonely."

I knew this would never happen. I asked for more of Claire's coffee, the smell of it bringing me back in time to her Braintree kitchen and laughter and teasing and the hubbub of family.

As I was leaving, and we were exchanging hugs and kisses, Phil said, "Lisa, after you leave, I'm going to call your father and tell him you stopped by. I'm going to tell him you look beautiful. And it's going to make him so happy to hear that, that you stopped by —"

Laughing, I cut him off and said, "No, no, Phil, please don't do that. Please don't call him. Please."

Taken aback, he said, "Why not?"

I said, still laughing, "Because he doesn't give a shit. He really doesn't. And that's okay. I've come to terms with it. And it really is okay."

Phil said, "No Lisa, it's going to make him happy and he's going to call you —"

I laughed harder. "Phil, he is not going to call me. I told you: he doesn't give a shit. That's why he stays on that mountain in Vermont. Away from family. And does what his wife wants him to do."

Phil said, "I am going to call him anyway and you'll see!"

I said, "You are wasting your breath! I love you both. It was wonderful to see you. Wonderful." I hugged and kissed them again, said goodbye, and hopped into my friend's car. That was the last time I saw them both.

Claire died suddenly, in January 2016. My sister Kris found out online a few months after the fact and was furious that no one had contacted us, but I was not surprised. Phil must have been lost without her. I believe one of his sons moved in to look after him. My father never moved to South Weymouth. He never came down from the mountain because he missed his family. He never called after I visited Phil and Claire. None of that surprised me, either.

I do miss Phil and Claire, and everything they gave me while I was growing up: They shared a house full of life. Of raucous, rippling laughter. They always gave without asking for anything — and my aunt worked full-time in a bank! My mother said she didn't know where Claire got the energy. I knew, though. Claire knocked herself out. She cleaned the house and prepared and cooked all the food - that food! - for one reason and one reason only: because she wanted to. She liked making people happy. She made my uncle happy. And he made her happy. For over sixty years. If my father ever made one single person happy, I don't know about it.

Indelible

WHENEVER I THINK OF DAVE, the first thing that looms is his 6'5" frame, clocking in at around three hundred pounds. He has a mustache and a beard that reaches to his sternum. He wears black jeans, black boots and a sleeveless tee shirt. When given a long-sleeved XXL tee shirt by a well-meaning aunt or new girlfriend, for Christmas or birthday, he accepted it because he was nothing if not unfailingly polite. After the gift giver departed, he immediately grabbed a scissors and cut the sleeves off. Over the sleeveless tee, he wears a black leather jacket. This is his uniform. Dress shirts, if you caught him in one, at a family wedding or reunion, didn't stay on long — first the sleeves got rolled up and then the shirt was discarded completely in favor of the sleeveless tee beneath. Every inch of skin that shows, with the exception of his face, is tattooed. I have no idea how many. One hundred? Two? I'll bet he lost count. On his arms, skulls. An eagle with an enormous wingspan. A crucifix. Prudentia, holding a mirror and a snake. An American flag. A large angel's wing under his left arm. Bracelets of thorns encircle both wrists. Like me, Dave was raised to be a devout Catholic. Like me, he stopped churchgoing in his teens, after being Confirmed. But his tats taken together are his own doctrine, his own personal mythology, all laid out symbolically on his body, belying the hulking, scary biker stereotype.

I can't remember him not looking like this, even when very young. The only difference is that as he got older, he put on muscle and weight. At seven years my senior, I looked up to him, usually from the vantage point of a book, awestruck. He reminded me of Paul Bunyan, if Bunyan had been adopted by bikers who made him trade the plaid for leather and the axe for tats.

"Hey Lis."

"Hey Dave."

"Good book?"

"Yes."

"Wanna see my new baby?"

The "baby" was typically a Harley.

He liked bikes. I liked books. We didn't have much to say to each other until we were in our twenties.

Dave Baldassini was my second cousin (or 3rd? I always get the lineage confused.) Technically, his mother, Aunty Lucy, was my Great-Aunt, but we never called her that. So maybe Dave was my uncle? But we always referred to each other as "cousin."

Aunty Lucy, married to my Uncle Johnny, had three children: Paul is the oldest, with an average, skinny frame. Dave is a fraternal twin: Susan is his sister. Susan is 5' or so, petite. You could not find two more physically dissimilar people.

After Dave's imposing physicality, I think of his fine, chiseled face. Behind that shrubby beard are high cheekbones and copper-colored, almond-shaped eyes. Above the eyes, many piercings in his left eyebrow. Many studs and small hoops in his left ear. These external accoutrements belied the fact that Dave was not a violent person. I said to him once, "It must be nice to be so big, to be the biggest person in a room sometimes." He paused and said, "No, it isn't. Because some jerk always wants to fight the biggest guy in the room, and I am usually the biggest guy in the room. And I don't like fighting."

He used to ride with the Hell's Angels, until, he said, "They started killing people." Then he joined the Red Emeralds, and he and other members were friends for over twenty years.

Aunty Lucy was the younger sister of my grandmother, Maria Philomena, on my mother's side. Phil, as my grandfather used to call her, and Archie, short for Achilles, as she used to call him, were the maternal grandparents that lived next to me growing up. Family lived within walking distance, or the next town over. After that, you had to jump a country, to Italy, Naples, specifically, to find more members of my grandmother's side of the family.

Phil was born in New York City, where I have lived for the past twenty-five years, where I have a now-explainable affinity. I don't know how the family wound up in New England. But I have always felt that my birth there was an accident of geography. New York City is my home.

When I was about fourteen and my grandmother was in her 60's, she developed Alzheimer's Disease and quickly lost the ability to recognize anyone, including my mother. That devastating loss was mitigated by Aunty Lucy, who stepped in to be my mother's "mother," which meant we all spent a lot of time together, and I got intimately acquainted with Paul, David and Susan.

Paul, the eldest, became a graphic designer and left home as soon as humanly possible, ran his own business and lived in Boston proper. Susan got married, then unmarried, so went back to living at home. When she wed for the second time, she and her husband got their own place. Dave got a job at the post office (Uncle Johnny was a mail carrier for thirty-two years) and lived in the finished basement.

While my Aunt Lucy was alive, Dave was the favorite. Like her, he was also gregarious and had a big personality. Aunty Lucy spoiled him. And though a grown man living in the basement does sound like he was enabled, or stunted or something, he did some cool things with the money he saved.

He collected vintage Harley Davidson motorcycles. He'd pick up ones that needed work, fix them, keep them for a time and then sell them. He showed them to me and I rode on them with him (more on that later).

He and his Red Emeralds' friends shipped themselves and their bikes to Europe - twice - and traveled everywhere on them. Munich. Portugal. Italy. The Swiss Alps. He said, "Lis, I have always wanted to do this. I have always wanted me and the guys to run down the Swiss Alps in our leathers and tats singing, 'The hills are alive, with the sound of music, Ahhhhhh...' at the top of our lungs in falsetto. SO WE DID IT. We laughed so hard we almost pissed our pants." I wish I had been there just to see that.

He kept his sister Susan safe. If anyone in the town of Quincy or surrounding towns, for that matter, was to give Susan a hard time, he or she would have to contend with Dave. And everyone knew it.

The Baldassini clan was a large presence in my young life.

I left for London at eighteen. When I turned nineteen, my mother called and said that Aunty Lucy had been diagnosed with a brain tumor. She was due to have surgery shortly, but it didn't look good. I flew to Boston, my mother met my shuttle from Logan and we drove straight to the hospital. Aunty Lucy had come through the surgery okay, and was fine for a couple of days afterward. But by the time I landed, she was in a coma. We walked into the hospital, took the elevator up and stood in front of her door. My mother said, "Do you want to go in and say goodbye to her?"

I thought about it. I thought about Aunt Lucy gesticulating in her kitchen as she told her stories. I thought about her lavishly praising Susan and David. I thought about her yelling to Uncle Johnny from the kitchen to shut off the television, stop watching Angie Dickinson and come to the dinner table. I thought about her incomparable pasta sauce. I thought about the baby powder smell of her when she hugged me.

My mother said, "She doesn't look the same. Her head has been shaved and she's bloated. When I saw her a few days ago, before she slipped into a coma, I told her you were coming and the first thing she said was, 'Lisa is going to see me and I have no hair!' Aunty Lucy was a beauty in her heyday. I've seen the photos. She resembled Rita Hayworth. I appreciated that sort of vanity after a brain operation.

I thought about my love for her. I thought about her curled red hair. "No," I said.

My mother said, "I have to go in. She was like a mother to me."

I said, "Of course. Take your time."

I waited outside until my mother came out ten or fifteen minutes later, looking ashen. "It's good you didn't go in," she said.

We walked to the car and drove to my childhood home. Aunty Lucy died the next day, at sixty years old. On the day of her funeral, her cocker spaniel, who had been an obedient dog all his life, ran out into the main street and was killed by an oncoming car. Uncle Johnny said, "He wanted to go with her. Never seen the dog run off like that before. Wanted to go with her."

At his mother's funeral, Dave was stoic, strong for everyone around him, particularly his father. I drove to the cemetery with Susan, who was in deep shock. She had to be, because she asked, "I don't understand why, if I come back here in six months and dig my mother up, she can't be alive like she used to be."

Trying to think of something she could comprehend at that moment, I said, "A human being is like a plant, or a flower growing in the ground. Like your Sunflowers in your driveway. They need light and water and oxygen, and if you deprive them of all of those things, they die."

Susan paused and said, "That's a good way to think about it."

After the service, I stayed in town for another week or so and then went back to London.

For the first seven or eight years I lived there, I missed nothing and no one. I graduated from LAMDA. I did a musical. I joined an alternative cabaret group to get my Equity card. We performed all over London, and at the Edinburgh Festival. I had adventures that my mother most certainly would have disapproved of. I married the man I was dating to stay in the country because there was no way I was going to go back to the U.S. No way. But when I told my mother about my pending marriage of convenience, she said, "Please do me one favor. Please don't give up your American citizenship." So I became a British resident and made a life in London.

Until the funerals started up again.

My Uncle Joe had died suddenly of a massive heart attack at the age of sixty, leaving my Aunt Jan, my mother's sister, a widow at fifty-five. I flew home for the funeral, which was very tough. Dave was there. My step-father, Steve, was very upset; he and Joe had been best buddies since they were in their twenties. Dave stood behind him in the church. When Steve began shaking with grief, Dave's large hands stretched out from behind him, covering his shoulders, steadying, comforting him.

The last time I had seen Dave, I was a teenager. I was now twenty-five. Dave sidled up to me and said, "Lis! You're in with the good-looking cousins." I laughed and we talked. He filled me in on the aftermath of his mother's death.

Only Dave and his father were left in the house. Uncle Johnny had always liked a drink or two or three but kept it in check. Until Lucy died. Then he hit the bottle and hard. I can only tell you what Dave told me: that there were too many nights when he had to put his drunken father to bed. That he told his father he needed to get help. And Dave was good to his father. He had learned from his mother how to make her meatballs, her pasta and sauce, most of her recipes. He cooked, cleaned and made sure, after he got home from the post office, that dinner was prepared. But Johnny's drinking only got worse. He didn't listen to Dave. And Dave got tired of putting his father to bed drunk, tired of cleaning up after him, tired of taking care of a grown man who should know better. Dave had never wanted to get married or have children. Neither did I. There's a reason for that.

So after months of this, one night, after his father had gotten home, settled himself in his favorite mauve, velveteen chair, clicked on the television to watch "Police Woman" and started in on the first six-pack, Dave was in the basement, listening to the familiar sounds coming from above, that familiar routine, and thought about what he had to look forward to in a few hours.

"So Lis, this is what I did, I had had it, I was done, D-O-N-E; so I went and got out my gun (a pistol), put one bullet in the chamber, cocked it, walked up the stairs into the living room. Dad looked up and said, 'Hey David.' And I said to him, while he was sitting there drinking down the beer, 'Dad. I'm not going to live like this anymore. I'm not going to watch you wallow in self-pity, and I'm not cleaning up after a drunk. So this is your choice: I put one bullet in the chamber. One bullet for you.

40

You Are All a Part of Me

If you want to kill yourself, I'm not going to watch you drink yourself to death. This way is much faster. Either, you put that bullet in your head now, or you let me drive you to a detox center. There is no other choice. So I'm gonna go downstairs now, and I'm gonna wait.' And I put the gun on the side table next to his beer, and I went back downstairs."

I said, "HOLY SHIT, DAVE!"

He said, "I know."

I said, "How long?"

Dave said, "Lis, that was the longest five minutes of my life. I was sweating, waiting to hear the shot — because that's what I thought he was gonna do. I thought for sure he wanted to die. Five minutes later, I heard noise, heard footsteps. He came to the top of the stairs and said, 'David. All right. Take me to detox.' And I drove him to the detox center."

I said, "My mind has been blown - no pun intended. Oh my god!"

Dave laughed, and I laughed with him. His father got sober and lived until he was eighty-one years old.

After the service, I stayed in town for another week and then went back to London. Two years later, my grandfather, Achilles, died on my birthday. I flew home for that funeral, too. I looked sideways at the receiving line I was standing in: my two younger sisters were no longer girls, they were women. I had seen my mother maybe six times in nine years. Time hit me upside the head. A few months later, I moved back to the U.S. and then to New York City. I also reconnected with Dave, who updated me on the family drama.

One of our phone conversations naturally turned to our respective love lives, a subject Dave relished. He was seeing a woman he had dated in high school, a redhead.

"How's it going?" I said.

"Not too good," he said.

"Why?"

"She wants me to wear long-sleeved shirts."

"Why?" I asked.

"Because, she wants to go to restaurants where they want you to wear long-sleeved shirts."

So Dave bought *one.*

"Well, that's… that's a concession…and I have to say, I'm impressed… actually, I'm shocked," I said.

"I don't know Lis, not sure how much more of this crap I can take."

Dave called a few weeks later. He didn't say hello. He didn't say hey Lis. What he said when I picked up the phone was, "It's O-VER!"

Stifling a laugh, I said, "What happened?"

He said, "She wanted me to go sailing. I said, 'yeah, I'll go sailing.' But she said I couldn't wear my boots. I said, what else am I gonna wear? She said Docksiders."

"Docksiders??"

"I said I'm not wearing Docksiders. So she said wear those white flat shoes…"

"Keds?" I said.

"Yeah, Keds."

"Do they even make those in your size?" I said, letting the laugh go free.

Dave said, "It's O-VER!"

And that was the last I heard about her.

There had been some business involving Dave and drugs: Susan, to her credit, got him clean. But this had caused a rift in the family, as some of the pious older members found out and no longer wanted Dave in their homes. They didn't care that he was clean. That hurt both Susan and Dave. The thing about twins is, one doesn't go without the other. So, if Dave wasn't welcome, then Susan also stayed away. I sided with my cousins for two reasons: they were part of my childhood, part of me and they were not hypocrites. They had always been candid about their respective imperfections, so consequently, I could be my imperfect self with them.

Once I moved to NYC, Dave began visiting me regularly, not least to partake of every cigar shop the city has to offer. Dave liked coming to Manhattan. He liked the fact that in a city where no one blinked, people outright gawked at him. He stayed at my tiny SRO on W. 43rd Street with my friendly British Blue cat Madison, while I stayed at Yash's (my then-boyfriend's) apartment across Times Square. When I came back the first morning, Dave said, "That cat hissed at me!"

Madison was sitting upright on the only table in the room, staring at Dave like he wanted to tear his face off. I said, "What did you do to him?"

Dave said, "Nothing," but what I heard was, "I'm lying."

I said, "You must have done something to him or he wouldn't have hissed."

"I didn't do nothing!" Dave said.

Madison was happy to see Dave go.

In the middle of settling the details for another one of his visits, our phone conversation took a dark turn.

Dave said, "Lis, you're shittin' me! You don't have even one? Not even a tiny one?"

"No," I said, "Not one."

"Not a flower or a heart or nothing?"

"No."

"Virgin skin? I can't believe you have virgin skin. I don't know anyone who doesn't have at least ONE tattoo."

I couldn't believe that we had never had this conversation, that the subject had never come up, that he had never asked before, and now that we were having this conversation, now that we were well into our 30's, I realized I could have lived without ever discussing tattoos with Dave.

"Well, you know me, and we are related, so now you know someone with virgin skin."

"Okay Lis, when I come there, you are getting INKED, baby, INKED. So, start picking something out that you like, because the clock just started ticking."

"Dave, one of the reasons I do not have a tattoo is commitment issues. I can't pick something I know I will want on my skin for the rest of my life. I just can't."

"I don't give a shit, Lis, you are getting inked in New York City in two weeks so you better decide on something. Virgin skin! Ha ha! Yippeee!!"

I hung up the phone. Damn. I loved my cousin, but not enough to get a tat. Yet there seemed no way out now that Dave knew I had *virgin skin*.

In preparing for Dave's visit, when he said not only would I get inked, I also needed to get leathers for bike riding, my imagination was failing me when it came to picturing permanent images on my body. So I repaired to the NYPL (New York Public Library) for inspiration. And I found something! A pencil drawing by Edward Burne-Jones of a siren for wallpaper design, of all things. I still have it somewhere. She is about 3" wide and 4" long, ornate, and beautiful. I could live with her. A Pre-Raphaelite siren I could live with.

So Dave came to town. He said, "Okay. Let's see what's going on that virgin skin."

He really was way too happy about this whole thing.

I pulled out the drawing. Braced myself.

Dave took the drawing, studied it. I paced. Played with Madison. Made tea.

Finally, he looked up from the siren and said, "Do you have any idea how much this is going to cost?"

"No," I said, puzzled. At the time, I knew nothing about tattoos. Cost. Artwork. The difference between a good tattoo and a bad tattoo. The difference between one tattoo artist and another. Nothing.

He said, "This is going to be like 500 bucks! More, maybe."

Wow. That was a lot of cash. Still, I wanted my siren and my siren I was going to get.

I said, "Do you have any idea how long it took me to find something I could live with? I had to go to the damn library for inspiration."

Dave snorted and said, "That sounds right."

I said, "What is that supposed to mean?"

Dave, "You and books. Still the same."

I said, "Don't do that. Don't deflect."

Dave said, "Can't you pick…?"

I said, "Listen! I am not going to have a smiley face tattooed on my ass just for the sake of getting inked! You said choose something and I have chosen. You didn't say anything about price or size… you didn't say there were any restrictions. So take it or leave it."

Dave looked conflicted. "Lis…"

I shook my head. "No way. It's MY SKIN."

Stalemate. But there was no way I was getting inked just for the sake of getting inked. Madison jumped up on the table we were sitting at and began sniffing whatever he detected in Dave's beard. With resignation, he said, "Nah, I can't afford it. It could be up to 700, ya know."

I jumped up and down with relief! "YAY!! I GET TO KEEP MY VIRGIN SKIN!!!"

Dave, annoyed, sat back on the chair that barely contained him, folded his arms and said, "For now, cousin. For now."

One of my favorite photographs of Dave and me sits on the blue hutch in my Upper West Side apartment. It was taken in front of Bethesda Fountain in Central Park. He has on sunglasses and an "America" tee shirt with the sleeves cut off, of course, and I have on sunglasses and a black leather jacket. We are both smiling. The photo was taken about six months after 9/11, 2001.

Dave knew I was in the city when the Towers came down, and, being a patriotic person, he said he wanted to see how 9/11 had affected New York City. I said, "Come," so he did. We toured the fire stations, and looked at all the memorials. Dave shook hands with some of the firefighters, didn't say much, other than, "Jesus Christ." We went to Central Park because he had never been there before. Then we grabbed lunch at a diner, a novelty for a non-New Yorker. The bill for that meal was $37 bucks. I had forgotten how much Dave could put away: steak, eggs, home fries, toast, chocolate milk. I had scrambled eggs and coffee.

Afterwards, as Dave reached for the Tums in his inner pocket, he said, "Where's Yash?" I said he had gone to Long Island, to visit his mother.

Dave said, "Let's go. We'll take the bike."

At the time, he still had the Suzuki. Fastest bike built, he reminded me. Did this faze me? Did I think twice?

No. I loved riding with Dave because he knew what he was doing. In forty years of riding he had never had an accident.

I put on the requisite leathers and a helmet and hopped on the back. Driving from Manhattan to Long Island is almost all highway, all straight roads. At one point, after going at what felt like a fairly high speed, Dave pulled over and said, "How fast do you think we were going?"

"I don't know," I said.

"Guess," he said.

"I don't think I want to," I said.

"GUESS!" Dave said, all excited.

"90?" I said, tentatively.

"180," he said.

I opened my mouth to speak but nothing came out.

Dave laughed and laughed, started the bike and off we went.

When I told that story to my mother to deliberately provoke her, she yelled at me, not Dave and said, "Don't you ever get on the back of his bike again!"

But of course, I did. Whenever a fleet of motorcycles pass me roaring on the highway or in the city, Dave appears in my head.

A sensitive stomach had always plagued Dave. He attributed this to his enormous appetite. He'd eat a ton, then throw up. Happened at my wedding in Manhattan. Happened at my sister's wedding. He never saw a doctor because he never thought it that serious. He'd take a few Tums, then go to bed. So when he got sick, we thought it was stomach-related, no big deal. There were two diagnoses: the first was Hep C, not good, and his kidneys were failing. He went on dialysis. We talked over the phone. I said, "How do you get Hep C?"

46

Dave said, "From a needle, a tattoo needle, I've had so many, who knows, or from some whore in a club." He laughed. I loved that laugh.

"What can I do?" I said.

"Nothing you can do, Lis."

I really didn't want to believe that Dave's tattoos were ultimately his downfall.

When his sister told me his kidneys were failing and she was going to donate one, I immediately said, "You are not in good shape. You'd never survive that surgery. Please let me do this." She cried and said okay. I didn't cry. A person can live with one kidney, for Christ's sake. And it was for Dave. Donating a kidney? No big deal. Dave was happy about that. Susan was ecstatic. I was happy Dave was wrong.

"See? I said. "There is something I can do." Relieved, we laughed together and Dave asked about my sex life, which segued into a series of raunchy commentary.

About a week later, I had just gotten out of a play and was standing on Broadway and 43rd, surrounded by a million noisy theatergoers. I got a call from my mother. Dave had liver cancer and had slipped into a coma. No kidney donation would help. Nothing would help. Susan was too distraught to talk. I walked the sixty blocks home to 101st & Broadway, with Dave's face and words and motorcycle and the hugs that he gave me that were so like his mother's all flying through my head.

You died on November 11, 2011, at fifty-three years old. You were told what you had was fatal, and you were okay with that. You said you had lived a good life. You were not okay with leaving your sister alone. Your casket was open. I kissed your beautiful face, your ice cold cheek. I tucked a Nat Sherman cigar next to your tattooed arm. My best friends Carol and Derek came with me to your service, and I needed them next to me in that pew, needed Carol's hand on me when I couldn't lift my head. You had a motorcycle-drawn glass carriage transport you to the graveside. Your chosen epitaph was, "I'm not here for a long time, only a good time." And damn you, I am still contemplating that siren tattoo.

FAMILY

I have difficultly imagining my life without my ex, though we divorced over ten years ago. He is part of my family, and I am part of his. There is the English family I am part of. There is my best friend in the world and ersatz nieces and nephews. There is the #1 most difficult friend who is also the love of my life. Go figure.

32 Highbury Place

GOD SAID, "GET OFF THE TUBE AND CALL." It was the only time a voice, an outer voice I swear I heard, spoke to me. There are, of course, other explanations: it could have been Buddha, Mohammed, a Martian, Satan, or I could have had a schizophrenic episode. Nevertheless, whoever it was said, "Get off the Tube and call." I thought of it as the Tube by that time, not the subway, nor anything remotely American.

There was a tiny box of an ad in one of the free magazines proffered at the mouth of most Tube stations. I needed a job and a place to live, so had been perusing the stack on my lap and finding absolutely nothing in my skill set, which was also absolutely nothing. I had graduated from LAMDA (London Academy of Music and Dramatic Art), and then was subsequently cast in the Academy's graduating musical, "The Pajama Game." The gig came with a small stipend. Very small.

I got off the train and called.

A posh, slightly harassed voice answered. This was Angela. She said she was a journalist. She sounded welcoming, trusting. I wondered why. The woman didn't even know me. My interview was for the following day at 32 Highbury Place, overlooking Highbury Fields.

I hate children. I had been forced, for what I now see as economic reasons, to look after my two younger sisters, Kris and Jen, every single summer in my teen years (until I got a real job, that is) and resented both my mother and them for what I perceived as a raw deal. Then, it was explained to me that I was the oldest. At thirteen, I was supposed to be "the responsible one." I had no choice.

Those summers completely colored my view on children. I was unable to go to summer camp, even if it was in my own town, unable to hang out with my friends. My time was not my own. What I could do was read, and hate my sisters. I did watch them; I did keep them safe. But

I never wanted to feel like that again: trapped. Caged.

Why I was applying to be a nanny was beyond me.

If I had had any sense, I'd have read a few books, maybe "Nanny 101," or "Nannying for Idiots," or even "What Not to Wear on Your Nanny Interview." But I read nothing, and showed up at the interview in my street clothes, which would have gone down perfectly well in theater circles, but not so much in nanny circles, or the mothers who hire.

I wore: black opaque tights, black suede heels, a tiny black and red plaid mini-skirt, a black sleeveless semi-sheer tank, and a short, black jacket. Designer Vivienne Westwood would have loved me that day, but she was not looking for a nanny; Angie was.

This is how Angie later described me:

The young woman standing on the doorstep could have come straight from a Hollywood film set. A mass of sheeny black curls cascaded down her back. Full lips were glossed scarlet against a perfect pale complexion. She wore a spray-on tight mini skirt and little black sweater leaving no doubt about her curves. She teetered on kitten-heel shoes.

I had taken a moment to glimpse through the sitting room window, as I always did when someone rang the front doorbell, making sure I wanted to open the door. To say I was shocked is understatement. I would never have imagined such a person as the owner of the warm, slightly shy voice on the phone answering my advertisement for a nanny for my sons Zek, 9, and Cato, 5.

Perhaps I should have taken pause when she gave me her name — Lisa del Rosso — which certainly has a touch of the flamboyant about it, or when I picked up the New York twang. But she sounded nice and enthusiastic and I needed a replacement nanny badly.

The door opened and a barefoot, lithe blond woman in leggings and a blue top greeted me, complete with a blond male child clutching her side.

"Hello, I'm Angela," she said. *"Won't you come in?"*

We walked down a hallway with a checked black and white floor, then through a heavy door into a mauve-colored kitchen. Angie left me for a moment, taking blond male child with her.

You Are All a Part of Me

I looked around, startled, and realized I was not in another home, or even another country; I was in another world entirely. Their house was a sensory-overload experience. The walls in the kitchen had writing all over them, great scrawls of pencil, up to say, four feet high. *The children were allowed to write on the walls?* In the house I grew up in, if I had deliberately put one mark on *any* of the walls that would have been cause for a good dose of corporal punishment.

There was an ugly, grey, unvarnished table that would not have looked out of place in the woods of Maine in lieu of a normal kitchen table, with long picnic benches to match. There was something called an AGA which heated the whole room and looked pretty old-fashioned and very cool. Colorful crockery piled up in and around the sink. Books, notes, magazines, newspapers and postcards covered every counter, shelf, and most of the table. From the kitchen, one could walk straight through to the sitting room, in an open-plan fashion. There, a worn, green leather sofa crammed with overstuffed pillows in African prints and a wicker chair worse for wear sat on a stripped pine floor. On the walls, a large, neon painting of two girls sitting next to each other with their knees up, showing their vaginas co-existed next to black and white photographs of what looked like parts of Africa.

I walked away from the neon vaginas and back into the kitchen. There were French doors that opened out onto an enormous, walled garden, at least 120 feet in length, which was surprising for London. More surprising were the chickens, not in a coop but roaming freely (the coop was at the very back, in a corner, I later found), and a large, panther-like cat being ardently pursued by a bowling ball-shaped white bunny.

I was definitely through the looking glass.

Angela called to me from the kitchen. "*Tea?*"

"Yes, please," I said, walking back in and sitting down at the picnic table.

But could this glamour puss so inappropriately turned out for the rough and tumble of our energetic, high-spirited and at times unruly boys, possibly be the right stuff?

Still, Lisa, 19, had journeyed across London and I should at least invite her in for a cup of tea, and a brief chat, and then it would be thanks, but no thanks, I decided.

Angela asked what I was doing in London, and I told her about LAMDA, singing, and the hope of pursuing some sort of performance career. From there, we segued into museums, theater and books. We seemed to have similar interests and be on the same wavelength, so I didn't feel intimidated at all, despite the fact that I really did not know exactly why I was there. And she seemed strangely…interested in me. This might have been because she was so used to interviewing people, but I didn't know that then. Angela has a gift for making people feel comfortable; that what they do in the world matters.

"Do you want children?" Angela said.

This was an interview question?

"No, I don't," I said.

"Oh really, why not?"

And I told her. She said they all sounded like sensible reasons.

Then blond male child came bounding into the room. *"This is Cato. He's five."*

What kind of a name is that?

"Ang, who's this?" he said, rubbing his eyes.

"This is Lisa, Cato."

And they call their mother by her first name. Of course they do.

Another, older child came in, with an unruly mop of bronze hair and a scowl on his face. He was carrying a soccer ball.

"This is Zek, and he's nine."

Not Zak, not Zeb, not Zeke, but Zek. Okay. If I had that name, I'd scowl, too. The boys kept inching closer to me to get a better look.

"So you're American?" said Zek, with an unmistakable note of disdain.

"That's right."

There was a pause. What did he expect, that I'd deny it?

His small chest was puffed out, like one of those little Blowfish.

"Americans are rubbish at football, y'know."

"You think so?"

"Complete rubbish."

"I used to play on a team," I said.

"Did not!"

"I did. Team won town champs every year I played, too. We were really, *really* good."

Zek paused. He looked at his ball. He looked back at me. *"Prove it."*

I said, "When?"

He said, *"Now."*

I looked at Angie. I really wanted to kick this kid's ass, and I'd do it in bare feet if I had to. "What size shoe do you take?" I asked.

"39, something," she said.

"Um… translate that?" I said.

"7 and a half, I think."

"Close enough. Do you have a pair of sneakers I can borrow?"

That might have been that, but within minutes of Lisa perching decoratively on the sofa, Zek, our elder son, came into the room. He heard Lisa 's transatlantic twang and burst out: "You are American! I bet you can't play football".

The years I played goalie in middle school, I found out I had incredibly fast reflexes, a perfect skill for that position. I also found out I could kick a soccer ball very, very high and very, very far.

Across the street, out on Highbury Fields, I continued to listen to Zek berate Americans and watch him stick his chest out, until I knocked the ball out of his hands.

"Go to the end of the fields."

"What?"

"Go to the end of the fields."

"Right, like you can…"

It was a perfect, early June day: not too hot or too cool. The grass on the field was a green I have only ever seen in the UK and Ireland, due to the rain; the sun was shining in a bright, blue sky. The English call this kind of day rare.

When I kicked the ball, it went so high and so far, I stopped watching it and instead watched Zek and Cato's heads go up, up, up, and then all the way down.

All was quiet for a moment. Then Zek called to me.

"I was wrong! You can play soccer."

We stayed out there for about forty-five minutes, playing and kicking the ball around. It was great fun.

It was a moment of transformation! Lisa kicked off her high-heels, asked if she could borrow a pair of sneakers and within minutes she was out on the green opposite our home with Zek and Cato, playing a makeshift football match. And, as Lisa later put it, she "kicked the crap out of them."

That impressed me as much as it did the boys, and during the "trial day" Lisa came to spend with us, I was won over by her artless friendliness, her obvious delight in the unorthodox way we lived, and her immediate rapport with the boys.

Angie hired me, and two days later, I moved in.

We all sort of fell in love with each other; Angie had no daughter and I had no family in London. Being the boys' nanny never felt like a job, it was more like being paid to play and wrestle and get mucky, like an older sister. It completed the circle of my interrupted childhood. Angie once told me, *"I've always said my children are the best form of birth control."* Except, I became that daughter and for over twenty years, they have been my second family. My life was changed irrevocably because I listened to a voice I swear I heard, and made a phone call.

Published in *Barking Sycamores Neurodivergent Literary Magazine* 2016

Confederates

ON THE STEAMY AFTERNOON OF MEMORIAL DAY 2014, I found myself standing in a Confederate cemetery in Fredericksburg, Virginia, among many miniature Confederate flags undulating in the breeze. We had missed the ceremony and re-enactment but I found a program on the ground that said, among other things "The Ladies Memorial Day Association, 148th Memorial Day Observance. On the walkway, see the wreaths presented by Confederate organizations and individuals to honor the Confederate dead."

It made me uneasy. My friends and I had just come from the Union Cemetery, where there were speeches and soldiers and a number of black people were present. I doubted any blacks would have felt welcome here. Then it occurred to me I was being uncharitable, so honor your dead, I thought, but must there be a proliferation of Confederate flags?

I periodically stay at a former plantation not far from both the Union and Confederate cemeteries, along with my friends: two Brits, a Dutchman and a southern amateur historian.

My friend Patrick Neustatter (one of the Brits) lives with his wife, Paula (the southern amateur historian), on a 35-acre expanse called "Belle Hill," circa 1815. I call it "the estate" to tease him, but it is far too ramshackle and welcoming to deserve such a snooty moniker.

I know Patrick through his sister Angie (the other Brit) and her husband, Olly (the Dutchman). I was once nanny to their two small boys in London, where I lived for ten years (though not all of them as their nanny) and met Patrick around the same time. So when they come from London to visit Patrick, I come from New York by train to visit all of them.

I didn't know a whole lot about Fredericksburg nor Belle Hill, but the first time I walked through Patrick's grounds, I noticed trenches and little markers. These were left over from the Civil War, and their history was explained to me by Paula, who researched diaries from the time period and spoke with descendants of people who actually lived in Belle Hill, as many of the county records prior to 1842 were destroyed by fire. This is from Paula's blog:

> "*During the winter of 1862-63 General Stonewall Jackson's troops wintered at Moss Neck and the division of Jackson's troops under the command of Lt General Ambrose P. Hill (for whom A.P. Hill was named) camped in the woods of Belle Hill, Prospect Hill and Santee. The trenches and gun pits dug by those troops 148 years ago are still visible to this day.*"

Paula said the biggest difference about the house is the way it looked in the winter of 1862-63, which was a trodden mess, to the way it looks now. It began as a four-room summerhouse, and she surmises it was part of a larger, 200-acre plantation nearby called Prospect Hill that bordered the Santee plantation.

Now, the house is a sprawling place with too many rooms to count, perfect for when loads of people come to stay for weeks on end. The grounds look like a bucolic, forested wonderland, complete with a lake and the most spectacular sunsets over the Blue Ridge Mountains, six counties away. One can see this from the dining room every single night. My envy knows no bounds.

Then there is the wildlife. Birds: cardinals, hummingbirds, mockingbirds, sparrows, goldfinches, mourning doves and more I cannot identify. Bugs and large flying creatures I choose not to identify. We came home from a dinner in Richmond a few nights before and no one had managed to remember to leave any lights on. As we pulled in, headlights blazing, it looked like three families of deer had been picnicking on the front lawn with their children and we had spoiled their party. They ran off, and we oohed and aah-ed. We city folk, that is. For Paddy and Paula, this is the norm in their fairly isolated, spectacular spot.

The average daily routine has been as follows: yoga with Angie and Olly at 9 am on the outside deck for an hour, to Hyperion at 11 for a coffee, then off for a walk somewhere for hours, then afternoon reading and talking and talking and talking and perhaps Tango (Angie and Olly) or taking photographs (Olly or occasionally, me), cocktail hour at 6, dinner at 7:30, then fighting over which movie to watch and Angie is the bossiest so she usually wins, then the older folks to bed before midnight while I go upstairs and try to write something, then fall asleep. Olly turned to me after one more blissful day and said, "I could get used to this, eh?"

I said, with mixed feelings, "Me, too."

There is a guesthouse on the property, where Angie and Olly are put so they don't cause too much disruption. This was originally the slave quarters/kitchen to the main house. Before the Civil War, Fredericksburg had a thriving slave trade. In fact, walking to the butcher's in the center of town I passed a stump of some sort, stopped and doubled back: it was a preserved slave auction block, with a plaque in front of it which read "Fredericksburg's Principal Auction Site in Pre-Civil War Days for Slaves and Property." It was dedicated in 1984 because that is how long it took to decide whether or not to put Fredericksburg's ugly past right on display, but dates back to 1857 in the selling of slaves.

Juxtaposed with the stump, Fredericksburg is quaint in an old town, small scale, preserved New England kind of way. It is charming, with antique shops, mom-and-pop restaurants and flowerpots dotting the sidewalks. There are even a few wonderful thrift and consignment shops (my personal weakness). The city seems keen on keeping older buildings alive and it is a pleasure to spend time wandering around with no particular destination. Fredericksburg also has a terrific, informative museum, comprising two entire three-floor buildings containing both permanent and temporary exhibitions (and free for educators, a nice plus for visiting adjunct professors). There is a Fredericksburg at War section, detailing the slave trade before the war, freedom after and struggle for equality; George Washington's Mason membership; while "Our Community" considers Fredericksburg's African American community via the Civil Rights Movement up to the present day.

On Memorial Day, Ang, Olly and I were taken to the Union cemetery for a ceremony. There was a man dressed up as Lincoln, a man dressed up as Grant, a woman as Mary Lincoln, etc.... There was a knowledgeable Civil War scholar who drew a diverse crowd and a soldier in Union garb standing sentient waiting to play taps. As we were leaving, Ang and I got to talking about the unfairness of war; that is, if you had enough money you could buy yourself out of fighting in the Civil War, so as usual, the poor and working class fight the battles others create. Then I said, Yes, but say this war wasn't fought, then what? The South secedes. There's no body of water between North and South so it's always a hostile border. And it didn't begin because of slavery per se but about the economics of slavery and control of that system, so then what? We still have slaves today? No. That war had to be fought and Lincoln was the right man for the job. And Angie said, Well, it's just like World War II. Do you let Hitler do a takeover, exterminate everyone except the Aryans and then what? Hitler takes over the world? That war absolutely had to be fought, and as Lincoln was the right man for the job, so was Churchill; bloody Chamberlain just would have let the whole thing happen.

Then we went off and had a lovely lunch.

History is history because it can be judged from a distance; and judged easily when it is not my head on the chopping block, not my brother's, not my sister's, not my family, not my friends.

Actually, before we went to lunch, Paula and Paddy wanted to take us to the Confederate Cemetery. It's a little bit of a misnomer; the Fredericksburg Confederate Cemetery, dedicated in 1870, is small and a larger non-denominational cemetery has been built around it. Lee, or someone, who looks like a noted Confederate leader stands on a hill. Its upkeep is the responsibility of aforementioned The Ladies' Memorial Association.

This is from the Memorial Day Speech, May 31, 2010, by Jerry H. Brent:

"According similar treatment to the dead was just as important to Southerners as it was to those in the north. By 1864, townspeople had begun to bury Confederates in the City Cemetery, in neat graves. But, after the war ended, the Federal government, quite understandably, was not about to foot the bill to so honor their recently vanquished foe. Thus it fell to private individuals and groups to find the means to create a cemetery for their fallen heroes. In 1866, the Ladies Memorial Association was organized to accomplish this important task. The plan was to raise as much money locally and within the state as possible, and then issue an appeal to be sent all throughout the southern states for funds. In 1867 the association was able to purchase the property that would soon become the Confederate Cemetery. Soon the work began of gathering the dead from the surrounding battlefields resulting in the graves of approximately 3,300 that you see before you today."

I understand all of this. There is a large amount of pride for the Confederate cause in Fredericksburg: It is their heritage, the sacrifices of their forefathers, the convictions of their ancestors and also, at the time, perhaps being exploited by the North economically. But skipping down, I got to:

"Thus, at first, all efforts were focused on the proper burial and memorializing of the dead. But once this task was accomplished, there began to be an interest amongst the veterans of the conflict to gather and relive old times and honor their fallen comrades."

Reading "veterans of the conflict to gather and relive old times…" on the Fredericksburg Confederate Cemetery website made me as uneasy as standing among all those tiny Confederate flags.

After Memorial Day, we all took a trip to Washington DC. As Paddy drove, Paula turned to me, pointed, and said, "Look up."

And there, waving in the wind, was an enormous Confederate Flag, right on the I95.

"The 90-foot-tall flagpole is firmly — and legally — planted in private property on the other side of a tree barrier from the highway near mile marker 134. The flag, measuring 30 feet by 22 feet, is a reminder that in Virginia, the battles of 150 years ago are still divisive and deeply felt." (Susan Svrluga, "Confederate Flag along I95 divides Virginia community")

This banner was raised by an activist group, the Virginia Flaggers, whose forty or so core members say they want to protect the Civil War standard. The group rejects the idea that it's a symbol of racism and hate. On the contrary: Barry Isenhour, who is active in the group, says that when he sees the giant flag along the interstate, he feels pride and reverence.

As he drives through Stafford County (Va.) for his work as a sales representative for a winery, Isenhour often thinks of all the Civil War battles that were fought in the area. He has ancestors who fought for the South, some of them buried in unmarked graves.

"I know there are soldiers up there lying under buildings, under trees, who have never been properly buried. It rends my heart," he said. "They are veterans. They put their lives on the line for the common people they love."

Aston Haughton, president of the Stafford County chapter of the NAACP, sees it differently. The flag, he said, "symbolizes racism, oppression. It reminds people of the days of slavery"

"It's a racist statement," he [Sanchez, a Californian living in Virginia] said. "I wish someone would put a flag up right next to it, or across from it. A Union flag."

There you have it, in a nutshell: a tale of two cemeteries.

What I have seen of Virginia is spectacularly beautiful, the people friendly, and I'd like to explore more of the state. Fortunately, I am a good houseguest (I do dishes, cook, and don't tear open bread through the plastic wrap on the side like a wild animal which leaves a gaping hole, like some other visitors I could mention, Angie) so I keep getting invited back to Belle Hill. Paula said, "You don't come here often enough." Perhaps on the next Memorial Day, it might be an idea for the re-enactors in the Confederate Cemetery and in the Union Cemetery to put down their fake guns and honor their dead together in neutral, de-flagged territory. Then they can all go off for a lovely lunch. Because the Civil War is over. Isn't it?

Published in *The Literary Explorer*, 2014

Things to Fix Around the House

THE BATHROOM DOOR REALLY SAID IT ALL. There was a massive crack in the center, which I had papered and painted over, then hung a mermaid made out of coconuts to mask the problem. From the inside of the bathroom, however, the crack was entirely visible. Because Yash had broken the door, he said he would fix it himself.

"I will."

"Okay," I said.

Weeks went by.

"Are you going to fix that door?"

"Yes."

"When? Time's a'wasting."

"I know, I know, I know," said Yash.

Months flew by.

"WHEN?" I yelled.

"I know, I know, I know!" Yash yelled back.

A year went by, and I wrote on the back of the door, "Yash broke this door and promised to fix it a year ago." Another year went by, and I crossed out 'a year' and wrote 'two years.' Three years later, I wrote, "Yash promised to fix this door many, many years ago and it will never be fixed. Until we're dead. And then, by someone else."

My brother-in-law Alan, Yash's older brother, once said he was supremely shocked when his seven-year-old adopted son took apart the alarm clock he had been given, wanting to see how it all worked inside. "No one," Alan said, "No one had ever done that in our family. We had no facility for wanting to know how things worked."

You Are All a Part of Me

Except Alan is no longer my brother-in-law, as I am no longer married to Yash: not for about a year and a half now. Yash had no idea what a marriage entailed, nor had any interest in fixing what was wrong. Some of our friends and family know our situation, but not all. No one at Yash's job knows, and since he still wears his wedding ring, there is no reason to tell. I still call him husband, and he still calls me wife. We are each other's "in case of emergency." We share the apartment, share meals together that I cook, but not the bed. The bed sort of looms each night, but dissolves into a nothingness, because the bed, or the lack of what goes on in the bed, is not discussed. Not yet.

Yash and I have known each other for eleven (as of 2011, when this essay was published) years. He is quite possibly the kindest man I have ever encountered. On one of our first dates, we walked past the Ben & Jerry's at the end of 43rd Street and 8th Avenue and there was a contemporary Jayne Mansfield-type coming out, wearing a pink, off-the-shoulder angora sweater. Everyone turned: men, women, children, pigeons. I said to Yash, "Did you see that woman?" He said, "Yes, she was carrying a double chocolate-dipped waffle cone with two scoops, strawberry and cookies & cream, whipped cream, and nuts." It was then I discovered Yash was obsessed with food and exercise respectively, and that he was someone I could love. When I took him to Cape Cod, to meet my parents, after the first meal my mother pulled me aside and said, in all seriousness, "I don't think we're going to have enough food to feed Yash for three days." I said, "That's okay, we'll go food shopping." And we did. Quickly.

Out of all the men I had dated, Yash was the one I felt the most comfortable with, exposing warts and all to.

We had a spectacular evening wedding, in late September. It was small, about thirty people, in the back garden of a midtown restaurant called Luxia. My mother gave me away. Yash's mother was in red, neglecting her walker, having a fine time. My man of honor was Derek, my best friend, who attended with his wife, Carol, and their adorable toddler children, Ian and Julia. A friend's jazz trio played all night long. Under the tree with the colored glass bulbs, we pledged our love to each other. After our vows and toasts, I said to all, "Everyone I love is in this room."

Yash had some troubles he didn't tell me about before the wedding, troubles I didn't know about until we began living together. Long before our engagement, he had begun finishing the bachelor's degree he did not receive after dropping out of college at twenty-one. It meant a lot to Yash to complete the degree and I was very proud of him for going back to school in his thirties. With his previous credits, he was told it would only take him a year or so. But he stopped doing his homework before our wedding and stalled afterwards. He gave me all kinds of reasons: he was tired, he had ADD, he couldn't concentrate. So he would not do the work, but would not quit, either. On beautiful Sunday afternoons, I asked him to go for walks with me in Riverside Park and he always declined, saying he had work to do. So I walked alone. Hours later, I would come back to find that nothing had been done. I was baffled. I tried pleading, cajoling, praising, shouting; doing anything to get him to do his homework and get on with his life. This escalated into screaming fights standing in front of his computer. To me, it felt like a mother and son dynamic, not a wife and husband dynamic. At one point I said to him, "What do you want from me?"

Yash said, "Well, after we got married, I expected you to help me more."

"How?" I asked. "What more can I do?"

This limbo stalled us for over three years; as a result, we never had the "honeymoon period" most couples have, and all I was, was incredibly angry with him. So angry I didn't want him in the bed, or to touch me in any way. This was not what I signed on for, I reasoned, he lied to me; this isn't fair! We had no social life, because in addition to the homework struggle that took up his spare time, we worked completely opposite schedules: I taught college writing, and he worked in a restaurant. My lonely walks got longer and longer, and the sunshine ceased making me happy. So I began having affairs, to make myself feel better. Each one, long or short, was disastrous in its own way; if not to me, then to the other man I chose to involve.

The situation between Yash and me did not get any better, though I hoped it would. We tried counseling three or four times, to fix our troubles, but nothing helped. One dubbed us "the irresistible force meets the immoveable object." The last of the counselors, a wonderful man, said, "You know, Lisa, Yash is a man who won't budge until he is standing on a cliff with his heels on the edge and the ground is crumbling beneath his feet." Despondent, I moved out. Yash still called me every night, and I let him, even though I was seeing someone else at the time. I took off my wedding rings, but Yash still came to visit, anxious and depressed. We slept together. He loved me, he said, and promised things would be different.

Months later, I moved back. After waiting for what seemed an interminable length of time for something, anything to change, I filed for divorce.

Joan Didion wrote, in *The Year of Magical Thinking* (and I paraphrase) that marriage isn't just about love: it's about time and memory and a past that you both share. I was there for both of Yash's parents' deaths; I read the eulogy at his mother's service. I said goodbye to her, shrouded in white, in her casket, and tossed a handful of earth into her grave. I sat Shiva with the family, and cooked and served because no one else could touch anything. My sister-in-law Abby said, jokingly, "You could rent yourself out for a lot of money, Lisa. You're good at this!" Yash has met my now-estranged father, whom I will never see again. Two cats have been put down, and a third is on the way; there have been countless Christmas Eve feasts, menorahs lit, birthday carousel rides in Central Park, trips to Europe, the West Coast, and summer holidays on the Cape.

The day I got my divorce decree, I cried, called my mother, who was alarmed as I do not cry, as a rule, so she talked me down off the ledge of personal and profound failure and I hung up, took a big breath, and then, a funny thing happened: all of my anger, all of my rage at Yash… disappeared. Vanished. It was like a stone was rolled away from my heart.

Gone.

Did getting divorced fix my marriage? Somewhat. Not totally. There are things we have not dealt with yet. Yet. I did tell Yash about the affairs and he has forgiven me, he says, unless he really thinks about it. Since the telling, other men hold no allure for me. It's like a spell was broken. As for Yash, he finished his degree. His troubles are getting smaller, and he works on them every day. He sees a specialist for ADD, so the onus is off me. He is… more considerate, and never says no to a walk with me. The divorce for him has meant that he no longer takes me for granted. But we have both changed profoundly, I think: there are no more expectations, because the words "wife" and "husband" no longer intrinsically carry any. We are kinder, more accepting of each other: more forgiving. We are not married any longer but choose to be together still. He is the person I want to come home to, tell my stories to, share my life with. Some of our friends and family think our situation is very odd. My sister said, "Getting divorced to get rid of your anger is a little extreme, isn't it?" But I didn't know, could not have known, that that would be the case. I thought that little piece of paper freedom would propel me out, ready to begin a new life. I had no idea that the divorce would be the key to shedding my internal anger, or my pain. That it would be the way to forgive Yash.

Last week, something broke in the apartment and the conversation went like this:

"The fixture is crooked and the chain is jammed," I said, looking up.

"What?" Yash said.

"From when you tried to fix the ceiling fan yesterday. The ceiling fan I told you not to touch."

Yash groaned, shook his head, and laughed.

"You know, husband, when I married you I accepted it when you told me you were not a handy Jew. You are skilled in other areas. I thought you had accepted that as well."

"Well," Yash said, "I just thought I could…"

"Could…?" I said, waiting.

You Are All a Part of Me

"Make it a little worse?"

I began to laugh, and Yash picked up the phone to call the super.

Published in *The New York Times*, 2011

My Mother-In-Law and Me

"You know," Libby said to me, "we're a lot alike, the Italians and the Jews. We fight, we yell, we eat... we fight, we eat, we fight... we fight...but we still love each other, ya know."

That was how I intended to end the eulogy about my mother-in-law. I just wasn't sure how the rest of it would go down, so I was nervous, squirming in my seat, sweating up a storm. Libby was both deliberately and inadvertently very, very funny. She could be razor sharp and deeply profane. While personal eulogies are no longer allowed in Catholic churches, I was hoping the Conservative branch of Judaism would have a sense of humor. Besides, I reasoned, once I was up there, no one could stop me. I intended to begin with the first time we met.

Her son Yash — not yet my husband — and I were coming from Manhattan to Long Island for a Seder, which would have been my first Seder except we were late. Very late. As in, we missed the entire ceremony and everyone was now in the downstairs living room watching a movie. Except Libby. She was seated on one of two red velvet-covered chairs that resembled matching thrones. Yash introduced us and left me alone on the couch to go and rummage for leftovers. Libby gave me the once over and the very first thing she said to me was, "So, why do you date my son, what is about my son that you like, out of all of the men in the world why would you want to date my son?"

I paused. Out of all the things I imagined she would ask me, this was not one of them.

"I guess I date your son because he has a great body. Yeah, a great body. That's why I date your son," I replied.

She said, "Oh, is that what young people go for nowadays?"

I answered, "I think that's what young people have always gone for, actually."

Libby tilted her chin down so that her thin, black-rimmed glasses slid down her nose and her dark eyes peered at me, as she said, "Ooooh."

Then she paused and shouted, "YASH! Get your girlfriend some food."

After that, we were thick as thieves.

So she was very unhappy, a few years after we married, to find out there was trouble between Yash and me.

"Please don't divorce my son, whatever you do, don't divorce my son, please, please, please," she begged.

"Okay," I said into the phone, alarmed.

My reasons for saying okay were: guilt, panic, and to stop her from crying. I knew I was lying but I wanted to take away the pain in her voice, the pain she was feeling.

The shakiness of my marriage between me and Yash was a disappointment to her because she loved me and I was part of her family. But change happens. Two years later, we were separated and Libby was dead.

I didn't talk to her specifically about Yash. She already knew his shortcomings perfectly well and a few times listed them in public, at family dinners, until, at the end of her rant, she would blame herself, saying that his failings were not his fault because she had never had any self-esteem and therefore could not instill it in her son. Then she would sob. Startled the first time it happened and angry the next, I spoke with Yash privately, urging him to tell his mother to cease the public displays and if she had anything to say to him she should do so in private.

But to me, she was always encouraging, personable, even deferential. After she was widowed, she became increasingly housebound and her phone was her weapon of choice. Though she did not drive, this was not the reason for the narrowing of her world. Her home was where she felt safe, where all her stuff was and the place she wanted to die. She had Meals on Wheels delivered as well as newspapers and library books. Her neighbors looked in on her regularly. All of her children and grandchildren visited often. There was no reason for her to leave. Because of her phone, she never lost contact with the outside world.

Sometimes when I got home from work, there would be eight or nine or ten messages on the answering machine. When we talked, the calls could last an hour or more. She always asked, what was new? What had I done today? What did I see, where did I go, what did I do? She seemed to live vicariously through her phone line; she read me articles and told me all sorts of Jewish jokes that she either found or her eldest son sent her, and sometimes, she would sing old songs from the 40's and 50's, and fortunately I could sing most of them along with her. Show tunes, too. It did not hurt that I knew all the words to "Brush Up Your Shakespeare" from "Kiss Me Kate." She saved most of her venom for President George W. Bush, calling him the worst name she could call anyone: "He's an anti-Semite, Lisa, just like his father. That ----" (Expletive.)

But mostly, we talked about family and food. She asked about my sisters, mother and my estranged father, the latter whom she referred to as, "that jerk" or, "that deadbeat." She talked about her grandchildren and how much she missed her husband. She knew I was from New England, so we talked about my love of Cape Cod and how much she loved lobster with a lot of butter even though she wasn't supposed to. When she asked what I was cooking and I said sauce or steak, she always said, "That sounds nice." She'd confess to me when she'd eat Chinese food on paper plates, and feel guilty about it, but that didn't stop her from doing it from time to time.

Mothers-in-law get a bum rap, rather like wicked stepmothers. They are traditionally meddlers, harridans, and they were the staple of Borsht Belt comedians. That was not the case with Libby. After being married and unmarried to Yash and knowing his siblings, I believe that in many ways she treated me better than her own children. Like grandparents who are better to their grandchildren than they were to their own children, so was my mother-in-law better to me. I don't believe she loved me more than her children; love had nothing to do with it. Rather, it was the distance — not directly responsible for my wellbeing, for my being successful in the world — that made it easy for her to be my ally.

When she died, I was the one to tell Yash. I was at his apartment that night, around eight o'clock, visiting the cats, and his older brother, Alan, called and told me. I burst into tears, then composed myself, grabbed a coat, walked down to the restaurant where he worked, told his manager because it was the height of the dinner hour, and told Yash. He seemed shocked, unable to take it in. We went home and I stayed with him. No one asked me if I would be going to the funeral, it was assumed I would be there. In fact, it never occurred to me *not* to go. I wanted to go, for both Yash and Libby. Once arrangements were being made, I asked Yash if anyone other than the rabbi would be speaking. Her eldest son would say something, he said. "No one else?" I asked. "No friends, no other relations? No one is going to talk about her sense of humor?" I wanted to speak; I wanted to represent what I knew and how I felt about Libby. After all, I loved her. Alan said, "Of course Lisa can speak."

So I stood up, in my grey Calvin Klein sleeveless sheath (as I write this line, I think of the play "Love, Loss and What I Wore" and how the Ephron sisters nailed perfectly the particular way the memory of women and their clothes works), and I told stories about Libby. People laughed, cried, laughed some more and afterwards, strangers grabbed me and said, "That is exactly how she was, you know."

I do know. Had she been there, Libby would have laughed the loudest.

Published in The Huffington Post, 2011/2012

Roses In His Cheeks

I THOUGHT HE WAS DEAD. I really did.

Out of the two of us, I always assumed I would go first, always. Yash only has things go wrong with him when he lifts too many big weights and then tears bits of his body that need to be repaired. Epilepsy can't be repaired and has no cure, so brain disorders trump athletic injuries. I win. I die first.

And that is what I was thinking, amongst other things, when Yash passed out in the chair, as I was trying to hold up his heavy body with one arm and a shoulder and staunch the blood with a cloth in the other hand. Neither was working. The gash on his forehead continued to flow and I had never thought about his weight before, but of course, muscle weighs more than fat, and so Yash was heavier than I thought he would be. He had also turned an alarming shade of wet sand: cold, skin clammy to the touch, underneath his eyes completely black, eyelids closed. This is what he'll look like dead, I thought, and he can't hear me and won't know me and will not respond to me. I wondered if all women who divorced men but continued to live with their former spouses still cared about them, dead or alive, but I did.

He had banged his head on that same, sharp corner of the book-shelf before, emitting the same cry each time, unusual for him, as he is an even-keel kind of person. The damage had always been minimal, barely a scratch, and it never occurred to either one of us to change the position of his desk or perhaps not store the stepladder underneath the lowest shelf. Most accidents happen inside the house, we sometimes said to one another in mocking, parental tones, and then burst out laughing.

This time, I heard the cry and said, "Oh, what did you do now?"

Yash stood up, blood spewing from his head, a lump rising and not looking well at all. I made him sit down at the kitchen table, got him some juice, and he said, "I feel kind of woozy." And he went out, just like that. I was amazed that it happened so fast. One second he was there, one second gone, and suddenly that silt-grey color, with no response to what I was saying. I sort of kept jostling him as best I could, holding him upright and with the same arm, I patted his back and continued talking to him.

"Yash, wake up, talk to me, you are not going to die on me today, no way, come on, wake up Yash, talk to me, no way are going to die on me today, wake up, wake up, wake up." And then I burst out laughing.

Stress does strange things to a person. Laughter. Why? Release? Disbelief at the situation I was in? Who knows? And while I was talking and laughing and rubbing Yash's back, I thought nine million things in those seconds or minutes he was out, about Natasha Richardson dying so young and vibrant over a fall she believed to be only silly, about being alone in the world without Yash in my life and that he needs to fight and come back from wherever he is now, just like I wanted him to do when we were married, fight for me, fight for us, but he didn't, couldn't, and why did I divorce him anyway and that's really mean payback, for Yash to die on me after I divorced him, really not fair at all and I have no chance of payback myself if he dies, I'm just left to suck it up for the rest of my life…

We are young, too young to be thinking about death, but since the epilepsy and even before that, I think about it more and more. I think a lot about quality rather than quantity, and because I have largely done what I wanted to do with my life, I'd be okay with it. Don't get me wrong: there will always be more stories to write and I would always elect the "more time" option if there was one, but I think that's the same for most people.

And then Yash woke up. Came to. Color back in his cheeks. "Hi," he said.

"Hi," I said.

Then I had a seizure. Now I know how I react to extreme stress. I had to rest on the floor, but didn't black out. I could talk through it, which was good because Yash was too weak to help me. He could only watch.

What a pair, I thought.

After we both composed ourselves, we went to the emergency room to make sure Yash did not have a concussion.

"I hope I don't get a needle," Yash said.

"I hope you do," I said, "because I thought you were dead."

"I'm sorry," he said.

"You should be," I said. And then I hugged him and never wanted to let him go.

He did not have a concussion. The doctor put some clear gel on his forehead, to close the gash. He did get a shot, for tetanus. I laughed only to myself. Yash told the doctor I had a seizure, which I brushed off, because there's nothing an ER can do for a seizure disorder other than admit me for tests, and I didn't want that.

We finally went home and considered filing down that edge of the bookshelf. We lay down on the still-made bed together, and I said to him, "I thought you were dead."

"I know," he said, "I'm sorry."

He closed his eyes, and I turned out the light. I kissed him and thought, I really hope I go first.

Aurora

MY ACTOR FRIEND, JT, was leaving his basement apartment in the Rockaways for six weeks in August to do a show in Massachusetts. His place was five minutes from the beach, I love the beach, and I was off until September, so asked if I could stay there to finish a play I was working on. He said, "Sure." He dropped off the keys beforehand. A few days after he had gone, I took the train from the Upper West Side to his place, which was about an hour away.

I had a small suitcase with me and set it down in front of the door. As I turned the key in the lock, I heard a "meow," looked down, and there was a small, striking, green-eyed, grey, long-haired Persian cat. JT had said nothing about a cat. To my knowledge, he had no cat. However, he also had an inner St. Francis of Assisi and animals of all sorts were attracted to him — squirrels, birds, mice, all city creatures — then he'd feed them and the animals never wanted to leave.

So I called him. "What's up with the cat?" I said.

He said, "Oh, the cat. Well, just put some food in a dish and leave it outside and she'll be fine."

I said, "What's the cat's name?"

He said, "I don't have a cat. I'm an actor; I'm not home long enough to keep a pet."

Baffled, I said, "You feed the cat. So she is your cat."

He said, "No, I don't have a cat. Just put some food out and she won't bother you."

And I should have known, when I opened his kitchen cupboard to find no human food but at least one hundred cans of cat food, that JT was a big, fat liar. Or delusional. One or the other.

I changed and went to the beach. Took a walk for a couple of hours. Then I went to the nearest market and picked up some human food for myself. I got back, ate and wrote till about 2 AM, then crashed into bed. A good day all around.

YE-OWL! YE-OWL! YE-OWL!

In JT's bedroom, there was a screened-in window above my head and that is where the same striking cat was, at four in the morning, YE-OWLING her head off.

I got up. I called JT. My intention was to wake him. Because if I am awake at 4 AM, then therefore, everyone should be awake to keep my miserable self company.

"What's up with cat?" I said.

"The cat?" he said, yawning.

"Yes, the same cat yowling her head off outside the bedroom window."

"Oh, the cat," he said. "Just let her in, give her some food, she'll sleep in the bed with you and she won't bother you."

Now, as he was saying this, I did let the cat in, and she seemed remarkably familiar with her surroundings.

I said, "*Sleep in the bed with me?* You let her sleep in the bed with you? Then she's your fucking cat!"

"I don't have cat! I'm an actor!"

"I don't give a shit what you are — you feed her and she sleeps in your bed! She is your damn cat!"

"No she is not!"

"What is the cat's name?"

"She is not my cat and she doesn't have a name!"

"She is your fucking cat and you need to name her!"

"She is not my fucking cat!"

JT and I have known each other for a very long time. Can you tell?

Meanwhile, the cat had perched herself on a black box of some sort and was tilting her head, listening to my raised voice. I watched her watch me. Then I looked closer.

I said, "Your cat is sitting on your fucking shredder, you asshole. The name on the shredder is "Aurora" and that is the name of your fucking cat!"

JT, by this time, was laughing/angry at the same time. "I told you she is not my fucking…!!"

I hung up on him.

And that is how Aurora came to be named after a shredder.

Aurora made herself at home. I let her out daily when I went to the beach, and by the time I came back, she had deposited presents for me in front of my door: beautiful, tiny, yellow and brown birds, black crickets, all dead.

I was a little concerned she was decimating the local wildlife.

The day after she slept in the bed, I was covered in flea bites; I don't know how long she had been living outside, but she was flea-ridden. So I searched online for a toxin-free flea bath, ran out and bought it, put on gloves, locked us both in the bathroom and soaked her down. It was horrible, kind of like the scene from the movie *The Miracle Worker* where Annie Sullivan tries to get Helen Keller to eat all those awful scrambled eggs — for hours. I had to de-flea her twice and each time, she looked at me with such pained eyes I felt like a guilty, bad person. But once her fur was all wet and stuck to her I saw how skinny she was, skinny like a winter squirrel.

Aurora had gotten to me.

So, I went on a research mission. Aurora had on a pink, faded collar with a heart on it, so she must have had an owner. I called JT. He didn't know. I asked neighbors. JT called the neighbors. They didn't know. I asked the man who owned the house JT rented the apartment from. He guessed a family had come in May, gotten the cat for their child, and once their vacation was over, put the cat out. This reminded me of a Parisian friend who told me when some families went on their August vacations, the sounds of cats locked inside apartments could be heard, until the cats were heard from no more. The cats starved from lack of food and water.

Because people are horrible.

About ten years ago, there was another cat, also grey and long-haired, that had turned up on my mother's doorstep in Boston one cold, wintry January evening. An old woman who lived at end of the street had died and her many cats scattered. My mother said, after the second night of the cat sitting erect and proud on the doorstep, "Don't feed the cat, Lisa, or the cat will never leave and I don't want a cat."

I understood. I was visiting from London and so could assume no responsibility for the cat. I could not take it with me. And as my mother said, she did not want a cat.

So after my mother went to bed, I put out a bowl of food for the cat and a box with a flannel shirt in it, so the cat would be warm.

Typically, I am a night owl: left to my own devices, late to bed, late to rise. In other words, not a morning person. But when I was awoken by the yelling rising from downstairs and up the winding staircase, I knew why. I covered my head with the pillow.

"Lisa!"

"I am asleep, mother," I groaned.

She burst into the guest room.

In the house I grew up in, there were no any locks on any of the interior doors, with the exception of my mother's room. I always thought this was strategically planned and deeply unfair.

"I told you not to feed the cat!"

I peeked out from under the pillow.

"I am not going to watch a cat freeze to death. I'm not."

"Now the cat will never leave!"

"Good!" I said, "Now you have a cat!"

She didn't speak to me for the rest of the day.

One of my sisters de-flea-ed the cat in our basement, then a few days later, my mother took him to the vet where he was treated for worms. I named him Felix. Within days, everyone in the house had fallen in love with him.

Felix turned out to be the best cat ever. He climbed trees, jumped in piles of leaves, waited like a dog by the door for my stepfather to come home every night, and slept with his belly facing the ceiling. My mother tells me Felix used to spend hours sitting on the mantle above the fireplace, looking at himself in the mirror, fascinated with his own reflection. She says Felix was "half-human."

A singular cat.

It is not often my mother is wrong, which is really very irritating. So the times when she is wrong, it's best to gloat and immortalize.

So, ha ha, mother!

Felix lived for ten more years, then was bitten by a raccoon (or badger? we were never sure which) and contracted Feline AIDS. After that, he wasn't to be let out of the house anymore, which made him really mad, to the point where he would jump up onto the kitchen counter, meow and meow and meow until he got someone's attention, then lift his leg and pee on the microwave. Then he'd take off and hide. But until that time, I had never heard of Feline AIDS. I had also never heard of Feline Leukemia. It was the former that killed him.

But because of Felix, I now knew that the longer Aurora lived outside, the more likely it was that she would contract something, so I found a vet in the Rockaways and took her to be examined and spayed.

The vet, a nice, portly man, laid Aurora out on a metal table. And what she did was stretch herself long, clearly enjoying a belly rub. Then he called the other people in the office, vets and receptionists and technicians alike, all who happened to be women, to come in and rub her belly, and the vet and the five women fairly cooed over my beautiful girl. After a few minutes, the vet said, "She's already been spayed. She was somebody's pet, but she's lived outside for a long time and she's thin, so we'll test her for AIDS and Leukemia. You can't let her out of the house." And then all of the other women, like a Greek chorus, turned to me and said in unison, "You can't let her out of the house!"

Put on the spot, I said, "Okay, okay! I won't let her out of the house." And that is how Aurora came to adopt me.

Back in the Upper West Side apartment was another cat named Madison, and Yash, my ex. I knew if I presented Aurora as a fait accompli, everything would be fine.

So I called him.

"Hello."

I said, "Remember that door you always wanted, the one that would separate your office from the rest of the apartment, the one I always said no to?"

"Yes?"

"Call the super and have a door put in. I'm bringing home another cat and have to separate Madison from Aurora for a couple of weeks so they don't kill each other."

"You're what?"

"Bringing home another cat!"

"Wait, when?"

"In about five days."

"Five days? I don't know if that's enough…"

"In five days, I am bringing home another cat. The door is up to you." I hung up on him.

Five days later, cat problem solved, I finished my play.

Aurora came home with me in a box via a bumpy cab ride, which she hated. Once in the apartment, she hid under the bathtub for two weeks, then gradually got used to her surroundings. I swore I would always look after her and never abandon her, no matter what.

Part of Aurora's typical routine involves either kissing my nose or whacking me in the face with her fluffy tail around 4 AM to wake me for cuddles. When I dangle string above her head, she stands on her hind legs and waves her paws in the air like a dancing bear in the circus. Her favorite toy is a large, red ostrich feather a former student gave me. My private students have posted her photo on Facebook and Instagram.

And that is how Aurora turned out to be the best cat ever.

Best Friend

AT MY GRANDFATHER'S FUNERAL, while I was delivering the eulogy in Immaculate Conception Church, I was surprised to see Derek, in the back, standing against the far wall behind the last pew. He just gave me the slightest nod, the "You will be okay" nod. And I was. It went smoothly. I even got a few intended laughs. People came up to me afterwards and said, "That's him, you captured him." But the only person I wanted to talk to was Derek. I waded through the mass of people to where he was standing and threw my arms around him. "How did you know?" I said. Because in my haste traveling from London to Boston, I had had no time to contact anyone.

"I saw the obituary in the paper. His last name, Nicoletti, is different from yours, but I remember you talking about him and you loved him so much and you are in there as one of the grandchildren."

Living abroad for a decade really sorts out friendships. Derek is one of two friends who wrote to me — actual letters and cards — on a consistent basis for ten years. I've kept them all.

We walked outside of the church for some air. We didn't say anything else. His company brought me enormous comfort.

A few years after my grandfather's funeral, we were going somewhere (me, Derek, and Carol, Derek's wife) with Derek driving, Carol in the passenger seat, me in the back. I don't know how it came up, but we talked about Derek showing up to the funeral, and I said, "I'll never forget that you did that, you know. I'll never forget."

He said, "Of course I'd show up. I know how much he meant to you."

There was a pause. Carol turned her head to look at Derek.

"Derek? Didn't… didn't your grandfather die on your birthday, too? Just like Del's? (a childhood nickname) died on her birthday?" There was another pause.

"Oh yeah, that's right. He did." Derek looked at me in the rearview mirror.

"I didn't know that," I said.

Derek said, "It was a long time ago. But yeah, I had forgotten. He died on my birthday, too."

There was another pause, and then Carol said, "That's just spooky."

✳

Derek is my second decent male role model after my grandfather, but I didn't meet him until I was seventeen, and he was nineteen, when he joined the theatre company I belonged to. Derek is about 5'6", broad and muscular. When he first walked in to audition, it was the height of summer. Derek, sporting a tan, wore tight blue jeans and a tiny, white, denim vest, unbuttoned. And that's it. I suppose he had on either shoes or sneakers, but I didn't notice his feet. Nor did any other woman in the place, as we all swiveled our heads and craned our necks to check out the "new guy."

We dated briefly and nearly killed each other. We are too much alike, except I have less patience. Mercifully, we went through a brief hate-ship phase, and a year later, best friends.

I don't know if everyone has one defining moment. But I know Derek's. When I lived in London, I could afford to come back to the U.S. once every year and a half or so. One of those visits occurred in June of 1987. I went to Derek's house, of course, which always seemed to be full of people and noise. The driveway sloped downwards and usually had too many cars for me to park in, with a big shiny Cadillac at the top. His parents could not have been more different: his mother, Ginny, was usually in the kitchen, loud, emotional, funny, Italian; his father, Arthur, who was a stonemason with his own company, was usually in the living room, quiet, wry, unprepossessing, English. Derek is the middle child. He has two other siblings: Leeann, who is younger, and Butch, who is the eldest. Derek's house contained life in a way mine did not; his family had parties for no reason whatsoever. Granted, there was a pool in the backyard, which invited parties. But it was always a welcoming place, and no one ever stood on ceremony.

You Are All a Part of Me

I left after my two-week visit. Two months later, on August 15th, I got a call from Derek. The night before, his father, while driving their shiny Cadillac, along with his best friend in the passenger seat and their wives in the back seat, were hit head-on and killed by a seventeen-year-old drunk driver. The wives survived, cut out by the jaws of life. His mother was hospitalized, in traction. In shock. Derek's father was fifty-four years-old.

I no longer remember what I said, but it doesn't matter, because it was totally inadequate. I knew I could not afford to fly back so soon for the funeral and Derek, also knowing this, said it was for the best as the funeral was going to be public. Arthur's best friend was the captain of the Braintree Fire Department. His death reverberated throughout the community. It was a big deal. It was in the papers. The media would be there. Cameras and reporters would be there. No privacy would be afforded to any of the family members. After the funeral, Derek told me it all felt totally unreal, like being in a dream state. Carol, who was his then-girlfriend, told him the funeral was the easy part. The aftermath to come was unimaginable.

I came back at Christmas and went straight to Derek's. He was in the basement, sitting behind his father's desk. I asked how he was. He said how strange it was seeing his father's slippers, knowing they would never be filled by his feet again. The shoes of the dead have resonance. In Joan Didion's "The Year of Magical Thinking," she said she could not get rid of her late husband's shoes, because he might need them when he came back. That is grief for you.

With tears streaming down his face, Derek said, "I'm over it. I've forgiven the kid who did this (the kid who killed his father, because he was seventeen at the time, only had his license revoked but could not be charged as an adult), I really have."

I sat across from him, said nothing and thought, "Oh, you have a long road ahead of you, my friend."

It took Derek approximately two to three years to adjust to his father's death. Not accept. Not move on. Adjust. He went to drama school, where after a few outbursts he was referred to therapy; went to

New York City to act; went back home to Braintree where he married Carol and eventually assumed responsibility of his father's company. Because Derek had been trained as a mason, too. By his father.

Because Arthur was an avid golfer — he taught Ginny to play as well — Derek and his siblings set up a foundation in his father's name that helps needy families in the form of an annual golf tournament. Derek still runs the masonry business, writes and teaches acting workshops, had two successful masonry shows on HGTV. And he has a killer pizza oven in his backyard.

But let me go back a bit.

It would be wrong to say that Arthur's death made Derek who he is. Rather, that tragedy enhanced what was already there, inside him.

When I first began visiting Derek's house, at seventeen, I was a little surprised and a little jealous. His house, the one filled with noise and people, was also filled with stuff: the newest CD's, or the best sound system or top-of-the-line fridge or cameras or shoes or accessories or clothes. Everyone in the house — Derek, Leeann, Butch and his parents — worked, and worked hard for what they got. None of them ever showed off. They were generous to a fault. The abundance of material goods just surprised me — and yes, I was jealous. It was also a permissive household, in that Derek and his siblings could have their respective girlfriends or boyfriends sleep over.

That would never have happened in the house I was raised in, unless I wanted to be thrown out into the street.

I guess I thought Derek was a little bit… spoiled? I mean, from my perspective, he had everything. At nineteen. His parents were together and they cared about him and loved him; rules of the house were manageable; he was materially satisfied with cars, money, and it looked as if he wanted for nothing. It looked *easy*. Perhaps because I had none of that, I thought he took it for granted.

That was not the case after his father's death. Derek did an awful lot of work on himself. A lot of introspection. He takes nothing for granted. His family comes first. He is fiercely loyal, protective and proud of Carol and their children, Ian and Julia. When I stay at his house, I am told by all who live there, "You're not a guest, you're different," so no Guest Pass for me. I am on the special Family Pass, and that is what I consider them to be: Family.

Ian and Julia have the distinction of being the only two children on the planet I actually liked when they were children. They are both in college now, both terrific. I am "Aunty Del" to them. I am not sure either one of them have ever called me Lisa, because Derek calls me Del, which is preferable. When Julia was born, eighteen years ago on Christmas Eve, I held her shortly after, all swaddled in pink, both of us looking at one other, until she shrieked and I handed her back to her mother.

Derek and Carol became Born-Again Christians, and his faith is part of what deepened him. He walks the walk, not just talks the talk. Though I am not of the same faith and I struggle, he has never tried to force his belief system on me. He has never tried to convert me. It is the same with our politics, which are sometimes oppositional. But we have always been able to talk to one another, listen to one another, respect one another. We both like solving problems. I like when he gets angry, because we have that in common. I'm glad he uses profanity, because otherwise, I would be the only trash mouth in our friendship. We are both masters at self-deprecation, and making others laugh is key. Time matters to him, because he knows all too well it is finite. His family matter to him. Excelling and working hard matters to him. Communication matters to him. He calls, he checks in, he tells me he's thinking about me — this when he keeps a six-day work schedule beginning with excruciatingly early mornings I cannot fathom.

People matter to him. I matter to him. And he matters to me.

Derek is the reason I moved to New York City from London. I have a list in my head of Hugely Important Life decisions that took three seconds to make. I believe moving to New York City is number 2. I was in a horrible relationship I seemed unable to extricate myself from, in between London and figuring out what I was going to do with my life, and Derek, who also trained as an actor at Trinity Rep in Rhode Island, called me up out of the blue one day and said, "I'm moving to New York

City for about three months to audition and see if anything's happening there. Want to come?"

Yes!

In New York City, we illegally sublet a large studio apartment in Manhattan Plaza, a rent-subsidized complex on 42nd Street and 9th Avenue. An actress acquaintance was going on a three-month tour, so there we were, living above The Little Pie Company, down from The Food Emporium, sharing one ID card to swipe in and out of the building using a very sophisticated system whereby whoever was home chucked the pass out of the window down to the other person down below, out of view of the guards. This was before either one of us had cell phones, so we had to be inventive.

There was a daybed and a sofa bed in the apartment. Only best friends can do this and make it work. One night, I woke up from a nightmare, something about giant termites eating their way through the walls. But the crunching sound continued, so I got up, bleary-eyed, followed it to the kitchen, and there was Derek, eating the most enormous bowl of cereal.

I said, "What the hell are you doing at 3 am, making all kinds of noise?"

Derek said, "Eating cereal."

I went back to bed and pulled the covers over my head.

Derek had no memory of this the next day. That is when I found out he was a sleepwalker and a sleep eater, and that we could no longer keep cereal in the cupboards because all of it would be gone by morning.

We spent our time getting headshots and resumes together, going on auditions, and trying not to run through the money we had brought to last us for those few months. We were actually thankful not to have that much money, because those delicious apple pie smells wafted up through our windows every morning from The Little Pie Company. Not being able to afford them kept us trim. Food Emporium is expensive, and Derek said if they did not have a cheapish brand called America's Choice, we would have starved (this was before Ruth Miller introduced me to the now-defunct Apple Market and Stiles fruit and veg market formerly on 9th Avenue between 41st and 42nd).

After the three months in New York City, Derek went back to Braintree — this was when he married Carol and took the reins of his father's business — then I went into a sublet with a man who laughed when I asked him to do his own dishes and let them pile right up to the faucet until it was not possible for water to flow. Three weeks later, I called Derek and said, "You have to get me out of here."

He told me he was coming to town for an audition, staying in a 6th floor walk-up on 451 West 44th Street, while the primary tenant, that same Ruth Miller, was in Maine at her other residence. Derek knew Ruth, an actress he had done a play with in Bangor. I came over to visit, sat down and said, "I'm staying."

He said, "I have to ask her first."

I said, "Okay, but I'm staying."

He called Ruth. She said she didn't want another roommate. I yelled from the kitchen, "Tell her I'm staying."

Basically, I squatted her apartment and she was going to have to come down from Maine and pry my cold, dead hand off of her doorknob.

Derek told her I was desperate, which was not a lie. Ruth said I could stay for two weeks and then she was coming to the city once the play she was in finished, and we would "go from there."

As Derek left he said, "You're on your own. But if it works out, you owe me your life. I'll just add it to the list."

That list just gets longer and longer, and includes but is not limited to leaving me hilarious voice texts upon the demise of my relationship with Kentucky to lift my spirits. Derek has shown up for me again and again and again. When he heard about Kentucky, he called. He texted. He kept me sane.

✳

In the summer of 2018, I went to his son Ian's high school graduation party. Derek and his very generous friend, Maryann, found a way to fly me in and out of Boston within forty-eight hours, right before I began teaching in the summer NYU Opportunity Program. Derek said, "Del, you have to be here." It was a glorious evening and I was so proud to be part of the enormous extended family for the night.

Last October 2019, I stayed with Derek for four days in order to attend my first mentor's memorial service, where I would be singing in a choir and giving a speech. I also wanted to spend time with them, as I don't get to Boston as much as I would like, though Derek and I call and text often. After the service, Derek had a party. With that pizza oven on his patio and a fire pit as well, his parties are extremely well-attended. There were a ton of people, and Derek makes a mean pizza — and a gluten-free one for me. We sat around his blazing fire pit, drinking, relaxing and laughing until everyone had gone except Julia, Derek and Carol. Derek asked me to read them the speech from the service. I did. They cried. I think it was the drink, but I was flattered. Then Julia and Carol went to bed and Derek and I stayed up until 3 am or so, and had one of those long, intimate conversations about love, sex, loss, friends, writing, theatre, finances, goals, dreams, life. What is the word to describe the feeling of never wanting to leave that fire pit, never wanting to leave him and his family and that oasis of a home they have made? The word that means feeling elation, and whole, and at peace? The word that means to be known, loved and accepted for the imperfect woman that I am?

Ruth

"YOU NEVER GRIEVED. YOU JUST DELAYED IT BY LEAVING," Dr. Silver said.

"I know," I said.

"Do you have some of her things? In your home. Do you have some of her things?"

I did. When I cleaned out her apartment, her son had said, "Take what you want, because the rest is going to the Salvation Army" (which was Ruth's favorite store). So I now had her cast-iron frying pan, the one she made me veggie scrambled eggs in. I had a black and white vase she used to put orange flowers in. I had an enormous painting called "Girl Writing" that was in her front room.

"Good," Dr. Silver said, as tears streamed down my face. "Things help."

❋

I lived in Ruth's rent-controlled apartment on 451 West 44th Street in the Hell's Kitchen area of Manhattan for four years.

When Ruth and I met, it was like meeting a version of my older self, and for her, meeting her younger self. She was in her sixties at the time, an actress, red-haired, about 5'3," attractive, brilliant, talented, formidable. We became friends immediately.

I really didn't care for New York City when I first came here. I kept comparing it to London, where I had lived for ten years. London was cleaner, slower-paced, less crazed, less people, less, less less. Derek had said to give it eighteen months, that I couldn't make a proper decision unless I gave the city a fair shot. But I was out-of-sorts and unhappy.

On one of those moody days, walking down the street with Ruth, I was complaining about this or that, and Ruth said, "Look at the way the sunlight hits the buildings."

I did, and saw that which I had not seen before and it was beautiful.

Another time she said, "Look up to see the architecture. The street level changes but above that it doesn't if it's not a new building. They're all so different. And look at the nifty details there. And the Dutch Gabling there. Gargoyles there. Gothic there."

Ruth had been married to two architects.

I did, and began noticing details that had eluded me because I was not paying attention.

When I began temping, before I could even think of moaning, Ruth said, "That's wonderful. You'll get to see different parts of the city you would otherwise never go to."

She was right. The Battery, Rockefeller Center, South Street Seaport, Wall Street, the intersection of Prince and Spring are not places I would just go to for the heck of it.

In her 87th year, she called and said, "I was thinking of something for you today so when I got home I wrote it down."

I said, "What was it?"

"Tell Lisa to remember."

Ruth has a complicated story, and this is the way she told it to me. I cannot remember how this subject came up, but I was in the comfy green chair in her sitting room, and she was at the dining room table. The distance between us was only a few feet. Ruth said she had been raped twice.

The first time, it was in Chicago around 1950, she was approximately twenty, living at home. She had a date with someone she liked, and he liked her. He took her to a dance, they went back to his place and he date-raped her; he "shoved it in me," she said, and thrusted her arm upwards for effect. She went home. She did not tell anyone. Who would believe her? She had agreed to the date. Whose reputation would be ruined? She went home with him. She was seething, furious.

"What did you do?" I asked.

Ruth said slowly, "I thought about it and thought about it, and finally decided I'd marry him, and make his life as miserable as possible."

If Ruth had said she had decided to murder him, I would have understood it better. This I did not understand at all.

The marriage produced two children. Ruth said she "cheated all over him." And he knew it. She said she'd pull into the garage after some assignation, and he'd be waiting for her, one time choking her so violently that she blacked out.

Eventually, she ran away to New York City to continue her acting career but said she always knew she would go back for her children. Her husband, who repeatedly told her he would never file for divorce, filed the day after she left. He sued for sole custody of both children and it looked as if he would win because Ruth had ultimately deserted. But the judge split custody, with Jamie, the son, going to live with the father, and Jan, the daughter, going with Ruth.

After the divorce, Ruth was back at home in Chicago and said her mother was making intimations about her becoming an "old maid" and what was she going to do about money and such?

Ruth had a degree, in English, I believe. She worked as an actress, but in repertory there is not much money. She began dating one Peter Miller and he became her second husband. She and Peter lived "in the islands" in Puerto Rico and ran a charter boat business, where people would book three-day trips, Ruth cooked (she was a wonderful cook) and Peter sailed. Her daughter was there as well.

In the photos she showed me, they look blissfully happy. There is one of all of them together — Ruth, her two teen-aged children, Peter — with palm trees and bare feet and smiles all round. In her heyday, Ruth looked like Ellen Burstyn: beautiful, pixie-ish. She continued to act as they sailed on and settled in Florida. The marriage lasted many years. But Peter Miller had a drinking problem and when he came into money, she knew that was the end because he had the resources to never stop. So, with her daughter now grown and off on her own, for the second time, Ruth ran away to New York City to act. She was fifty-two. A friend of hers told her that at fifty-two, she was too old to move to New York City. Ruth said, "I am never going to be any younger than I am today."

At fifty-two, she was cast in the Broadway production of "Come Back to the Five and Dime, Jimmy Dean, Jimmy Dean" by Robert Altman (she called him "Bob") via an open call. She played a teenaged version of one of the leads, and the leads were played by Sandy Dennis, Karen Black and Cher. Kathy Bates was also in that cast (Ruth also appeared in the movie version). Opening night, for the after-party, Ruth was panicked. She had no idea what to wear: all of the women in the cast had money to buy fabulous clothes and she did not. So she went the vintage route and pulled out a black, velvet, glittery coat to show me what she had worn, almost twenty years before. The cast picture from "Jimmy Dean" now hangs on my wall.

When she told Peter she lived five minutes away from the Salvation Army, he said, "You'll never come back."

She never did. And why would she? That apartment on West 44th Street was rent-controlled.

When she got the Bonkers candy commercial plus two spin-off commercials, she earned enough money to buy herself a house in Maine on a quiet road with a bit of land. I visited her up there the week before 9/11 and asked why she chose what I thought was a very isolated spot. This proved to be accurate, when she lived through an ice storm in January 1998 with no heat, electricity or water for a week. She said what most people say: she had gone on vacation there and had been happy. Derek and Carol visited once. He said it was too depressing to ever go back. The land was covered in overgrowth, so walks were impossible. For any kind of supplies, entertainment, errands, one had to drive. The house was not situated close enough to other houses to have any neighbors nearby. I did not visit again.

Something happened between Ruth and Jan, her daughter. Or rather, nothing happened, it's just that one day, Jan decided to stop speaking to her, and that lasted for about thirty years or so, until Ruth's death. Ruth never knew why and Jan never told her. Jan never gave her the chance to make it up to her, to say she was sorry, to make amends. She would not take her calls, would not talk to her. Jan did, however, cash the checks Ruth sent, on birthdays and holidays, without thanks. That really used to piss me off. I told Ruth to stop sending the damn checks. She didn't listen at first, because she felt guilty. She thought the reason for this estrangement was because she was a "bad mother." She had run away, after all. But she had come back and had gotten custody and raised her, so to me that made no sense. I suggested we both go to Brooklyn, where Jan lived, and sit on her steps with a box of doughnuts — you know, to be friendly — and wait until she either came home or came out and then confront her. But Ruth would not do this.

We were talking one night in the apartment and Jan's name came up. Ruth's face crumpled and she put her head into her hands and wept. "I just can't believe I'm not going to see her for the rest of my total life." I put my arms around her, held her. Because that was all I could do.

Years later, after Ruth stopped sending checks, after Jan siphoned a few thousand dollars out of one of Ruth's bank accounts and Ruth found out and then wrote her out of the will, I had dinner with her nephew, Evan, who was in from LA. The subject of Jan came up, mainly because it wasn't only Ruth that Jan stopped talking to: it was almost the entirety of her extended family. Evan had inadvertently run into her in a Brooklyn coffee shop. He relayed a disturbing allegation as to why Jan stopped speaking to Ruth.*

I said, "Okay, Ruth does not know that. Ruth has no idea that is the reason why. She thinks it's because she was a bad mother and she ran away from home when they were little."

Evan said, "She does?"

I said, "Yes! She does! What else would she think? Jan won't tell her. Ruth isn't a fucking psychic, so…?"

"So?" he said.

"Is Jan going to put on her big-girl pants and fucking tell her? Or is she just going to wait it out until Ruth is dead, thinking that will solve her problems? Because guess what? Death changes nothing. It doesn't change what happened. It resolves nothing."

Evan said, "I don't think she's going to tell her."

I said, "Motherfucker." Then I looked at him.

Evan said, "Well, I'm not going to tell her." Then he looked at me.

"Don't look at me," I said, "I'm not telling her! I can't do that."

He said, "Then no one will tell her."

"No," I said, "Because it should be Jan."

Bitch.

Yes, bitch. No, not nice and perhaps grossly unfair. But consider the following: I didn't like seeing my closest older friend who eventually turned into my closest elderly friend cry over Jan who would not pick up the phone but who would go and bank her checks. I didn't like it when we were walking back home through Times Square after seeing the play *The Heiress* with Cherry Jones and Ruth stopped dead in her tracks, her face drained of all color and said, "Oh my god. That's my daughter." She raised her arm and pointed a finger toward a woman with auburn hair standing on the sidewalk. I had no idea what to do. My heart was pounding. I waited to follow Ruth's lead. The woman turned toward us. Then Ruth said, "That's not my daughter. My daughter is pretty." She righted herself. I exhaled. And we both walked home without discussion.

I didn't like it when Jan stole funds from Ruth when she was in her 80's and on a fixed income, because, as I well knew, if Jan had just asked her for the money, Ruth would have given it to her. I disliked that Ruth told me stories of Jan's brilliance when Jan's behavior toward her mother was stupid, stupid, stupid, because not talking solves exactly nothing. I dislike that she hurt my friend for over thirty years.

Bitch.

Granted, Ruth was not the easiest person to get along with. She holds the Number #1 spot — still! —as my most difficult friend. She was highly opinionated, to the detriment of her career. We both agreed that we were brats, that we liked being brats, and she taught me my current M.O.: You don't have to do anything you don't want to.

But where we differ is I believe there are times and places to think very loudly rather than speak.

In 2005, the very fine actress Lois Smith was in "The Trip to Bountiful" at The Signature Theatre. I was over at Ruth's for dinner, and all excited, I told her. "And it's right down the street! And it's only 25 bucks! And we can get tickets right now! And, and, and, it's Lois Smith,

I love Lois Smith!"

Ruth was making a salad in the kitchen, facing the window, concentrating on shredding lettuce with her hands as I bounced around her. "No," she said, without looking at me

"What? Why?"

"Because I don't want to," she said.

I shook my head the way I do when I get out of the ocean after a swim and there's water in my ear.

"I don't think I'm hearing you right. Great play, great actress, great price. What am I missing?"

Ruth stopped her shredding and turned her head toward me. She said, "I don't want to go because Lois Smith had the career I should have had and I'm jealous." She was half-smiling when she said this, but her voice sounded sad.

So we did not go to see Lois Smith in "The Trip to Bountiful."

Ruth had told me a few stories about her theater beginnings in New York City. Remember, she was fifty-two when she came here. Sam Shepard auditioned Ruth for his first play, "Buried Child." She told him, among other things, that she didn't understand the play and hated the title. She was not cast.

Edward Albee auditioned Ruth for "Who's Afraid of Virginia Woolf?" She told him she liked the play, but had no idea what it meant or what he was trying to say. She was not cast.

Ruth refused to audition for "Steel Magnolias" because, she said, it was "maudlin."

Ruth and I have a friend in common: JT, the professional actor who refuses to believe he had a cat for a pet in the Rockaways. He told me that at one point in time, he was casting a production of "The Fantastics" and it came down to two actors for the part of El Gallo. Both were equally attractive, good actors, had beautiful baritones, and comparable resumes.

"How did you decide?" I asked.

"I did some research," he said. "I asked around, asked all of my contacts, of which there are many, about both actors. And what I found out was, one was a pain in the ass: to the crew, to the rest of the cast, no matter where he went or what play he was in. The other, I heard good things and 'easy to work with.' So 'easy to work with' got the part."

That makes total sense to me.

Maybe that is too simplistic, too pat. But I have seen Ruth in a few plays, and she is the kind of actor who you swear is eight feet tall onstage until her 5' 3" frame is standing beside you. She knows exactly what she is doing, what she wants, why she is saying every single word. She is invested in the play, and if she didn't understand the play (or the title) she wouldn't take the role.

Off stage, that overused phrase "does not suffer fools gladly" is Ruth in spades. As I said, she had a brilliant, inquisitive mind. She read constantly. With that, she could be highly critical, sometimes caustically so.

Three shorts about Ruth's inner critic:

I was diagnosed with epilepsy while living with her. During that unfortunate period of time when doctors were trying to sort out my meds and dosages, I was still having complex/partial seizures. So I had no choice other than to stop singing. Stop performing. Having no other creative outlet open to me, I went back to writing, something I had always done but never taken seriously. It was just fun. Up to that point, I had been writing theater reviews. Fun.

But then I was invited to a writers colony in the Hudson Valley, got some encouragement from an editor along the way, and began a novel about my experiences volunteering for The Samaritans in London. I also tried my hand at a few essays.

"Can I read something you've written?" Ruth asked.

"Of course," I said. It was a Friday. I handed her a couple of essays, went out for the night and came back two days later.

I walked in late Sunday. "Ruth?" No answer. No one home. I took off my coat, hung it on the rack, opened the fridge and poured myself a glass of water. Walking into the sitting room, I saw my essays on the table. I put my glass down. *Good*, I thought, *She's read them.*

Until I really looked, that is.

Both essays were totally covered in red ink. Markings, comments, corrections, question marks. I felt like I was back in sixth grade. And isn't red pen against the law now?

Steaming, I sat down. I didn't recall asking for a critique. If that was what I had wanted, that is what I would have said.

I did not show Ruth any further writing — with the exception of my plays, because I cast her in them — for the next ten years.

So when she complained that other friends had been given my work to read (published work) and she had not, I always said the same thing: "You red-inked the first essays I ever gave you. Think I'm risking that again? Wrong."

I finally gave Ruth a folder of published essays in 2016. By that time, I had a healthy enough "writer ego" to withstand her opinion, and she knew better than to even look at a red pen this time round.

She thought they were great. In particular "The Worst Thing That Happened" she said was one of the best things she had ever read. Inside, I jumped for joy.

❋

Sometime during 2015, in Maine, two new friends entered Ruth's life. A couple in their 70's: Paul and Ann. Ann runs a small art gallery. I am not sure how they all came into contact with each other. But Ruth met Ann first, they became friends, then came Paul.

Both knew that Ruth went back and forth from Maine to New York City, so they exchanged cards, phone calls, and Paul took beautiful photos he framed for Ruth, some of which she hung on her walls in the NYC apartment.

After about a year, Paul, who told Ruth he was "writing" and had aspirations to be a writer, asked her if she would look at some of his stories and tell him what she thought. He had already sent out a story to a publisher (rejected). He asked for her opinion, and said, "Be honest with me. I can take it."

Ruth said to me, "I don't know why he asked me. We've never talked about writing. We've talked about books, but not writing. So I said... okay."

He sent her a stack of short stories. She must have called me at least ten times while she was reading them.

Ruth said, "Not only are they dreadful, but they also don't make any sense. In one story, he has a character who is an award-winning hiker stranded in the desert having brought nothing with her to survive. They aren't even...they are not even stories, Lisa. They're ideas not fully formed. In another story, he writes about sex and uses words like 'behind' and 'fanny' and 'ass.' I couldn't read them all. I couldn't finish them. What am I going to tell him?"

Ah.......Um....

Ruth said, "I have to tell him something."

I said, "Well, he asked for your opinion (**in my head, thinking, stupidly! stupidly!**) so you have to tell him, just try to let him down easy."

Ruth sent back the stories to Paul with a letter. One thing she said was, "Do not under any circumstances, send these out for anyone to read. They're not stories." And she gave him a long critique. Told him what she thought about the story with the sex, the hiker, etc... was very specific. She also gave him some advice on how to fix them (but to me, she said he wasn't a writer and there really was no hope, and yes, I do agree that part of the problem is everyone thinks they can write in the same way everyone thinks they can teach, which gets right up my nostrils.)

A week later, having had no response, she called me, full of guilt. So she sent Paul a funny note, not as an apology but as a way to move on, to resume the friendship.

Five days later, she received a communication from Paul. Ruth called and read it to me. I can't remember the exact quotes, but here's the paraphrase: Fuck you, lady. No more friendship. How dare you. Don't you ever come into OUR GALLERY (Ruth: "Now it's 'our gallery'? He has to bring Ann into it?") because you are not welcome here. Don't write me. Don't call me. Don't contact me ever again.

It took Ruth two days to respond. She gathered every single card, letter, and photograph he had sent her throughout their friendship. She put everything in an enormous manilla envelope. And she wrote a note to Paul in bold, black letters which said:

**YOU SENT ME YOUR BABIES AND I DIDN'T SAY GOO
GOO.**
 EGOIST!
WHY WOULD I WASTE MY TIME?

✳

Her daughter published a mystery thriller, a genre Ruth enjoyed. She bought and read it. She did not tell me what she thought, nothing. A couple of years later, she found out that Jan had published her second book. What she said to me is the following: "I didn't know, but I wish I had. If we had been in touch, if things were different...the first book wasn't that great; I could have helped her with the second..."

 As Ruth got older, the depression she suffered from worsened. But, having had a bad experience with one therapist, she swore them off, and refused medication. What she did instead of seeing a therapist was bake. And in addition to being a wonderful cook, she was also a *wonderful* baker. It's no accident that I dropped ten pounds when I stopped living with her. Because at any given time, the following could be found in her fridge (and everything on this list was made from scratch): chocolate cake with chocolate frosting, Whoopie pies filled with hand-whipped cream, rugelach, brownies, lemon bars, orange cookies with bits of nuts, chocolate chip cookies, cinnamon rolls, pudding.

She ate what she baked and gained weight; the weight made her more depressed ("I look like a barrel") and to combat this, the more she baked. She had gout a few times, which vexed her. But that did not stop her from baking.

We were roommates for four years, and then I finally moved to my own apartment (far from the baked goods) on West 43rd Street, then four years later to a bigger apartment on the Upper West Side once I married. She was part of my New York life for nearly twenty-three years, and we saw each other at least once a week when she was not in Maine (the hot summer months) and talked on the phone daily.

So in June when I told her via phone that I was moving to Sarasota in the fall (which I did, when I took a semester off in 2016), at first she said, "I can't think about this right now. I'm going to do that when I get off of the phone."

I said that was fine.

The next day, she called and said, "I can't imagine coming there in September or October and you not being there. I'll never see you again."

I said, "Of course you will. That's why you have a sofa bed, so when I fly up at Thanksgiving, I'll have somewhere to stay."

Ruth laughed. Thanksgiving was either at her apartment, or mine; we traded off years, invited people who were at loose ends and called it a "Misfits Thanksgiving." She and I usually spent Easter and New Year's together, and Christmas if I was in town. I have notes and cards and letters and egg cups and jewelry from her; I also have many many books, Christmas ornaments, vintage gloves and scarves, and oddball presents like a small wooden block that says "GOD IS WATCHING YOU" because the atheist in her found it hilarious. That was the same year I gave her "The Patron Saint of Television" which was a small, plastic figurine that Ruth took great pleasure in nailing to her wall next to the television set.

In July, Ruth went into the hospital. I can remember where I was standing on 110th Street, the green on the leaves of the trees above my head, near St. John the Divine, when she called and told me about the cancer. She said, "When will your book come out?"

I said, "Next year, I think."

She said, "I hope I'm alive to see it."

Ruth went into hospice and died in her home in Maine on Friday, August the 5th. It was so fast I just… went into autopilot. I was nearing the end of teaching a six-week intensive for NYU that ended on August 11th. As requested, I cleaned out her apartment on Friday the 12th, had dinner with her son on Saturday the 13th and flew down to Florida on Monday the 15th. Never was I so relieved to get on a plane and flee. When I came back to the city six months later, her death hit me all at once. It was and still is an enormous void.

You Are All a Part of Me

Ruth never wanted to face living in New York City when I was not going to be in it. Now, she doesn't have to.

*Which I am not at liberty to divulge.

The following are vignettes I wrote for her adored nephew, Evan, to keep him in the loop of our "adventures," as Ruth called them. I never showed them to her.

Fairs with Ruth

RUTH AND I RENT A STALL at the annual 44th Street Market in Manhattan, which takes place on the first Saturday in June. We have been doing this for over ten years. Everybody on the block sells their own junk and the junk is really, really good. It's a long day, from early morning to early evening, especially if the day is very warm, or very cold. I was told years ago that the 44th is the best street fair of the year. Judging by the money I've made and stuff I've bought, my day at the 2010 street fair makes me believe it more than ever.

8:30 AM. I set up first and wait for Ruth (she is in her early eighties and still living in a sixth-floor walk-up on 44th, so she takes her time). There is a large table, a red cloth to cover it, two chairs, and we divide the space between us: mostly on the table but also on the ground and on a clothes rack. Everything is clearly priced with neon tags. Though the fair does not begin till 10 AM, you're a fool if you don't get out there early. A man comes over to look at my stuff, still in boxes, and I recognize him as the guy who cleaned me out of silver from the previous year: the silver man! He is an early bird. A Russian woman also comes over at the exact same time and they both fight, actually grapple with each other to get to the silver jewelry box, nearly knocking over the whole table. I tell them to knock it off, back off, and step away from our table. As the Russian woman yells at him, he collects a handful of jewelry. He smiles, hands me two hundred dollars in cash, tells me I have exquisite taste, and leaves. The Russian woman is furious, says that is not the way things go, that is not the way things go! She leaves in a huff. I am very, very happy.

10 AM. Ruth and I are underway and the day is looking to be a warm one. I tell her about the silver man and she says I can go home now;

I'm ahead of the game. I go for a walk to check out the other stalls. Ours is always the best and that is my unbiased opinion. I begin at a colorful stall; the woman running it looks Filipino, fifty-ish, and beautiful in a sexy-mama outfit. As I look through her bamboo rail of clothes, she says, from behind me, "I have a Gucci skirt but I don't know if you'll fit into it." I say, "Okay, if you don't know if I can fit into it, then take your hands off my hips." She does, I say thank you and leave.

11:00AM. Back at our stall, a small, gnarled, mean woman tries to barter with me for a vintage Bakelite clamper cuff. "15," she says.

"No," I say, "It's worth 20 and it's too early to knock my prices down."

"But I have to re-sell it," she says, "so I only want to pay 15."

"But I don't care what you want," I say.

Woman puts cuff down and huffs off. I turn to Ruth and say, "I'd rather eat it than sell it to her." Ruth nods in agreement.

Generalities: One of the pluses is that if people are mean, you don't have to sell, say, the pair of shoes they really want, because you don't have to; you have the power. There are people who do not want to spend more than two dollars on any given item. "Two dollars? Would you do it for two dollars?" No. Put that down. "What is the original price?" I don't know; I stole it, okay? Now put that bag down. "How much are shoes?" Ten dollars. "Ten dollars! How about five?" How 'bout no? These people wind up leaving empty-handed.

There are women who will buy clothes of mine that I know and they know are at least two sizes too small for them. The rule of thumb seems to be the tighter, the better. "What size is this skirt?" It's a 6. "Do you think it will fit me?" says the size 12, 4 foot-eleven woman, trying to get it past her knees. "Um…" I say. "I'll take it," the woman says. She leaves happy and I am left flummoxed. Ruth looks disgusted and shakes her head.

1:00 PM. I visit a lovely Austrian woman's stall and become obsessed with a pair of handmade black angel's wings. Enormous and beautiful, soft to the touch but powerful looking, I try them on. Another woman comes over and says, "You look like a black angel!" I love them but they are a little expensive, so don't buy, and tell her I'll come back. Instead, I buy a white shirt, a coat and a shawl from the Austrian, as her taste is wonderful and she is really, really nice. I go back a while later and some-one else has bought the wings. I am an idiot.

2:00 PM. I try on two long stands of vintage pearls: one grey, one white. They cascade down past my belly button, and I think that perhaps the man I am dating might like them on me, naked and straddling him. I buy them immediately.

3:45 PM. I go to the deli to get something to eat (egg salad in a con-tainer). I am wearing a short black skirt, a low-cut black top and wedge-heeled sandals. On the way back, a hot Mediterranean man, about 6'5" and 250 pounds of muscle, tells me how beautiful I am. I thank him and keep walking. He follows me, sidles up to me and says, "No call, no lunch, no dinner, no nothing?" Then he stands in front of me so I can't possibly pass him. He tells me he is looking for love and when can he call me. I am just his type. He tells me all about himself; no, tries to *sell* me all about himself, and finally I take his number so he will go away. He tells me again I am his type and he is looking for love with me. He asks to see my eyes behind my big, black Prada sunglasses. He tells me he is a very serious person, and I have two days to call him before he is no longer at that number. He tells me he is a personal trainer but is soon getting his own business. I am very aware of his body and think that this man, if we were in close proximity, could snap my neck like a twig. That has never been a very romantic proposition for me. The man is simply too big. He waves as he walks away, still shouting out for me to call him.

5:30 PM. JT shows up between his off-Broadway shows and hangs out. He is in his early 60's, small in stature and still boyish; once, a friend remarked JT reminded him of one of Santa's elves. I tell him about the hot giant who wouldn't leave me alone, the Russian woman who got angry with the silver man and almost knocked over our table, and the preening woman who tried on all of my dresses (and actually bought two) while her boyfriend held up a large mirror for her; a mirror, I tell JT, that he carried with him. From home. For her. Like palm fronds, no? I say. JT laughs. Ruth and I complain that we are exhausted. He commiserates, until we tell him how much money we have made. Then he says, "I have no sympathy for either one of you." Ruth, who had earlier sagged in the sun, despite her big, floppy sunhat, winds up and punches him in the arm. She could've easily been a boxer. JT continues to laugh. Ruth makes it up to him quickly, because he offers to help get the remaining junk back upstairs. We need him.

6:30 PM. We start packing up, exhausted but satisfied. Ruth made some money, and I got rid of a lot of stuff and also made 500 bucks. We haul all our leftovers up to Ruth's six-floor walkup then go out to eat and drink a lot of wine at the 44th Bistro. Ruth says, "This is the last year we do the street fair!"

I say, "You've been saying that for ten years!"

Lunch with Ruth, Part 1

I AM SEEING RUTH TOMORROW (I have Fridays off, so this is "our day") and we always do the same thing: meet at the giant Salvation Army on 46th Street between 10th and 11th Avenue at 11:00 AM (late for her, early for me, so we are both equally cranky), she on her floor (bric-a-brac & books), me on mine (clothes); I go up to the 3rd floor (her floor), grab her and give her a hug and a kiss, then go back to the 2nd floor (my floor); three hours later she comes to find me, with two bags of books she bought, and I have an armful or cartful of clothes. She complains that she can't find any clothes for herself because she is "shaped liked a barrel." I tell her to stop. Then she tells me all the things she baked over the previous week, and I roll my eyes. She shows me all her books: silly books, picture books, literature, cook books, for a dollar ninety-nine each, three dollars total because Janice at the cash register upstairs likes her. I nod in admiration, thinking that maybe having an elevator in Manhattan Plaza, her new home, is not the greatest thing in the whole wide world for a hoarder. I show her really expensive DVF silk shirts, a sweater and a dress, for a dollar ninety-nine each. She nods in admiration, I buy them all for 20 bucks then later sell half for $$$. We love the SalAr!

Then we are hungry. Ruth picks a new place each time, because her neighborhood transformed from a gritty, drag queen-hooker-actor-cheap haven (when I lived there) to an expensive restaurant haven. Last time, she picked a place where a hamburger cost sixteen bucks (I could buy five outfits for that money at the Salvation Army) and I nearly fainted (menu limited, and what I can eat, also limited). But that was after we fought over four other places, and both lost. We said yes to the 5th place, because fatigue won out. And, okay, the sixteen dollar hamburger (locally sourced, locally stroked bullshit) was great. But came with no fries. Instead, "Duck-fat potato chips" in a teeny-tiny ramekin. Bullshit.

We're not going back there again.

Ruth mentioned a restaurant where the interior looks like a beauty parlor, is foofy, pink and one could imagine getting a manicure. When I asked what kind of food they served, she didn't know. I don't think that's why she wants to go there, although she is picky about food. I have been in diners with her when she sent bacon back because she wanted it crisp. Twice. And she wasn't nice about it, either. The third time they brought it out, it was burned black. I'm sure someone stepped on it in the kitchen as well.

So next week's choice should be interesting.

One of Ruth's favorite lines is "It's an adventure." It is mine, too. So even though we do the same thing on Fridays, it doesn't matter, because it's all an adventure.

Lunch with Ruth, Part II

AFTER WALKING FOR THREE MILES IN THE RAIN, we found this week's new lunch place called @Nine, a Thai place Ruth said looked elegant from the outside. The restaurant had big, white letters on the plate glass, advertising OPEN FOR LUNCH, which I did not think was very elegant, but never mind. It was painted black inside, with a chandelier and blaring pop music, but the window table was available and prices were cheap. My meal tasted like someone had flicked their cigarette ashes into a can of pineapple juice and dumped it on brown rice. Ruth liked hers. She said, "So we're not coming back here again."

I said, "No, we're not."

Sample lunch dialogue, somewhere in the middle:

Ruth: So what else is new?

Me: I think I've told you everything. I'm going to Virginia in May to see the English, and…

Ruth: No men?

Me: Um…no.

Ruth: None?

Me: No. Well, I have heard from the ex-stockbroker…

Ruth: The jerk?

Me: Yes, the jerk. I ran into him a while ago, out of my neighborhood and thought Damn, what is he doing here? Since then, he's been texting and emailing me. Two days ago, it was: "We never rescheduled. Need some LdR time."

Ruth: Who's LdR?

Me: Me.

Ruth: Oh yes, of course.

Me: So that means he wants sex and I don't so that's a no.

Ruth (nodding): So…

Me: I'm thinking of hiring a matchmaker.

Ruth: Are you looking?

Me: I…just don't want to weed through loads of men. I want someone else to do that for me. And I refuse to go online.

Ruth: (Rolling her eyes): Online. Never.

Me (deftly): When do you think you'll go back to Maine?

Ruth: Well…

Lunch with Ruth, Part III

THERE ARE ROUGHLY SIXTY-FIVE EATERIES in proximity of Ruth's apartment, and sixty-four of them, we fight over. Usually it is so early when we meet I have no had breakfast – caffeine, yes, but food makes me nauseous in the wee hours of the morning. It takes time for my system to wake up. So after we've been in the SalAr for hours, what I want is eggs and turkey bacon/sausage and coffee. In short: a diner.

We settle on the Manhattan Theater Diner. We sit in a booth in the window. Our waitress, who is Hispanic, takes our order. Ruth asks what the soup of the day is and the waitress rattles off a selection. Ruth makes a face.

"I'll have a quesadilla."

This is not what you should order in a New York City diner.

The waitress says, "It comes with soup."

Ruth: "I know, that's why I asked you what the soup of the day was."

Waitress: "You don't like any of them? The chicken noodle is good."

Ruth: "Well, I make my own, you know."

Waitress: "No, no, it's really good."

Ruth: "Okay."

Waitress: "Do you want some lemon with that?"

Ruth: "What?"

Waitress: "Lemon. With your soup."

Ruth: "Why would I want lemon with my soup?"

Waitress: "In my country, when we have chicken soup, we have lemon to squeeze in the soup."

Ruth, in a perfectly deadpanned voice: "Not in my country."

The waitress leaves. I feel as if I am in a Seinfeld episode.

To start, there are two small containers of coleslaw and a few pickles brought. Then our food comes. I get my eggs and turkey sausage and coffee, which tastes delicious. Ruth's quesadilla is enormous, and cut into four parts. We talk for hours. We have fun. We laugh a lot.

The waitress comes and asks if we need anything else and we request the checks. She asks Ruth if she wants to take the rest of her quesadilla home, as she only ate half (and it was an enormous portion). Ruth is silent.

I say, "Do you want to take that home?"

Ruth makes that face again. "No."

Then she addresses the waitress. "I didn't like it. It was bland. How can someone take all those ingredients and make it taste bland?"

This is why you do not order a quesadilla in a New York City diner.

The waitress leaves. Ruth tries the coleslaw. Hates it.

Ruth tries the pickle. Hates it.

We put our coats on.

I say, "So is this another place we can't come back to, because you didn't like the food?"

Ruth says, "No, no. We can come back."

She puts her hat on.

"And the coffee was bitter," she says, "It tasted bitter."

I say, "Great, you hated everything."

Ruth says, "The chicken noodle soup was good."

We get outside, and she takes my arm to walk. She says, "I don't want to be that kind of a person, but I just am! The kind of person who complains a lot! I just am!"

I say, "YES YOU ARE!"

I walk her home, slowly. We hug each other.

I'm seeing her next Friday.

Theater with Ruth, Part I

Ruth and I are going to a play on Saturday, a matinée, instead of our usual Friday date. Called "The Velocity of Autumn," it stars Estelle Parsons and Stephen Spinella (the latter whom I love onstage, the former I have seen only on film). This was Ruth's idea, largely because Parsons is eighty-six, like Ruth, and also because the tickets were five dollars each. This is the synopsis:

> "The Velocity of Autumn swirls around Alexandra, a 79-year-old artist in a showdown with her family over where she'll spend her remaining years," press notes state. "In Alexandra's corner are her wit, her volcanic passion and the fact that she's barricaded herself in her Brooklyn brownstone with enough Molotov cocktails to take out the block. But her children have their own secret weapon: estranged son Chris who returns after 20 years, crawls through Alexandra's second floor window, and becomes the family's unlikely mediator. No sooner are the words 'Hi, Mom' uttered than the emotional bombs start detonating. The Velocity of Autumn is a wickedly funny and wonderfully touching discovery of the fragility and ferocity of life."

There was no periodical nor author attached to this screed on their website, though the play was previously done in Washington DC.

This word — "touching" — means Ruth will hate it.

I hope there is an intermission.

It has been a long time since we went to the theater together, at least fifteen years. For the eight or so years I lived with Ruth in Hell's Kitchen and then in my own apartment up the street, I used to take her to the theater all the time because I was reviewing off-Broadway shows for Time Out NY and other magazines. I could take a friend for free, so I took Ruth. She loved theater, she was an actress, seeing theater was expensive, she was my friend, and she was good company. Unless…

There was one play at Playwrights Horizons, which is an excellent venue for showcasing new, top-notch work; and in addition to the play being a family drama, everyone seemed to be having sex with everyone else in all kinds of configurations. And everyone got naked: men, women, teens.

I personally love equal-opportunity nudity, because it happens so rarely, both on-stage and on-film, and I get tired of female objectification. I deal with it daily; I don't see why smart people have to also put it onstage.

But I was aware that Ruth, seated on my left, was getting fidgety, rustling her program and the like. I take notes when reviewing; it is a job, after all, and I am there at the request of the theater company. So I am generally unaware of anything other than what is happening onstage. About a third of the way through, the lights came up on a scene and the mother (40's) was in bed with her daughter's boyfriend (20's); she was naked from the top up, and the boyfriend was completely naked, half-reclining on the bed. The first thing I thought was, "Wow, the boyfriend is extremely well-endowed."

The first thing I heard was, "JESUS CHRIST! I CAN'T STAND IT!"

Slamming of pocketbook on lap, slapping of hands on program on lap on pocketbook.

"I CAN'T STAND IT! THIS IS JUST BULLSHIT, BULLSHIT!"

We were in the middle of the row, in the middle of the play, nowhere near intermission.

"Ruth! Stop it! Stop!"

"I can't stand it, I can't stand it. This is nonsense: it's all sex and gratuitous and it's all bullshit and nothing else and I can't stand it."

She was *in the zone* and I don't think she even heard me. In fact, I know she didn't, because the next thing that happened was "I'm leaving," and she got up, squeezed by all the other people in the row and left. I followed her, I think because she was upset and just at that moment, clearly insane. It took her a while to calm down. I did go back to see the show again so I could finish the review. I said my friend was feeling ill and we had to leave early.

That was the last time I took Ruth to a play I was reviewing.

Theater with Ruth, Part II

RUTH WAS WAITING FOR ME outside the theater, all dressed in red.

"I got here *early*," she said. She looked disgusted.

"I'm sorry," I said, breathless, "but the express trains weren't running and a trip that usually takes seven minutes took me twenty-five. Fucking Saturdays!"

Ruth waggled the tickets at me in her cobalt blue leather-gloved hand.

"It's alright, it's alright. Come on. I have to get a hearing device."

The seats were great – 7th row Orchestra. We sat down. Ruth looked me over – my hair was up and I had on a white and black print coat, coral beads, a black low-cut shirt, black pants, sandals — and said, "You look very pretty! Are you going out tonight?"

"*No*, I'm going to the theater with my friend," I said.

Ruth said, "I know, no one dresses up for the theater anymore."

I said, "But we do."

Ruth said, "Yes, we do. So I decided to wear my red coat today. And red shirt. And pants. And handbag."

I said, "And you look great. I almost wore my red coat, too. I love your gloves."

Ruth said, "I'm the only one in Manhattan wearing gloves today."

I said, "Well, yes, because it's 72 degrees."

Ruth said, "Do I know that coat?"

I said, "Yes. It's old. But I haven't worn it in awhile because it's been too cold. My cousin called this morning and said by the end of next week, it's going back down to 40 degrees."

Ruth said, "It isn't. Who said that?"

I said, "It is, and the weatherman, apparently."

Ruth said, "Oh my god! The snow's just melted in Maine; they just got rid of it all!

I said, "What are you doing for Easter?"

Ruth said, "Not my favorite holiday."

I said, "Not mine, either. But I could make a dessert and bring wine to get you soused, and we can have a party."

Ruth said, "When is Easter? Oh… It's a week from tomorrow. That's fast."

I said, "That's right. And if you don't plan, nothing happens."

Ruth said, "Don't I know it. We'll talk after the play. Oh, there's going to be a talkback with the producers afterwards. Do you want to stay for it? That might be something I'd like to do."

I said, "Um…don't you want to see if you like the play first?"

Ruth said, "Oh yes, because if I don't like it, I'll be talking through it, saying 'Get me the Hell out of here.'"

And she laughed.

I thought, Oh no.

Fortunately, there was no nudity involved. Ruth liked it well enough not to talk through it; the performances were great, though we both agreed the play was over-written and a lot should have been cut. Ruth thought it would be better as a one-act play. I told her I loved Stephen Spinella, and Ruth said, "I couldn't stand him when he first came out, but then he grew into it. Does he always act like that? All…fruity?"

I said, "No."

We did stay for the talkback with the producer, director, and play-wright. Mostly, everyone in the audience just wanted to talk about their own experiences and hear their own voices; I felt bad for the playwright who was just standing there like a lemon. So I raised my hand and asked what inspired him to write the play. He took a moment and said, "Oh. Wow!" And then he told his very interesting story. Ruth leaned over to me and said, "Good, because even though I can't hear anything, I can tell he was dying to say something and liked telling about the play."

By that time, Ruth had to give her hearing device back, and so I translated the talkback for her ("You can just tell me all of it later") because she refuses to get a hearing aid. She is not old enough yet; nor is she old enough for a cane or one of those wheeled pull-carts that might make grocery shopping easier.

We walked out into the afternoon sunshine and she asked if I was going home. I said yes because I had work to do and also I was desperate for a walk on this spectacularly beautiful day. I hugged her goodbye on the corner of 45th and 9th Ave. and she said, "Easter. Let's talk about Easter." I said, "Okay!"

I forgot to tell her that Easter is all about candy, and chocolate in particular, which is the most important thing. I'll tell her tomorrow.

Best night of 2015 with Ruth

At the beginning of November, a Canadian friend of Ruth's came into town to stay with her for a few days — not sure of the name, will call her Judy — and Judy had gotten a recommendation to a play at The Signature off-Broadway. Ruth called to ask if I could book tickets online, as neither of them had devices resembling the 21st century. I did and because the tickets were all twenty-five bucks, I asked to go with them. It was pissing with rain that night so we all met in the foyer. Judy was grey-haired and Ruth's age. She went off to find the woman who recommended the play, leaving me and Ruth to pee, get a hearing device (for Ruth) and find our seats.

When we showed the man our tickets, we were informed we were up in the galley. Ruth, motioning, said, "I hope you don't expect me to climb those stairs."

No. The man said there was an elevator and to hang on while he fetched someone to clean it out. We waited and waited...

The man finally came back and said, "We're going to put you in the stalls instead."

Yay! An upgrade to better seats! We were very happy. We sat down. The lights went out. Ruth fiddled in the dark with her hearing device, leaned over and hissed, "There's something wrong with this! It doesn't work!"

This happens all the time.

Ruth waits until the lights go down to turn on the hearing device, whether it's a movie, a play, a puppet show. She can't see the dials, so it never "works."

There was nothing I could do for her in the dark, other than say sorry. The play began. And what a play!

"Night is a Room" was a new play by a playwright in residence, Naomi Wallace; her residency at the Signature ended once "Night..." closes. The play is a three-hander, set in Leeds, England. Scene 1: In a backyard, a very glamorous wife is talking with an older, dumpy, poorly dressed woman. The wife has tracked down the birth mother of her husband and this is what she wants to give him for his 40th birthday. But she has to convince the mother, who gave up her son when she was fifteen and works as a domestic. The mother is nonplussed about the whole thing. It was a great scene, interesting premise, and the mother finally agrees but asks the wife that the first time she meets her son, the wife not be present. Fair enough, as it will be emotional, difficult, etc...

Scene 2 opens six weeks later on an enormous front room mostly painted yellow, in a state of redecoration. Within minutes, the son, a gorgeous Patrick Wilson type, has gotten his wife off by slipping his hand down the front of her pants and she comes loud and, I must say, quite happily. Clearly, the husband and wife, him light, her dark, beautifully matched, still love and enjoy one another and have been married fourteen years. There is chatter afterwards, their daughter calls from abroad and then, the mother arrives for tea. The mother and son have already met by this point.

Everyone sits down and the mother spills something: the son goes to the kitchen to get a cloth and the mother stops the wife from cleaning up to thank her and tell her she was right, meeting her son was the best thing that has ever happened to her. The son comes back, they all sit down and the mother says to her son, "Tell her you are leaving her to move in with me and never coming back here."

The son tries to explain to an uncomprehending wife that actually, he and his mother have been fucking each other for the last six weeks and he's leaving her for his mother.

I thought, YOU HAVE GOT TO BE FUCKING KIDDING ME. THIS IS BULLSHIT!

I was also glad Ruth's hearing device allegedly malfunctioned.

The mother says to her son, "Do you love your wife?" He says yes. The mother says, "Then you have to leave her with no hope." So the son and his mother come to the very lip of the stage and have an extensive, grotesque make-out session with tongues and saliva all over the place.

The mother then exits. And the husband and the wife have the most fantastic fight, with the husband saying there is a syndrome, GSA (genetic sexual attraction) with children who meet their birth parents as adults and it happens more than people think, blah blah blah; the wife is having none of it. She wants to know when, where, exactly what was done. The wife gets all the best lines and the culmination of this fight was her line, shouted at a high pitch: DID YOU LICK YOUR MOTHER'S CUNT! The husband doubles over and holds his stomach. The wife turns to the audience and says, "I'll leave that one for the moment," which got a big laugh.

We left at intermission.

But before that...

When the lights came up, Ruth turned to me and said, "I didn't hear a thing."

I said, "That's good, that's good."

We exited down the ramp, around the corner, out the door, completely surrounded by people, when Ruth turned to me and said, "But I did hear the line DID YOU LICK YOUR MOTHER'S CUNT!"

In the loudest voice possible.

It was awesome.

Ruth, on a roll, returned the headset and told the girl, "This doesn't work. Mark that down right now," while tapping the top of the desk with her fingernail.

We went and had a coffee in the Signature bar and waited for Judy. Toward the end of intermission, a woman attached to the production and wearing a headset came over and said, "Will you be going back in?" and Ruth said, "No, it was awful."

I laughed and said, "Ruth..."

She said, "What? It was."

Judy came back and the first thing she told us was "You weren't the only ones to leave." The friend who recommended it also came over to our table, and as she walked up, I knew from the large, bright, blue hat tilted on her head and her Cubist jewelry and her wraithlike figure and the unmistakable disdain on her face that she was (in keeping with the rest of this story) a snooty, Upper East Side cunt. The kind of woman who sees things not because she wants to, but because she thinks she should, she gets to be relevant, and tell all her friends to go see crap "culture."

The friend said, "Well, I just loved it."

I said, "Well, goody for you." Then the woman left.

Judy turned to us and said, "The second act didn't get any better."

The three of us put on our rain gear and said our goodbyes. The two youngsters were going out to eat but I can't eat at 11:00 PM. I hugged Ruth and then said to Judy, "It was a pleasure meeting you. But please tell your friend her taste is in her ass."

Ruth looked at me, looked at Judy, and burst out laughing.

Students and Teachers

The only reason I am at all effective as a professor at NYU — or anywhere else — is because I had brilliant teachers. Teachers who literally changed my life. I have written about some of them in the past, but the one who really is responsible for setting me on a path died in 2018 at the age of 100. I spoke (and sang) at her memorial service in 2019, revisited what I had written, and the new version is included here. The rest has been my bizarre path, experience, adventures.

All the Sounds of the Earth Are Like Music

THERE ARE SOME PEOPLE YOU CAN NEVER THANK ENOUGH. What they gave was so extraordinary and immeasurable, the words "thank you" just seem puny.

Until I met Mrs. Hodges, I had no confidence in myself, largely because of my home life. During the 4th grade at Pingree School in Weymouth, I was the only child in my entire class whose parents divorced, and the other children avoided me as if what was going on in my family was contagious. I hunched over and wore baggy clothes because I had developed early; I crossed the street to avoid boys and their remarks. I sat at the back of all my classes, afraid to speak, though I made honor roll every semester. I pretty much stayed that way, ingrown, like a toenail, throughout middle school. But I always loved to sing, so in the 10th grade, I took Mrs. Hodges' concert choir class.

I had heard that Mrs. Hodges was a great accompanist, arranger, and had a daughter at Juilliard. I had also heard she was formidable. A taskmaster. She looked like a sensible New England woman, with her beige shoes, beige twin-sets, and pearls. She knew how to get the best out of a choir, stressing one pure sound, not a bunch of soloists competing to stand out. She hated contemporary music, but thought The Beatles were okay. I sang everything she handed out: Bach, Handel, Purcell and made it my business to learn the new music as quickly as possible.

After a while, she started to notice me. Gave me solos. Made me sing the Bach-Gounod Ave Maria in a small show choir while quaking in my heels. Eventually, she called me after class and encouraged me to train classically. We had no money at the time, and I knew my mother would consider voice lessons wasteful. Mrs. Hodges said she'd have a think. Twenty-four hours later, she called me after class and said she

127

had found a patron of the arts who helped gifted students, and that this patron wanted to help me. So for the next three years, every Saturday, I went into Boston and trained with Nancy Armstrong, the phenomenal teacher and singer with the Boston Camerata. I was totally hooked. I told my mother I wanted to be a professional singer, and she told me I'd change my mind.

During my sophomore year, Mrs. Hodges, who directed and conducted the senior musical, which that year was "Oklahoma," also cast me as one of the leads. Although this did zero for my popularity, it gave me a heck of a lot of confidence. Mrs. Hodges encouraged me to enter vocal as well as choir competitions, which I won (presumably, based on vocal talent, although in a District competition, where all singers had to perform in quartets, in the comments section on my sheet, the judge wrote, "Nice hair!"). When I performed in other theatre companies' shows, she would attend and ask exactly one musical question, then send me a card of congratulations by mail. I still have them. For "West Side Story," in which I sang the role of Maria, she hunted me down backstage during intermission and asked, "Was that you, hitting the high C during the quartet?" "Yes..?" I said, afraid. "Good for you!" she said, and then departed.

By the time eleventh grade began, I had decided to apply to music schools in order to pursue a performing career, a decision my mother was very unhappy with. But by that time, I had so much confidence in my ability, I don't think anyone or anything could have stopped me. I was granted early admission to The Hart School of Music at Hartford University and based on my audition plus scholarships — countless recommendations Mrs. Hodges wrote for each and every application — my first year was free. But I was so well trained that I was bored by Christmas, and then my brilliant former history teacher, Gerry Cavanaugh, who I am sure was tired of listening to me complain, suggested for the second time that I study abroad and sent me pamphlets to schools I had never heard of. This time, I listened to him. And even though Mrs. Hodges had been integral in getting me to this point, I did not involve her in my decision making. There were boundaries. Our relationship was teacher/student. I always called her "Mrs. Hodges." Not "Liz." Those boundaries persisted after I graduated from high school. I was unsure as to whether she wanted me to stay in touch.

I took the bus to New York City, where auditions for LAMDA, London Academy of Music and Dramatic Art, were being held. It was a post-graduate course, and I had no bachelor's degree. My two monologues were trash. But after I sang Pirate Jenny, the principal, Roger Croucher, who was running the auditions, said, "You have quite a mature voice for someone so young." I said, "Yes, I do." I was accepted to LAMDA and moved to London the year I turned eighteen.

When I was in my twenties, I found out it was Mrs. Hodges who was the patron who wanted to help me; it was Mrs. Hodges who had done all of those years of funding. I was astonished. Never mind why — she had done it selflessly, without wanting to be acknowledged. And because of all this subterfuge, I had no idea how to thank her.

I stayed in London for ten years. That part of my life was transformative. I worked as a performer, made friends who I now consider to be family, had adventures, built a life. And I am telling you this because although the singing got me to London, I would not have gotten **anywhere** without Mrs. Hodges' belief in me.

She reached in, grabbed me, took me, willingly, and changed my life in an amazing way, like a miracle worker.

One of the first essays I published in 2010 was about Mrs. Hodges. I decided to find her, though I was a little apprehensive; I thought she might be disappointed in me, because I was no longer a singer. I tracked down her address and sent her a copy of the essay along with a letter. She called me and said, " I knew it was you from the handwriting on the envelope. I was delighted to get your letter."

After, "Tell me everything," she said, "Call me Liz."

I said, "Um… I can't. It's too weird."

I told Mrs. Hodges about London, about New York City, about the epilepsy, about becoming a writer and then a professor. She said she was very proud of me and that "not many keep on going."

After that, we kept in touch mainly via phone.

Here is one thing about the personal essay: it forced me to examine my life under a microscope, not only the choices I've made, but the opportunities and doors that were opened **for me** by others. So after analyzing my time in high school, I finally realized what Mrs. Hodges had done for me.

In 2018, I called her to wish her a Happy Birthday and also to tell her my first book, *Confessions of an Accidental Professor* had just been published.

After the congratulations, she said, "I turned 100. 100 years is long enough, I think. Otherwise, people get sick of you."

I laughed at this.

"I don't know how long I have left. I suspect not too much longer," she said, "But you know what? When I was in assisted living, every Saturday night I organized a sing-a-long. And I would play piano. So I became that lady in assisted living who played the piano."

And we both laughed.

I said, "I wanted to tell you that the book is dedicated to you. To you, and Gerry Cavanaugh and the teachers who changed my life. I'm sending it to you today."

"Oh my goodness… how…sweet…" she said, her voice cracking.

"No, it's true. You have no idea what an impact you had on my life. So now that you're 100, this is a good time to tell you."

She said, "I didn't know that's what I was doing at the time. I just… did it."

"I know," I said. "That's what makes it so wonderful."

"I'm… I'm so glad you called. I'm so glad to hear your voice. And I love you," she said.

"I love you, too."

She got my book and her daughter Priscilla read the whole thing aloud to her, because Priscilla is awesome. Mrs. Hodges called me afterwards to tell me how much she liked it. And we stayed in touch until the end.

❄

I will never get answers to the questions I want to ask Mrs. Hodges. Why me?

Why help me?

Maybe it was not such a big deal at the time, funding my voice lessons and sending me to Nancy Armstrong in Boston.

Maybe I was a glaring mass of need.

Maybe prepping me for all of those auditions and musicals and solos made her happy. Made us both happy. God knows I loved the light she shone on me.

She couldn't have known, when she stepped in as the unidentified "patron," that by doing so she redirected the path I was on. Because the only path I knew for sure was that **I would** get out of my town no matter what. How? No idea.

Mrs. Hodges provided me with the "how."

There are some people you can never thank enough. What they gave was so extraordinary and immeasurable, the words "thank you" just seem puny.

But those are the only words I had for the woman who gave me the life I've lived, the life I've had. I got to say the words "Thank you" out loud to her and dedicate a book to her. Lucky me for stepping into the concert choir class of Mrs. Hodges.

Published in *Writers on the Job,* 2014/revised for Mrs. Elizabeth Hodges' memorial service, October 2019

The Accidental Professor

HALFWAY THROUGH THE INTERVIEW, I asked, "Do I have this job?"

The Chair of the English Department, Michael Frew, answered, "Do you want this job?"

I have made all of the major decisions in my life, for better or worse, in under three seconds.

"Sure, why not?"

"Great," Michael said.

"When do I start?" I asked.

"In a week," answered Michael, handing me the Grassroots book.

Then he said, "Don't tell the students this is your first time teaching. Put 'professor' on your syllabus. And get your BA as fast as you can. Don't tell anyone you don't have it."

I said, "Okay."

He said, "Good luck."

An hour later, I walked out onto East 43rd Street, squinting in the blazing September sunlight. I had no idea why I had said yes, what made Michael hire me, or what on earth made me agree to show up for the interview in the first place.

I had always thought I would be a performer: I was a classically trained singer who studied in London and had performed in straight plays and musicals alike. When I moved to New York City, I planned on doing the same thing. But one Monday, on my way to a temp job, I blacked out on the Times Square 42nd Street subway platform. It was all very dramatic and embarrassing. I had roughly a five second warning before the blackout; it began with a complete body sweat, light-headedness, and once the tunnel vision began, I stepped away from the edge of the platform and got to a seat that I sort of keeled over onto. I was all dressed up and it was quite early in the morning; I am sure people thought I was some kind of yuppie drug user. No one paid attention (this is New York rush hour, after all). When I came to, sweaty and disoriented, I knew I didn't have the energy to get back to my sixth floor walk-up on West 44th Street. I got on the train and made it to Union Square. The building I worked in had a nurses' station. When I opened the door, the nurse on duty took one look at me and said, "You need oxygen." I tried to explain what happened and instead she put a mask over my face and said, "Breathe." After that, she gave me some juice and told me to lie down. Three hours later, I came to. She asked me what had happened, and I told her. She said, "I don't know what is happening to you, but I do know that the next doctor you see must be a neurologist. And you should try to see one as soon as possible."

It took a long time to diagnose, but I had epilepsy. I knew no other singers who had this condition, no actors (but recently did find out that the astonishing Cherry Jones has epilepsy). The meds I was put on, three times a day, induced only one thing: sleep. It took two years of firing doctors, trying various medications, dealing with side effects and finally consulting a homeopath for me to both lessen my seizures and regiment my life in order to live somewhat "normally.s"

Two years away from performing is a long time. I was also terrified I would have a seizure onstage, while singing…it was something I could not control. And what if I was across the country, far from my (next) neurologist?

At twenty-eight, I stopped.

Having no other creative outlet open to me, I turned to writing, something I had always done but never taken seriously. I self-published a tiny "zine"; a writer's colony in the Hudson Valley then invited me for a residency; I began writing theater reviews for Time Out New York and another small, city publication. As far as a degree was concerned, LAMDA, where I trained in London, is not an accredited school, so the credits did not transfer. Empire State College, down on Varick Street at the time, offered something called "life experience credit": writing extensive, detailed essays on what one learned for college credits, so a twenty-eight-year-old woman wouldn't be starting her BA from scratch, as if she had not lived.

In 2004, I began my BA in Creative Writing.

A gal needs money in this town, however, so I was also working coat check at an Asian-fusion tourist trap called Tao, in mid-town. My boss, Deb, was a crazy woman with an undisclosed medical condition that forced her to run outside periodically for marijuana breaks during a shift. She could be moody, cranky, sarcastic. But the job was fantastic in terms of cash, so I put up with her and the extremely drunk but exceedingly generous tipping crowd.

One night, Deb's brother came in. She introduced him. "Hey Steve, this is the new girl." To me, she said, "This is Steve, my twin. Irish twins, except we're Jews. Hahahah!!" Steve looked at her and rolled his eyes. We shook hands. Steve seemed calm, unlike his sister, with a pleasant, doughy face. He asked me a few background questions: where was I from, what was I doing. I told him about London, and he said what everyone says, which is, "Will you sing something?" I said, "Sure Steve, in the coatroom, in front of all these people, is what I live for." He laughed. Then Steve left, and Deb said he was a professor at Berkeley College (a name stolen from Berkeley California), here in Manhattan.

The next night, Steve came back. He asked me a few more questions, about Empire State College, and the tutoring I was doing in the writing center, not because I wanted to (I didn't) or because I liked it (I didn't) but because my writing professor chose me. Steve nodded. I told him I didn't think I was very good at it, the one-on-one I found quite boring. The students who came in were adults and what I could do for them was minimal. Sometimes they would try to complain about their professors (which I stopped); some had ESL difficulties that I was not equipped to deal with; and one man showed up daily for two weeks until he brought me a beautifully boxed amethyst earrings and necklace set, and asked me for a formal date. I said no. He refused to take back the jewelry. I gave it to my Aunt Janet, who looks nice in purple.

I really didn't care for the writing center at all.

A few days later, when I got home from school, there was a message from Steve on my answer phone.

"Hi Lisa, this is Steve. The college I teach at is looking for a professor. I told my chair person about you, so he's expecting a call; his number is 212-xxx-xxxx. His name is Michael Frew. Go in for the interview and mention me. I think you'd be good at it. Okay, see you later."

I was…a combination of furious and flabbergasted. How did Steve get my phone…oh, he asked Deb. That bitch! She didn't tell me. And he didn't even *ask* me first! He didn't *ask* me anything! And that is what I said when I called Deb yelling. She said, "That's how my brother is."

Fantastic.

I called Steve.

"This is Steve."

"Are you out of your goddamn mind??"

"Who is this?"

"It's Lisa. Are you out of your goddamn *mind?*"

"Oh. What's the problem? I thought you'd be good at it, so go to the interview."

"Steve, I don't have a bachelor's degree! No master's, either! I've never taught before; were you smoking shit OR WHAT?"

"But you went to LAMDA, right? And you did graduate?"

"Yes, but…"

"And you're tutoring, right?"

"Yes, but…"

"Lisa, I don't have time for this; GO TO THE INTERVIEW! FREW WANTS A CALL I ALREADY SET IT UP SO CALL HIM!"

And Steve hung up.

Hating everyone and feeling bullied, I called. My interview at Berkeley College was the following day.

Michael Frew was a tall, dark, bespectacled man: very mild-mannered, Clark Kent-looking, and very pleasant. We sat down in his office, and he began explaining the course: Writing. He showed me the book, Grassroots With Readings. He told me there would probably be a lot of students but not to be alarmed. He told me a few of the problems that could come up, mentioned controlling the class, discipline and what the college would not tolerate with regard to student behavior. He asked very few questions. I asked fewer, due to shock.

When I say I knew absolutely positively nothing about college teaching, I mean I also knew nothing about how colleges work, nothing about how one college can differ so widely from another, nothing about who gets to go to what college based on race, class, location, economic bracket, nepotism, etc...

Scratch that, I knew less than nothing.

Later, after I had made my three-second decision and had the book in hand, Michael showed me around the college: classrooms, copy center, administrative offices, lounge. At the time, Berkeley College was comprised of mostly Black and Hispanic inner-city students, very few white students and approximately 2% foreign students; the median age was about twenty-four years old. For this reason, I assumed Berkeley had something to do with the state school system, and that it was, therefore, affordable. When I found out I was completely wrong on all counts, that Berkeley was a for-profit college with a high tuition, I couldn't understand how the students could afford it. I was told Berkeley had a very high placement rate; that is, internships that lead to jobs, good jobs, or just jobs in general. That may have been true at the time, but as of April 2015, the New York City Department of Consumer Affairs was investigating Berkeley, "over concerns about students' drop-out and loan default rates, and the way students are recruited in the first place" (Harris 1/New York Times/"New York Consumer Agency Investigating Four For—Profit College").

At the end of my tour, in the lounge, I overheard a few male teachers talking about their class comportment. The conversation went like this:

Male teacher #1: You gotta be a real dick at the beginning of the semester, or the kids will think they can walk all over you.

Male teacher #2: Oh yeah, you're right. Never let them know you're a human being for the first half of the semester.

Male teacher #3: I don't smile for the first three weeks.

You Are All a Part of Me

Male teacher #1: Well, I don't smile for the first six weeks.
Male teacher #4: Well, I'm a Nazi for the first six weeks.
Male teacher #2: You have to be. You really do.

This was actually the best indirect advice I received, and it was particularly relevant as a woman. Michael said that in general, there are some male students who simply don't like a woman in charge, "Particularly if you're pretty," said Frew, and he empathized with what some of his female teachers went through. So I decided I would be initially terrifying, then segue to tough but fair.

The first time I stepped out onstage, in a leading role, was as Ado Annie in "Oklahoma." It felt *easy*. Like gliding on water. Like I belonged there. I had so much confidence at sixteen, and portraying a woman completely different from myself was very freeing. I liked the yellow dotted Swiss dress the costume mistress had put me in for Act 1, the lavender gown with the huge skirt that flared out as Ali Hakim and Will spun me for Act 2, and how my hair had been rolled back and braided, which reminded me of Judy Garland's Dorothy in The Wizard of Oz. I felt in command, I liked the audience's attention on me, and I knew what I was doing.

The first time I stepped into a classroom, in front of a roomful of thirty students, I thought I was going to have a heart attack. It was a shock how close the students were: almost right up my nostrils. Thirty pairs of eyes watched me, and waited. I, in turn, sweated. Then I breathed.

Costumes can be a miraculous help in terms of stepping into a character: that first day, mine was a black suit. A black, fitted, fine-wool-with-a-bit-of-stretch killer suit with a tailored jacket and slightly flared trousers by Elie Tahari, bought with the last 950 dollars of hard-earned coat-check money. That suit became, very quickly, part of my professor "act," just like Ado Annie's dresses. The suit said the professor is smart, funny, attractive, knowledgeable, a leader, trustworthy, and takes no bull. It also said, this is the only suit I own, so I will be changing out the top, belt, shoes and jewelry, and will be wearing it to teach every class. That suit was my talisman. It gave me confidence. A strut. It made me stand up straight.

I looked out at all of the students seated in that large classroom, all of those eyes, waiting, and my LAMDA acting training kicked right in. In a big, booming voice, I said, "Hi. I'm Professor del Rosso. Welcome to Writing!"

Published in the book, *Confessions of an Accidental Professor*, 2018

The Worst Thing That Happened

I STEPPED OFF OF THE WOODEN WALKWAY, my feet hitting chilly sand. Just ahead, the vast indigo ocean beckoned. Intoxicated by its beauty, I breathed in deeply and then exhaled. I could smell, could taste the fall coming, and it felt exhilarating. A few hours ago, the Long Island sun was overpowering and crowds of people impeded any walking I wanted to do. It seemed millions of rambunctious children were everywhere, watched over by cranky adults, disgruntled by too much sun, sea, and Labor Day beer. Now, the beach was all but deserted, save for what looked like a father and his three young daughters at the shoreline, still aching for a swim, their towels and things in a pile behind them.

This was the time I liked the beach best, just after dusk, with a fiery sinking sun to the west, and the leaching of all color, leaving only the palest shade of grey in the east. There is comfort for me in this particular kind of isolation, and I have never felt afraid on a deserted beach. I don't swim in the Long Beach waters at night, though, because the darker it gets, the more the waves resemble long, black, white-tipped fingers, eager to pull me down with their undertow.

We had arrived at the cabanas later than planned, which turned out to be a good thing. At a particular point in the late afternoon, suddenly everyone departed, off to other parties or barbecues. No more baseball games broadcast from radios. No more crying children. I could hear the gulls again. Sitting across from me at one of the sun-bleached picnic tables, Miguel, my brother-in-law and a school psychologist, asked what I would be teaching my writing students at Berkeley business college for the last two weeks of the quarter, now that I was decamping for NYU (New York University). I told him about the class's last topic, which was to write an essay about something that had changed them. There was one student in particular, Nina, who had joined the class quite

139

late: a month into the quarter. She was a heavy woman, not very tall, Dominican, about twenty-five years old. She was a single mother with a two-year-old daughter. Her essay described being sexually abused by her father from the age of two, which robbed her of the ability to speak. This reminded me of the author Maya Angelou, but Angelou stopped speaking by choice, believing her voice was responsible for her rapist's death.

Months passed before her mother took Nina to a doctor, who discovered sores on her mouth and vagina. When he told Nina's mother he suspected abuse, she responded by saying that could not possibly happen in her house. So the abuse continued until Nina was three and a half, until the family moved to the United Sates, into an apartment so small, everyone slept in the same bed: her mother, father, Nina and her younger brother. Still Nina did not speak. Her father had been selling drugs to support the family, and Nina still does not know exactly what happened, but one night her father was doing something behind the house, and when he came in, her mother screamed at him, slapped him in the face and threw him out. After many months passed, and Nina was sure he was not coming back, she began speaking, both in Spanish and English. She ended her essay with something like, "I can finally talk about it; I can finally speak."

Miguel cleared his throat. He had his arms folded and a pained look on his face.

I said, "I don't know, Miguel, but when I finished that essay, I wished I had a degree in another subject that would have been more helpful, or..." I paused. "That I was you."

He laughed. "How did you respond to her?" he asked.

Nina had passed in her essay late, after the term had ended, so I critiqued her over the phone. It was extremely well-written, and I only asked for a few changes. Then, because I guessed the answer was no, I asked if she had sought counseling. Her friends had suggested it, and she knew the weight correlated to the abuse, blah, blah, blah, she said, but no. No counseling. I strongly suggested it as well, and from a specialist in sexual abuse and incest. I told her to keep writing, not as therapy but to make sense of what happened to her. She said she had been through a lot in her life, and I said it sounded so. It was her ambition to write a book before her life was over, and I said she definitely had one in her, she was a wonderful writer. And in a split second, two things occurred to me simultaneously: this was the first time in ten weeks Nina sounded confident, like she was on a path and she knew where she wanted to go; and that it was odd for her, at twenty-five, to use the words "before my life is over."

Then she said to me, "I tested positive."

" Positive for what," I said.

" HIV," she said, "I found out when I was pregnant."

I could not bring myself to ask whether her daughter was positive or not. Instead, I said something like...

"Oh!" Miguel said.

I shrugged my shoulders. "That's right. 'Oh!' is exactly what I said. I got off the phone with her, and I just wanted... I wanted..." I shook my head. What I had done for Nina was nothing.

"Well," Miguel said, "You encouraged her to keep writing, and to get counseling. You gave her permission to write about it: a safe place where she can go to, yes, to make sense of what happened to her. Or, to just get it out so she doesn't have to hold onto it."

I was silent. To me, it sounded puny.

Miguel, clearly reading my thoughts, continued, "Believe me, in my job, I wish I had the power to do more than I can do. You know?"

It was then I went for a walk.

Standing on the shore, I tiptoed to the water, then raced back to the sand as the incoming tide chased me, a game I used to play as a child that made me breathless with laughter. It was coming in fast. A few feet away from me, the three girls, in the water now, were jumping up and down, splashing each other, shrieking, and appeared to be climbing all over their father intent on mock-drowning the poor man, who was laughing despite the fact that he was clearly outnumbered. Suddenly, I saw the pile of towels and clothes that the family had left once safely on shore slide by me, lifted up by water. One more wave, and their belongings would be gone. I raced in to save them and in the process, lost the game. The tide had won. But the girls, running toward me, squealed with gratitude. "Thank you! Thank you so much!"

"Thank you," their father said, sounding relieved.

"No problem," I replied.

As I turned to walk further on down the shore, I heard one of the young girls say to the other, "Wow, that would have been the worst thing ever, right? If we had lost our stuff?"

"Yeah," the other girl said, "I don't care about the towel but my favorite tee shirt I just got and the other stuff, that would have been the worst."

I continued walking, my soaked shorts clammy against my skin. I thought about what the girls had said. I thought about Nina. I thought about fathers and daughters. The chill in the air had gotten sharper and there was a wind that no longer belonged to summer. I looked up. The stars were coming out, obscuring the red, bloody sky.

Published in Sowing Creek Press 2018
Published in the book, *Confessions of an Accidental Professor,* 2018

Tripping

It was the week of February 14th, 2014, the week where New York City had three major snowstorms, cancelling school, delaying flights and stranding passengers. Among them was Evan, Ruth's nephew, in for a visit from LA who suddenly found himself in a winter wonderland for not two days but seven. Keeping him entertained was easy: Evan liked my company and I liked being taken out to dinner. On the Thursday evening of that week, I had my coat on and my hand had almost reached the doorknob when my phone pinged. A new mail. It was after 10 PM but I didn't hesitate in looking, as my response to my cell is Pavlovian: it pings, I must pick up, look, check, scroll.

This mail was from a student. Julio [not his real name] was from South America. He was in my freshman writing class for the second term in a row: an attentive, present, A-student, bilingual in Spanish and English who was also quite open about his obsession with the intricacies of extracting oil from marijuana leaves for the best possible buzz.

His mail read: Professor, I really really need to talk to you right now I mean its okay if your not around but I really need to talk to you right now.

Damn it!

I replied: Julio, you have 5 minutes.

And I sent my number. Took my coat off. Paced. The cell rang.

"Hi professor."

"What's going on, Julio?"

"Um…I'm at my father's….apartment on East 71st and….there are like a lot of people here? In the apartment. And….we made a lot of noise and the neighbor…downstairs…"

Julio was speaking in a slow, irritating way, very unlike him.

"Julio, are you on anything right now? Because you don't sound like you."

"Um…I'm having, like, a really bad acid trip…"

"That's just… fantastic."

"Yeah…it's never happened before…before tonight.."

I said, "So, your neighbor."

"Yeah, the neighbor…downstairs…complained? And this apartment….my father…it took him a long time to get the apartment…he's not an American citizen…and he…"

I said, "Okay, so it's a co-op and you woke the neighbor and you're afraid the neighbor will complain to the co-op board and your father will lose the apartment and then you'll be screwed. Is that close?"

"Yeah…I had…I'm sorry, there was no adult, I have no adult I can talk to here, and so you were the one that I…"

I said, "Julio, how many people are in your apartment?"

He said, "There are two people in the bathroom, and four in the kitchen and a few in the bedroom room and I think someone is under the table in the main hall…"

"Okay, Julio, this is what you're going to do. Are you listening?"

Julio said, "Yes. I am listening."

"Good. You're going to get all of those fucking people out of that apartment! All of them! Except one. You pick one friend to stay with you through your bad acid trip to make sure you don't decide to sail off the roof of your apartment building. Get it?"

"I would never throw myself off the roof, I wo—

"PICK SOMEONE, THE ONE WHO IS THE MOST SOBER, TO STAY WITH YOU! And get everyone else out."

Julio said, "Okay."

I said, "Good. The neighbor who complained: was it a woman?"

Julio said, "Yes."

I said, "Excellent. Tomorrow you are going to go out and buy the biggest, most beautiful bouquet of flowers you can find, and you are going to *handwrite* her a note. You are going to apologize for the noise and say that you and your friends were excited by the NYU snow day and didn't realize how loud you were. And before you go down and present those flowers to her, you are going to *comb* your hair so you look decent. And I

144

promise it will be okay. But you have to do exactly what I tell you to do."

"Okay, okay professor."

"Contact me when everyone's out of the apartment."

"Okay."

"Okay. I'm going to dinner now."

I hung up, put my coat back on and reached for the doorknob. The phone rang. It was Julio. It crossed my mind that I would have to use the words "murderous rage" in a future essay, or play, or short story, or something.

"WHAT NOW JULIO?"

"Um...professor? There are two friends out getting peet-za? Should I wait till they get back to tell them to go home?"

I said, "No, no, no! They have cell phones! You have a cell phone! Call and tell them not to come back!"

Julio said, "Oh. Yeah. Okay, I'll do that."

Fifteen minutes later, with a large glass of wine in front of me and the bottle nearby, I relayed the story to Evan.

He said, "Oh, well, if you need to go to his apartment, take me with you. I went through so many bad acid trips in the 60's, I know exactly what to do."

I said, "I have never done acid, nor did I live through the 60's. And we are not going to that apartment!"

Evan said, "You saved a student tonight. Here's to you!"

I said, "I think that's a bit dramatic."

Evan said, "You did. Is he the first student who's contacted you with a problem?"

I said, "No."

Evan said, "More than a few? Many?"

I said, "Yes."

Evan said, "It doesn't surprise me. But NYU should really be paying you more, you know."

I said, "It's harder for the foreign students. Most of them have no one here: no family, no adult supervision, possibly an apartment to escape the dorms, a lot of money and Manhattan is their playground. At eighteen, nineteen years old. Sounds great. Total freedom. And it is great – until something bad happens."

Evan said, "And they contact you."

I nodded. "It's the part no one tells you about. Part counselor. I did tell one of the heads of the department, Kingsley, that I thought the best training I got for being a college professor was volunteering at The Samaritans suicide hotline and counseling center in London."

"What did he say?"

"Kingsley said, ""Well, you're better equipped than the rest of us.""

Evan said, "What?"

My cell pinged. "It's Julio," I said.

"Read it out loud."

"'Professor I did what you said and everyone is gone except two friends. I am okay and later we'll all go back to the dorms. You have no idea what you did for me tonight."

Evan said, "You know exactly what you did for him! He should take you to dinner."

I said, "That's a brilliant idea! Wait…"

I replied to Julio: I know very well what I did for you tonight, and as my reward, you are taking me to dinner. Pick a Spanish restaurant that you like, one where you won't complain about the food. It must serve wine. You will not be drinking, because you are under age. But I will be.

"Okay! I sent it."

Evan shook his head. "That's…that whole thing is crazy."

I poured myself another glass of wine. "It's an adventure."

❋

The next day, I got a mail from Julio: Professor! The flowers worked! She said what a nice boy I was and of course she understood we were excited about the snow day and when my father comes to town, we should all have dinner together. She even wrote me a note back! I'll text it to you.

I replied: I told you it would work.

146

You Are All a Part of Me

✳

Two weeks later, Julio and I were sitting across from each other at a Spanish restaurant in the Village. I had a glass of red wine in my hand. He had a glass of water.

I said, "Sorry you can't drink."

He said, "That's okay. I'll be drinking later on anyway."

I said, "Of course you will. Why didn't that occur to me?"

Julio said, "Do you like the food?"

I said, "I do. It's delicious."

He said, "I come here with my dad when he's in town. We're both Spanish food snobs, so it has to be good. Authentic. This place is good."

I said, "It is."

Julio said, "I told my friends I called you, the night of the acid trip. They said, 'Are you out of your fucking mind, calling your professor?' I said, 'No, you don't understand. I called her because I knew I could.' Then I told them about you. They said, 'She sounds cool as shit! Can we take her classes?' I told them, 'No, you can't. Her classes are all full. Too bad for you.'"

I laughed.

Julio said, "Thank you."

I said, "You're welcome."

Published in the book, *Confessions of an Accidental Professor,* 2018

Floridians

Florida is such a physically beautiful place, filled with lush vistas and astonishing sunsets that regularly take my breath away. It has a rhythm that is easy to sink into, one that lulls a person into believing she can live on permanent vacation forever. Lured by the weather and the luxury of wearing shorts year-round, people flock there from other cities, states, and countries — or perhaps those are the ones I gravitate toward, the ones I befriended. Or, the ones who befriended me.

Until I got thrown out of the state, of course.

The Man From Kentucky

HE WALKED ME TO MY MOTHER'S CONDO, but I wanted to say goodbye in the parking lot, rather than in front of her door. I was fifty, after all, not fifteen.

I had planned on not seeing him again, thinking that our differences were insurmountable.   We had had three great dates, but that last walk on the beach, with humidity rising and grey storm clouds rolling in on the Gulf, I thought that a number of things I tried to talk about, namely my book and agents and publishers, he either ignored, or did not or could not respond. I couldn't tell which. And if this sounds like I am a snob, you are right: I am a snob, and not only because I am a professor at NYU and have lived in London and New York City for a combination of thirty-two years.

So, in the parking lot and eager to get rid of him, I quickly stuck my hand out (those three great dates were also chaste) to say goodbye.

Easy.

Except, he did not respond in kind. Instead, he took my hand, kissed it and said very slowly, in that pronounced Southern accent, "Lisa, all I want to do is to make love to you and I really DIG YOU." When he said, "dig you" he made a bird-like motion with his hands and pointed at me. Then he turned and walked away.

I have no idea how long I stood there. Could have been a minute, could have been two. I know I can draw the back view of his broad shoulders in the grey tee shirt he was wearing, along with the black shorts and black and grey sneakers until he was in the distance, then no longer visible. Had he turned and glanced over his shoulder, he might have wondered why I looked as if I had just been hit by a bus.

No man had ever said that to me.

Let me rephrase: no man has ever said that to me and been dead serious about what he was saying.

151

This man was *serious*. And he lived in Florida. And I live in New York City. And we are complete opposites.

But after he said, "Lisa, all I want to do is to make love to you and I really DIG YOU," my response was entirely physical. I felt something give in my heart and something give in my shorts at the exact same time. It was the equivalent of a meltdown.

Uh-oh.

And from that moment, I knew that whatever it was that I felt, it was unfinished. I got on the plane back to NYC, thus ending my March spring break, and he began texting me.

Every single morning.

This man was *serious*.

I woke up to those texts, and at first, I thought it was delightful, then unusual, then nuts, then unsustainable, and then I so looked forward to them that one day when he was late, I missed that communication terribly.

In the Age of Technology, I would call this WVT- Wooing Via Text.

He had told me his fiftieth birthday was May 17th. Well, my term ended on May 9th, and wouldn't you know, I have summers off. So I casually mentioned I had some time off and if he could get free for a day or two, maybe I could come down and see him for his birthday. We looked at some dates. Then I got this text: "I think so highly of you I rearranged my whole vacation [normally a week in August] so I could spend time with you."

Did I mention that I have made all of the major decisions in my life, for better or worse, in under three seconds?

1. Moving to London
2. Moving to New York City
3. Becoming a teacher.
4. Booking my flight.

He also asked his boss of twenty-one years to borrow a small efficiency apartment on the beach, only for me, not for him, and this was granted.

You Are All a Part of Me

My mother of seventy-three has recently learned how to text. This newly-acquired skill of hers is now the bane of my life. After all this transpired with Kentucky, which is my nickname for him and where he comes from (his given name is Mike), this is the following annotated text conversation I had with her:

Tuesday, March 22

Mom: Don't you think you are moving a little fast with a man you hardly know?

Me: I have two months to get to know him via text and phone. I can't get to know him in person unless I spend some time there or he spends some time here. I am not staying with him (he, like me, has a roommate). So, if after a week, we hate each other, or our worlds are too different, then at least I will know. And he will, too. If I don't at least try, I'll never know: nothing ventured, nothing gained.

Tuesday, March 29th

Me: Kentucky called a little while ago and I actually feel a whole lot better now. He arranged the rental with his boss and it is free: he has the key and is checking the place out tomorrow. If it's awful, he'll arrange something else. I am not used to a man saying, "I'll take care of it" and actually taking care of it. The fact is, I have done everything for myself for such a long time, I no longer trust any man to do anything. But surprisingly, Kentucky has taken care of it, and, like, wow. I think I'm in shock.

Mom: Good for him. I hope you have a lot in common with him. I'm sure he's a nice guy, but I wonder if he has your love of books, plays and the arts to keep you interested. You are a very smart woman!!

Me: Probably not. But I had all that in common with Yash and the marriage didn't work. You also are a very smart woman, and you and Steve [my step-father] are very different. The marriage works. Maybe opposites attract? I don't know.

Mom (after a pause): Good point.

And if this sounds like my mother is a snob, you are right: she is a snob, not only because she got all A's in school and the one time in her life she got a B, she sat down and cried, knowing my grandfather would punish her when she got home; but also because she was a taskmaster with me about grades, homework, activities, college, etc... She expected a lot, and because of that, I thrived. She wanted the best, still wants the best for me.

But love is a complete and total mystery.

＊

Every year for the past fifteen years, on spring break, I have gone down to visit my mother and stepfather in Venice, Florida, where they have retired. And every year, I have been going to the Venice Avenue Creamery shop to buy iced coffee, which is both delicious and giant-sized, roughly 16 ounces for two dollars (unheard of in New York City). The shop is airy and white with Flamingo-pink wrought-iron seats; it smells yummy, because they make their own cones on the premises, and the menfolk behind the counter are always pleasant, chatty, complimentary, and sometimes flirtatious. I walk in feeling okay and leave with the over-inflated ego of a super model — that's how skillfully these men wield their flattery. In that vein, Kentucky, the manager, is usually the one who waits on me.

We have talked and flirted, and talked and flirted. For years. And for years, while also noticing the absence of a wedding ring, I have wondered why the man never asked me out for a drink, a meal, or even an ice cream cone. One year, he had a cross around his neck, and so I thought he was likely a deeply religious person who was looking for another deeply religious person, which I am not. Or, he was celibate, like a priest, which I am not. A year later, no cross. So I remained puzzled, yet pleased when he told me I was beautiful, and kept leaving the shop with only my giant-sized coffee.

This past March, I went down for my annual visit. I went to Venice Avenue Creamery. Behind the counter, Jimmy, a striking man of sixty-nine with white hair, a white goatee, bright blue eyes and a southern accent, went in immediately: "You need to be coming here every day. Please do."

"You need to move down here; we need you down here."

"If I were thirty-five years younger, I'd chase you all over the state of Florida."

"You're just beautiful."

Kentucky, meanwhile, ran around getting my coffee, nodding with Jimmy in agreement. When he handed it to me, he said, "You're beautiful."

I left with my coffee.

Halfway through my visit, during a Venice Avenue Creamery stop, Jimmy, while appraising me from top to bottom, said, "Miss Lisa? I'm going to ask you something that I shouldn't ask but I'm going to ask anyway."

I said, "Okay."

He said, "I've noticed you wear no wedding ring on your left hand."

I said, "Right."

He said, "You're not married?"

I said, "No, I'm not.

He fairly shouted, "WHAT IS WRONG WITH THE MEN IN NEW YORK CITY?"

I laughed. Then I said, "Well, the men in New York City by and large want twenty-one-year-olds, and that's not me, and I don't care!"

He said, "They must be out of their minds. If I were a younger man…"

By that time, I had gotten to the register, and Jimmy asked if I had children. I said I was divorced with no children. And Kentucky, who had been silent and I hoped, listening to all of this, stuck out his hand as if to shake mine and said, "Divorced, no children, no baggage!"

I laughed, shook his hand and said, "Me, too!"

As he was ringing me up, he said, "You come down here every year, right?"

I said yes.

He said, "We should get together and go out."

I said, "That would be great."

On Thursday night, I met him for dinner, which happened to be St. Patrick's Day, so the city was crazy-busy. We went to one place and the noise level was apparent from the sidewalk; once in, I asked the hostess, "How loud is it out there?" She said it was pretty loud, and it would take ten minutes for a table.

"Let's go," I said to Kentucky.

"Okay," he said. As we crossed the street to go to his first choice, he said, "Lisa, man, you've really got it together."

I said, "What makes you say that?"

He said, "Most women don't."

The date was great, because it was a proper date. Much later, when we said goodbye, I kissed him, but he was smiling at the time, so no kiss. No reciprocal kiss.

I went in. I paced the guest bedroom. No kiss bothered me. So, I texted him.

On Friday night, I met him for a drink, then a walk, and we wound up sitting on a bench by the sea under the moonlight. We talked. And talked and talked. Kentucky initially began as a basketball player and went to a college in Michigan on a basketball scholarship, and all was well till he blew out his knee. No more scholarship, so no more university. He went to college in Sarasota, but never finished. Later, I found out that even though he has no degree *and I have three*, as a manager he makes far and away more money than I do. This is the way it is now in America.

It was a beautiful night. We were on the bench together for perhaps an hour, perhaps more. And he still didn't kiss me.

Walking back to the car, he was still talking until I said, "Shut up and kiss me."

Yay!

He unlocked the ice cream shop (the manager is the one to befriend as he is the one who has the keys) and we ate Key Lime Pie frozen yogurt (in addition to the cones, they also make all their own ice cream, toppings, etc… on the premises) standing behind the counter. He said something about being nervous the night before, or jittery, or intimidated, which made me laugh, so I kissed him again, which was nice. And I liked his arm around my waist.

When we said goodbye, no kiss.

WTF??

Saturday, the day I was leaving, Kentucky asked if he could see me for a walk or breakfast or both, so we went to the beach and walked.

On days that involve me getting on a plane, I am irritable, anxious and distracted. I love arriving, but hate traveling. I hate packing. I hate airports. I hate everything traveling involves.

So on the beach with those billowing storm clouds in the distance, impatient that Kentucky didn't get every reference or detail I threw at him, I decided I wouldn't keep in touch and instead remain friendly. I'd stop by for iced coffee when I was in town. But I didn't think he was the man for me.

Until we said goodbye.

Published in *Unmasked*,2018

Angel on the Beach

KENTUCKY WAS AT THE AIRPORT TO PICK ME UP when I arrived. We hugged, and kissed cheeks. There was small talk in the car for the 45 minute ride to the city, and we first stopped by my mother's to say hello (and pick up some things I had left there), then grocery shopping, then to the efficiency apartment (where I couldn't help but notice that the king-sized bed took up most of the space) to unload and unpack, then en route to dinner, we stopped at a disappointing yard sale (my call). Arrived at the restaurant — Robbi's. The table had a bright light that bothered my eyes until Kentucky reached up and unscrewed the bulb. I do appreciate a tall man. After that, we ordered oysters, shrimp, two glasses of wine (for me), iced tea (for him, as he does not drink) and conversation flowed. The more we talked, the more I liked him, and I had had two months of texts and conversations to get to know him beforehand. We went back to the apartment, and Kentucky looked nervous, like he didn't know what to do next.

I said, "What's the time?"

This was, in fact, a ruse.

He said, "8:15."

I said, "Time to get naked." (Sidebar: I am not a romantic.)

And we did.

I don't think I can explain chemistry, any more than I can explain love. The first time with anyone is usually awkward, getting to know another person's body, likes and dislikes, touches and tastes. Not so much with Kentucky. There was fun and pleasure and joy. There was also a lot of laughter, thankfully the kind you do with each other, rather than *at* each other. Because that would have sucked.

The second day went by in a blur. There was not much sleeping. We walked on Golden Beach (yep, it is really called "Golden Beach") less than

100 yards from our rental, and then swam. We went out to eat. We held hands. We talked and got to know each other better. This was to be our daily ritual.

On our third day, after our walk and swim, we emerged from the sea and were standing on the shore, huddled in towels and then in an embrace. Kentucky is tall, 6' 1", which as I said, I like very much. I have to reach up to get to him.

In my periphery, a slim woman I had seen on the beach the day before approached us. I guessed she was about seventy. She was all in white: white hat, white long shorts, white long-sleeved jacket. She had short, dark hair and dark glasses against her pale skin. We both turned to look at her and she said, in a heavily accented English, with a wave of her arm, "You have the ocean here" and then another wave in our direction, "And you have true love here. What more could a person ask for?"

We were so surprised all we could do was grin like idiots. After introducing ourselves, Kentucky began explaining about how we met and I asked her name but not much else. We parted, and I have to say, my first impression of Inge was that she was an enigma, and something else I couldn't quite put my finger on. Not everyone would walk up to a couple she did not know and say that. I wondered what her story was.

The next day, we were on the beach in the same spot, same routine. Inge saw us and approached. Again, she was almost completely covered and all in white. She asked us a few questions, I asked where she was from (Inge is from Denmark — I had incorrectly guessed Germany — glad I did not say that out loud) and then she heard I had lived in London, was from New York City and realized I was not living in Florida so our path to sustaining true love would not be easy or immediate. I motioned to her rings and said they were unusual and beautiful.

She said, "Yes, well, Phil. We were dating, together for many years, after my first husband died and he was divorced (since the late 1980's), then last year I was diagnosed with breast cancer, so I had a mastectomy."

She brushed the left side of her chest with her hand and that is when I saw the smooth where her breast once was. And as she talked, her voice remained absolutely steady, calm, but tears ran out from under her sunglasses and down her cheeks. "I said to him, we had discussed it before, well, why wait? We decided to marry, because of time, you know. No more waiting. Why wait? You know, there is so much preoccupation with money, and I don't worry about that — yes, it's fine to have but it is not the point, not important. The point is, why wait? What is important is this." She motioned to the two of us.

And when Inge left us to go back into her cottage, we sat down next to each other on the sand and looked out onto that vast, deep sea, and I burst into tears. Last time I cried was a few years ago, at someone's funeral. I hate crying. Hate it. Kentucky hugged me tightly, but didn't say anything. Good. Then I didn't have to explain.

It's not as if I have never known anyone who has gone through cancer or disaster or trauma or loss, and I had just met Inge. Perhaps it was because there was little to no emotion in her voice as she brushed her hand down the smooth of her chest, while tears ran down her cheeks. Or it could have been what she had said the day before. Possibly, my state of mind? I don't know. But I do know that she reached down and pulled something out of me, and I felt inexplicably connected to her.

We ran into Inge and Phil the next day, having wine on their gazebo. They are also complete opposites, which is delightful. Phil is a short, stout, deeply-tanned, affable Cuban-New Yorker and though Inge is reserved in manner, she has no trouble displaying public affection to Phil, which makes him blush. They asked us to come for drinks the following evening at their place in Venice Villas. We were greeted at the door by Inge's pug, Petunia. I brought wine, sunflowers and white daisies for Inge and a note, saying I thought she was a wonderful woman and if she didn't mind, I'd like to stay in contact. Inge was touched, and we talked. She mentioned they were going on a cruise to Europe in August and were looking forward to it. She asked when I was leaving and when I would be back. I said we had been talking about August, but that depended on whether we could find a place to stay. Phil asked what dates I was looking at. Conversation rolled on about all sorts of things: dogs, Italian food, teaching, parents, ice cream, New York stories.

Inge said to me, "You are so vivacious, so lively. A different background. You are not just boring, 'I am from Ohio' or 'I am from Florida.' It's very good."

We had a terrific evening.

On the day I was to leave, Kentucky and I had a last walk and a swim on the beach. I saw Inge motion from the front of her cottage, and she walked toward us with a camera and took a photo. While he stopped at the gazebo to rinse his feet with the communal hose, Inge asked me to come to her patio. She said, "We are going on a cruise in August to September so, we want to say, to offer you to stay here? But there is a catch."

I knew already. I said, "Look after Petunia."

She said, "Yes. Then we don't have to board her."

Inge's villa is thirty steps from the beach. From her front door, there is a view of the ocean. There is a gazebo to watch the sunset from. There is a grill outside. It is a spectacular place to write. And it is a spectacular place to be with someone you might find true love with.

She ushered me into her house. She took a calendar from her desk and put it on the bed. "We are leaving here, on August 14th and back September 7th."

I said, while my heart skipped and pounded in my chest, "My course ends on the 12th. I can fly down on the 15th and stay until September 2nd."

She said," Perfect. And maybe Mike can stay here the night before and look after Petunia. But you discuss it with him first."

I said, "I really think Mike will be fine with all this" which might have been the understatement of the century.

I walked outside, called to Kentucky and waved furiously. He came to the patio and all I could do was point to Inge while she explained that she was giving us her cottage for two and a half weeks. This time, it was Kentucky who looked as if he had been hit by a bus.

We fairly skipped back to the efficiency, and all Kentucky kept saying was, "Oh my God, Oh my God, Oh my God! She loves you! Oh my God!"

Ten minutes later, I booked my flight back to Florida for August 15th, 2016.

No One Is From Here

I HAVE NOT SEEN IT, BUT AM NOW OBSESSED. For weeks, I stare at the horizon until I'm blinded, yet still no green flash of light.

I've been living in Venice, Florida, in a tiny villa on the beach since August 2016 and am addicted to the sun sinking into the Gulf of Mexico the way an alcoholic is to beer. I have to have it, and have it every day.

In Manhattan, the sunset is marred by buildings set into the stone of a grid system, barely glimpsed between city blocks. The beaches on Long Island are better. The beaches in Provincetown, Massachusetts, better still. But perhaps it is the proximity here, and the closer I am, the more intoxicated I feel. Awed by the beauty of Venice Beach, by the way sky, sun and clouds change shape and shade and color nightly, I let it fill me, wishing I could drink it, that it would pour into me, and I could hold it a bit longer before it fades to black.

But I still see no green flash of light, despite Paul insisting that I must. Everyone I know here has seen it, and until I do, I am odd woman out.

Then I get chilly and walk the ten seconds back to the tiny villa and make dinner. Unfortunately, this blissful routine will soon end, as I have to find another place to live due to rising rents, just like New York City.

So I enjoy all the sunsets I can for as long as I am able.

After I had been living at Venice Villas for about a month, Doug, the handy man, banged on my door at an ungodly hour of the morning.

"Exterminator!"

"Hang on one minute!" I said, grabbing my robe and putting away the Murphy bed.

I let them in. Doug is wraithlike, with the tanned skin of a Floridian, a long, grey ponytail, and bright blue eyes that match the grey tee shirt and jeans he wears daily. He appears to be sun-bleached, except for his skin. He is trailed by the exterminator, a large man with dark hair and a goatee, carrying a giant metal canister. I make small talk to avoid thinking about my Medusa-like hair and bathrobe-clad presentation.

"The cockroaches here are different from the ones in New York City," I say.

"Palmetto bugs," the exterminator says, "They fly, too. I've seen the ones in New York City. Big."

"Are you from Florida?" I ask.

At this, the exterminator stops spraying, puts down his canister with a clang, straightens up, looks at me and says, "Oh. No one is from here."

Unlike New York City, where anyone who moves there is desperate to become a "New Yorker," with time I will discover that in Florida, not being "from here" is not only a point of pride, but also a badge of honor to be flashed whenever possible.

"Where are you from, then?"

"Dallas, Texas," says the exterminator with pride. "And we got bugs there, too, thank goodness. I'll never go out of business."

Doug pipes up with, "No bugs in the east."

I said, "I'm from New York City, and trust me we have bugs."

"Further on up," Doug says, "Vermont. I'm from Vermont. Too cold for bugs in Vermont."

They have both seen the green flash of light as the sun dips into the gulf, because I asked them. They are surprised I haven't yet.

Inge, my Danish friend who also lives in Venice Villas, has seen it, along with her husband Phil, who is also a New Yorker. My parents, both New Englanders, have seen it "many times," they inform me. The man I am dating, Kentucky, who has lived in Venice for thirty-four years but spent his formative years in Kentucky and lives mostly in KENTUCKY-emblazoned tee shirts, hence his nickname, has seen it. My friend Yadira, who is Cuban, has seen it. Matt, a press photographer from Houston, has seen it, too.

Obviously, it must be me.

On my nightly walks, I can go in one of two directions: toward the Venice Fishing Pier and the Brohard Paw Park, or to the South Jetty and past Paul, whom I befriended. Paul is tall, black, charismatic: when he sets up his camera, people want to be near him, and he draws a crowd. Sometimes he has an entourage, sometimes an audience. I tease him and tell him he has a fan club, which makes him laugh.

I asked him how he came to photograph the sunset every evening.

He said, "I was a corrections officer in Upstate New York, and one day, there was a riot at the prison. My partner lost an eye. And I died next to a trashcan. I literally died. As it all went to black — I didn't see any white light, there was nothing — I thought, 'I'm going to die here beside a damn trashcan.' I don't know how long for. The next thing I remember thinking was, 'Why is someone beating my chest? I've already been beaten and kicked in the head.' But it was EMT's bringing me back to life. After that, New York retired me, pay and pension till the day I die. So now I live here: two blocks from the beach, apartment $675 a month everything included, I found my hobby photographing sunsets, and life is beautiful. Look at it," he says, pointing to yet another spectacular sunset, "Just beautiful."

I thought, Is that why people come here, to escape into the sunsets? And is that what I am doing, escaping New York City and Ruth's death? Running, like a coward?

I said, "It's just beautiful."

Paul told me to look for the green flash of light "through the prism" as the sun sets into the Gulf of Mexico. "The clearer the horizon, the better the chance," Paul said, "But it doesn't happen very often. If you blink, you miss it."

Yes, but he also said he has seen it "dozens of times."

When I tell Kentucky all this, he asks if Paul has hit on me.

"No. Why?"

"I'm just surprised he hasn't hit on you, is all."

"I've never gotten any vibe like that from him. He's just a nice person."

"I know men, so I'm just saying…"

"Okay, well, I answered you so can we go get dinner now?"

And I forget about this line of questioning, because it never entered my mind.

165

One night, there is an odd-looking man next to Paul, and as I walk up, Paul looks at me and says, "This is Marc/Rumi."

I say, "Sorry?"

Marc/Rumi says, "You can call me either one, whatever you're comfortable with."

Paul says, "Marc spent many years in India. He's an old hippie." And he gives Marc/Rumi a squeeze.

And in fact, Marc/Rumi is wearing some kind of blue sari bottoms and a roomy tee shirt. He is reed-thin and fragile-looking, and has frizzy white hair that puffs out on either side of his head. His age… I have no idea. His face is weathered, his black eyes bright. Later, I find out he is seventy-one.

I ask, "Where do you come from?"

Marc/Rumi says, "Oh, I'm not of this world. I was raised in France and Germany then brought here, but out there, somewhere, is where I belong."

He points to the horizon, and continues.

"I don't feel like I'm from anywhere, this man-made growth is so alien to me, I'm thinking of moving to Hawaii to one of the islands. There's too much growth here, I'm anti-growth. It's not to do with nature. So I'm from everywhere and from nowhere."

I take this as my cue to depart immediately.

The next few times I see Paul on the beach, Marc/Rumi is not with him.

In the interim, I meet the owners of the tiny villa, Therese and her husband. They live six blocks away and are retired, like most of the people who live in Venice, where the median age is sixty-four. Therese has had a stroke which has left half of her face immobilized, and her younger, unkempt, spattered husband, who looks like he just came from painting a house, kids me that the tiny villa is "probably a palace compared to what you had in New York City." He leans against the Murphy bed wall as he says this, looking pleased with himself. He is wrong and actually it is the other way around, but I'd hate to correct him and shatter his shining, know-it-all moment.

They tell me the water tank needs to be replaced and this may be "an inconvenience." They also tell me the toilet needs to be replaced because there is a leak and the plumber will contact me. This also may be an inconvenience. The following day, the plumber does call, but I am out cycling. I call him back. He tells me to call his office and schedule an appointment. I do, and the woman on the receiving end says she has no idea what I'm talking about, and "Why are the owners leaving it to you when they should be doing this themselves?"

Good question.

We get everything sorted and I have a date with the plumber the day after, which is a good thing since I clog the toilet at 4 AM and the plunger is inadequate, ineffective. I give up and go to bed, hating everyone.

Kevin the plumber is not from here. He is from Upstate New York. He is a nice man who doesn't make me feel bad about clogging the toilet and tells me that the most expensive toilets recline.

"Really?" I say.

"Oh yeah, top of the line. That's what I have at my house. Reclines. Leather. Big television screen at the back."

Call me crazy, but I want to be on the toilet seat for as brief a time as possible.

We chat for a while. I ask how long he has lived in Venice. He says, "I came here to visit friends in 1997. After two weeks, I went home, packed a few swimsuits and came back. I've been here ever since. Never go back. No point."

He fixes the toilet. He tells me he has to come back another day to replace the water tank. "That will take a few hours," he says, "but what's worse is I need a permit because it's the city of Venice, and that means an inspector is going to come and you won't have any idea when he does. He doesn't tell us. He just shows up."

That's three days of being inconvenienced. I say, "Can you do me a favor?"

He says, "Sure."

"When you calculate the bill, charge the owners a lot of money. Because I am not the owner, I rent this place. And for my trouble, the owners are raising the rent three hundred dollars come January, because it's high season. Because they can. And I will no longer be able to stay here."

"What are you paying?"

I tell him.

"Jeeez! That's my mortgage payment."

"I'm sure. Add three hundred bucks and that's my January rent."

Kevin says, "That's not fair."

I say, "I know."

He says, "Do you want me to leave some cash on the water heater that you can find later or something?"

I laugh. "That would be swell, but no. Just whatever it is you're going to charge, stack on a few extra. You're a plumber. You can do that."

We arrange the water tank for the following Monday. His office calls to confirm the plumber will be there between 10 AM and 2 PM.

I go on the hunt for an apartment. Most require 1st, last, security, background and credit checks and HOA checks, all of which cost money.

That evening, on the beach, I explain my plight to Paul and ask about the apartment he lives in. He had said it was "$675 all-inclusive, two blocks from the beach." Like all rent-obsessed New Yorkers, I have remembered that number, which is why I am asking.

He gives me his landlord's number. "How is your French?" he says.

"Non-existent," I say.

"His name is Axel. He's French. Mention my name."

In my periphery, I see Marc/Rumi coming toward us but it is at the tail end of this conversation, so Paul explains my situation.

Without even a pause, Marc/Rumi looks at me and says, "You can have my apartment. I'm moving to Hawaii. It's $650 a month and it's two blocks from the beach."

It can't be that easy, I think. Impossible.

Marc/Rumi says, "First, you should come and see it. Here's my number. Call me tomorrow."

The next day, I call. Marc/Rumi says, "When are you coming? I'm at the library and about to leave."

I say, "Take your time, forty-five minutes."

I cycle over and it's five minutes from my tiny villa on the beach.

Marc/Rumi meets me outside and asks me to park my bike in his shed. Another man walks by: this is Gary, the landlord. We are introduced and shake hands. He says to take his number, as Marc/Rumi has spoken to him about me. I oblige.

We walk into Marc/Rumi's place and he takes his shoes off. The interior is white, filled with light, and there is a small kitchen painted yellow to the left, with a table and chairs just outside the archway. There are archways through to each room, no doors. The eating nook blends into the sitting room, where there is a futon, television and DVD player. Walking through, there is a bedroom and a bathroom off to the left. Sliding doors in the bedroom lead to a spacious patio shaded with orange blossoms dangling down from an unidentifiable tree. There is a grill to the left and a few chairs scattered round. The whole place reminds me of flats in Seville, very Spanish stucco. I love it.

"Shall we take a walk?" Marc/Rumi says, "Because there are complications, as there always are in life."

We begin to walk. It's November 15th and I am still in shorts and a tank top. Marc/Rumi is in his baggy Indian pants and a tee shirt.

"It's warm," he says, "I am unhappy I didn't wear a top more suited to the weather."

Marc/Rumi leads the way down the backroads to the beach. As the sun beats down on us, he says, "You walk fast. It's Manhattan. I don't want to disrupt your natural gait, but I don't think I can keep up with you."

I say, "No, no, no. I came here to slow my gait. I will adapt to you."

I slow and I listen. He says, "I grew up in Germany and then France and then when I was about ten, my father, a diplomat, was posted back here in the states, in Chapel Hill, North Carolina. I was very unhappy to come to the states. I loved France, and loved the European way. My father took me to DC with him when I was about fifteen. He had some lobbyists to meet with, so he introduced me to another senator and I wound up interning on Capitol Hill for the summer. I decided to learn everything I could: so I listened when people didn't think I was listening. No one really pays attention to a teenager. I asked questions. I read, and asked more questions. And when I had learned all that I could, it was enough to despise politics for the rest of my life. It doesn't matter what party is in power. All politics is the same, the way man works and the way the world works is all the same."

At some point, Marc/Rumi had decided to "opt out" of mainstream life, without a proper job. He lived in Israel on a kibbutz. He had been homeless in New York City, but "in those days, you could sleep in the park and no one would bother you." He lived in India in an ashram for ten years. His spiritual awakening occurred there and he is a devotee of Meher Baba. Where he felt most at home was India.

His father retired to Venice, and Marc/Rumi came back to look after him because he was dying. That is how Marc/Rumi wound up living in Venice.

But there was something else as well, a brain injury, I think? A brain injury due to a fall. Two falls. Marc/Rumi does not connect this to what he did with his life. He does not say, "Because I had a brain injury, I could not work, therefore…" The way he lived his life was by choice, and about that he is very clear.

Many years ago, he also published a small book of poems, and still writes poetry which he sends to me and a few others, though not for publication. He signs them "Ruhi Ruki Rumi."

I have never been free
Even the years of wandering & searching
When I was strong & had courage
Wrote some beautiful poems i wasn't free

How to explain this to express it I don't know
There was always the human limitations

You Are All a Part of Me

The confinement of my body
The prison of my mind

All I did with my life was to learn stories
To have experiences to realize nothing
Not in Meher Baba or any God any country
Did I find I was free & happy & suffering ended

Ruhi Ruki Rumi

Each time I see him, more of his story is revealed, but there are gaps because there is no particular chronology. I do ask questions, as he does about what is going on in my own life. He does not subject me to a monologue. But in terms of timeframe and trajectory, Marc/Rumi is elusive. He is like a painting by Braque, three-dimensional and fragmented.

Marc/Rumi has a Section 8 voucher that is being transferred from an apartment in Sarasota to an apartment building not on Maui, but one of the lesser-occupied Hawaiian islands, and his caseworker said that should happen on January the 1st. He says he is leaving everything behind and how much furniture do I have? I say I have a table. And two suitcases full of clothes. Books. A piece of coral and a perfectly intact conch I dug out of the sand on Venice Beach during one of Hurricane Hermine's lulls. He asks if I want the futons and I say yes, so we negotiate a price for the two. I tell him to sell the telly and the DVD player. He is leaving the pots and pans and such, so I don't have to start from scratch. He says, "It won't take you long, with your personality, to get established here."

He asks if I have lights on my bicycle. I say yes.

"On the front and back?"

"Yes," I say.

"Good, because the police will stop you in high season and give you a fine if you don't, for your own protection. The snowbirds come down here and are horrendous drivers. They don't pay attention. It's best you stick to the back roads, get to know them. Safer that way."

171

I tell him one of the reasons I like it down here is I can ride my bike as a means of transport and for fun on the daily. I can't do that in Manhattan because people drive like maniacs.

We reach the beach, take off our sandals and walk to the water. He talks about the unspoiled nature of the islands in Hawaii, what Venice used to be like and what it is now.

"When I first got here," he says, "the water was emerald green. Conch shells washed up on the shore every day, and the beach itself was much smaller. Then they dredged the ocean, widened the beach and I don't understand why man is so stupid. Man is greedy, and only sees dollar signs."

It was then I began to feel like I was walking with Gandhi. Marc/ Rumi only needed a walking stick, really. And perhaps glasses. He is smart and thoughtful and soft-spoken, slight but strong. My first impression of him being an oddball only tells me one thing: that I am a judgmental idiot.

He tells me how he met Gary and the nature of their relationship. From the first, Gary, who identifies as a Christian, says that God wanted Marc/Rumi to live in his building, so Gary has looked after him in terms of housing, and for many years has functioned more like guardian angel than landlord. Though Marc/Rumi does not use the word "guardian angel," that is what it sounds like to me. Gary likes to help people. So does Marc/Rumi/Gandhi. So do I.

As we leave the beach, he asks me a few questions: how I came to be in Venice and why. He knows New York City well. Because he was homeless there, he never wants to go back. He leads me to an outdoor shower area, and as we rinse our feet, he says, "Are you interested in Paul?"

"In Paul?" I reply, stupidly.

"Yes, in Paul."

"Uh, no," I say.

"Well, you better tell him, because he thinks a lot and gets romantic ideas."

"I should…?"

"Well, he's attracted to you."

I say, "The only thing I thought Paul was attracted to was his camera."

"Naive. That's all right. I was young and naive, too."

I really hate it when Kentucky is even halfway right about anything to do with men in relation to myself.

We cross the street, and walk back to the Spanish bungalow. Marc/Rumi/Gandhi makes tea.

"I may just leave at a moment's notice, would that be problematic for you?"

"Not at all," I say. I am good at a moment's notice.

We part and I ride home. I feel remarkably calm and happy. I leave a message for Gary, walk the beach, take photos with the iPhone, eat, do yoga and go to bed.

The next morning, Marc/Rumi/Gandhi calls and says, "Gary got your message but couldn't get back to you. I spoke with him and he said you can have the apartment. He doesn't require first, last or security deposit; he would appreciate a month's notice in the event you are going to move out. He doesn't advertise, he rents only by word of mouth which is why he never has any problems."

I say, "Wow, thank you so much," and stutter a lot.

Marc/Rumi/Gandhi says, "You can come and visit me whenever you want."

"I will," I say.

And now I will be here in Florida for the duration. An apartment means permanency, of sorts. Commitment. Belonging.

A few nights later, while on the beach at sunset, that other-worldly green color appears in a burst. It makes me gasp, and so I stay on the beach, savoring the pleasure of the scarlet-streaked sky in all of its vast gloriousness, eventually deepening to indigo. I am finally linked to those who are united in their independence, those who have chosen Venice and its stunning vistas to settle, for now. I can't wait to tell Paul and the rest of my friends, all who are not from here.

School Maze

BEFORE ARRIVING AND LONG BEFORE my friend Ruth died, I applied to the Sarasota County School Board (SCSB) in the hope of teaching in private, charter or public schools. All transcripts, recommendations, references, work history, CV, cover letter, and $75 dollar fee were taken care of, and I was reliably informed it would take six weeks to determine if I qualified to do any kind of teaching whatsoever. That brings me to the end of September.

End of September: I receive a letter stating I can obtain a provisional certificate which says I am qualified to teach grades 6-12 English, provided a school hires me first and puts in the paperwork. That is the only way to get a provisional certificate. The teaching jobs advertised online, in the paper, anywhere and everywhere will only hire teachers who have a certificate to teach. If that sounds like a Catch-22, it is.

In the interim, I answer an ad for the Hershorin Schiff Community Day School, an all-faith private school, for substitute teaching. When I arrive, I am surprised to find I am in a room with mostly elderly people. Later, I will come to understand that elderly people, with much leisure time and little need of solvency, are my primary competition.

We fill out forms. We are all told that unless we are fingerprinted, no one gets hired. We are also told that once we get fingerprinted, everyone is hired.

They also need: Driver's License, Homeland Security forms, W9, work history, references, recommendations, CV, all manner of other forms to signature and swear up and down that I am not a pedophile, vagrant, transient, grifter, homeless person, bum, felon, squeegee-windshield-wiper-street-thief.

When I ask Kentucky why so much bureaucratic red tape, he says, "Because Florida is the toilet bowl of America."

My mother takes me to get fingerprinted.

You Are All a Part of Me

We walk through the door that says "Granny Agency/Fingerprinting," leaving us both mightily confused. We sit in the lobby. A woman comes out and commences the fingerprinting, also in the lobby, in full view of everyone, asking my height, weight, eye color, hair color, etc…I ask her about the Granny part of the signage, and she says their agency places nurses in residences, and every nurse has to be fingerprinted.

"Oh," I say, "I get it. That kind of security makes total sense."

She says, looking relieved, "I'm glad you get it. Most people don't."

Some $60 later, I am good to go for the Hershorin School. Except I am told they also need to take a copy of my Social Security card, and I did not bring that with me to Florida; I left it, inexplicably, in New York City. I call my ex, pleading stupidity, and ask him to send it to me along with my expired passport and "The Plot Against America" because in the unlikely event Donald Trump becomes president, I might have to re-read that essential Roth fiction.

My ex complies. That takes six days.

I am offered a few days of subbing, and I accept. The teachers at Hershorin call the subs directly; they are responsible for covering their own classes, and have access to the list of substitutes. The day before I am to go in, the teacher calls and cancels.

Two weeks later, I am called again to sub for two days for a classroom full of 3rd graders. This fills me with dread. But this time, the assistant principal is the one to call, and she says, "I know you prefer older children, but we really wanted to get you in here." I accept.

After two days of subbing for the 3rd graders, I am much wiser. This is what I learned:

1. Subbing is glorified babysitting.

2. My inclination never to have children was correct.

3. Corporal punishment in schools should be reconsidered.

4. Fathers of the 3rd graders consider substitute teachers hostage audiences as well as their dating pool.

5. Were I to stay on permanently, I would become an alcoholic in a matter of months.

I answer an ad for Imagine Academy, teaching 9th grade English. It is in Northport, miles from nowhere. My mother drives me to the interview, which lasts about forty minutes. The principal is impressed with my CV and says things like: "You could teach AP college courses if they are ever offered here again," and "It would be good to have an MFA on staff." I depart, hopeful.

The next day, the same Imagine Academy is splashed all over the television news, all over the net, all over the front page of the Herald Tribune, because two students threatened to blow up the school.

I take this as a bad omen and no longer am interested in the job.

A week later, the principal of Imagine Academy, whose first name is Cher, calls and asks to see me again. My mother thinks it is worth the ride and takes me.

Cher is again impressed and I am almost persuaded to work at Imagine until she says, "How do you feel about working with the parents of students?"

I think, How does "No" sound?

I say, "Parents?"

She says if a student is falling behind or disenchanted or problematic, I would contact the parents and we would "work together" toward a solution. In my experience, teaching is hard enough without parental involvement. This was one of the beauties of college teaching, at least the colleges where I have taught — not a parent in sight.

Cher calls me the next day and I decline the job.

That night, I do not need drugs to help me sleep.

Kentucky introduces me to the principal of SKY Academy, another charter school. We meet in a bowling alley. He looks like he could be one of Mark Wahlberg's brothers and is wearing jeans, an AC/DC tee shirt, a long chain with some sort of pendant on it, and a baseball hat. This guy is my kind of principal. His name is Steve Smith. Steve tells me that there are so many steps to becoming a sub it's crazy, everyone has to go through them, but once I'm in, with my degrees and experience, I will work. He makes me feel a lot better about my prospects. He gives me his assistant principal's name and number and tells me she will help me with whatever I need. Her name is Michelle Sooklai. When I meet her, six weeks later, I am delighted to find she looks and sounds almost exactly like Roseanne Barr.

Michelle tells me to register online with SCSB. I tell her I did that. She tells me to register as a sub and not to tell them it is for a charter school, or SCSB won't certify me. I go back to the site, and there are twelve steps, rather like a twelve-step program for AA. There are forms to prove I am not a pedophile, an online eight-hour SUB course I have to take, work history, CV, privacy policy, references, recommendations, a $20 dollar application fee, a $38 dollar drug test, a certificate from a physician stating I am physically fit to teach, and a $90 dollar fingerprinting.

I call Michelle and tell her I have already been fingerprinted. She says Hershorin is separate from them and SCSB has their own mandatory fingerprinting set-up.

I think, Fuck me.

I delay.

A week later, Steve contacts Kentucky and asks why I dropped the ball. Annoyed, I write Steve an email: "I have limited funds right now, and honestly feel hard done by having to pay ninety dollars for fingerprints when I already paid sixty for fingerprints — it's not my fault Florida agencies refuse to share information. They behave like the CIA and the FBI. So if you want me, you pay for the fingerprinting."

Send.

The next day, I receive an email from Michelle. "Please come in at your earliest convenience to pick up the money order for your fingerprinting, and I will make the appointment. What day and time works for you?"

Bingo.

With every single step completed, on Monday, November 7, I take all of my documents plus my photo ID, as I was told, as I have a checklist, up to the SCSB in Sarasota. The officious, insufferable bureaucrat at the desk says, "Where is your Social Security card?"

I say, "Not with me, as I was told only to bring a photo ID."

She says, smugly, "We can't certify you without your Social Security card. Company policy."

I say, "Well, should I not bother to do any of this now? I can come back later in the week."

She says, "No, you can do everything else and bring the Social Security card back as soon as possible."

The fingerprinting is in the same building. The drug test is in Venice, where my mother lives and where I live currently, in a tiny villa on the beach. The officious bureaucrat says, "You have 48 hours to complete the drug test, or you can't teach for us for a year."

I say, "No worries, I'm on my way."

I complete the drug test.

On Tuesday the 8th, Election Day, I had three appointments and could not get to the SCSB.

On Wednesday the 9th, because the U.S. elected a fascist to be our next president, I am up all night fielding phone calls, texts, emails, FB messages, WhatsApp messages and the like from distraught students, liberals and foreign friends, talking them down off many ledges. I did not get to the SCSB.

On Thursday the 10th, Kentucky drives me to the SCSB early in the morning, before he went to work. I am glad that the final step would shortly be over and I could begin with SKY Academy.

I leave Kentucky in the car, as the card business would only take minutes. Inside, the same insufferable, officious woman is at the desk. I give her my name and hand her the card. She stands up, goes into the next room and takes a copy. She comes back, hands me the card and has me sign a piece of paper.

She says, looking at her computer screen, "The name on your Social Security card contains your middle name."

I say, "That's right."

She says, "Your middle name is not on your license."

I say, "Correct. Because I have not used my middle since I was fourteen years old."

She turns her chair toward me and says, "They have to match."

I say, "What?"

She says, "The names have to match. The one on your Social Security card and the one on your license."

I say, "Are you joking?"

She says, "We can't certify you until they match. Company policy."

I say, trying to contain myself, "What do you suggest I do?"

She says, "Well, you could change your license…"

I say, "No, I can't. I have no permanent address."

She says, "Or you could change your Social Security card."

I say, "Is that even possible?"

She says, "Yes. The office is a few miles away. This is the address."

She pulls out a sticky note and scribbled something down.

I say, "And the Social Security office will drop the middle name from the card?"

"Yes," Ms. Smug Insufferable says, "It takes about a week."

"Thank you," I say.

As I walk the corridor to the front door, I remember a beautiful silver flask that I have somewhere in the apartment in New York City, and curse myself for not asking my ex to add it to the parcel along with my Social Security card and expired passport. However, I reason, I likely would not have had it in my handbag anyway, thinking I'd have no need for whisky at eight o'clock in the morning.

I get into Kentucky's car. Starting the engine and pulling out of the parking lot, he says, "All set?"

"Yes," I say, with my eyes fixed on my lap.

He says, "What's wrong?"

I say, "Nothing."

He says, "What is wrong?"

And I burst into tears.

There is something quite wonderful in having my mother furious on my behalf; it's like a boxing coach in my corner, sending me out for another round, convinced I can take more beating though I am bloody and bruised and my ear has been bitten half-off. Thrilling, really, to hear her voice, her response on the phone when I call her from Kentucky's car.

After I end the call with her, Kentucky does for me what I did for my liberal friends and relations on Election Night: he talks me off of the ledge. Back in Venice, after eating a container of pineapple, I go to the Goodwill in search of knives (unrelated to this story — I mean kitchen knives, for cooking) and wine glasses (because one of my guests broke one). After about a half an hour of mindless, cheap fun, my phone pings and it is my mother. She says, "I'm at lunch with Jan and she remembered there is a Social Security office in East Venice and…"

I say, "I'm calling right now."

A period of recalibration for body and mind follows for a New Yorker when she moves to Florida. There are adjustments to be made. One of them is that New York is the capital of the Service Industry — we run on tips, and charge enormous amounts for delivery and such even before we get to the expected tips. Florida, on the other hand, is the capital of the Retirement Industry. So most have "Retirement attitude." The living is easy. The pace is glacial. The driving is treacherous. No one expends energy to answer a phone here, not even a funded help line. So I am amazed when an actual person picks up the phone at the East Venice Social Security office.

I say, "I need to change the name on my Social Security card."

She says, "Do you have your original or a copy of your birth certificate?"

I say, "Fuck, no."

She says, "What?"

I say, evenly, "I am trying to register to become a teacher. I am a teacher in another state. The only thing holding me back right now is my cursed middle name. I need it dropped from my Social Security card so it matches my license. Can I do that at your office?"

She says, "All you want is to drop the middle name?"

I say, "Yes."

She says, "You can do that with your driver's license and the card at one of the windows here."

I saiy, "What time do you close?"

She says, "3:00 PM. But we're closed tomorrow for the holiday."

Crap! Veteran's Day!

I say, "Thank you."

It is 1:45 PM.

I call my mother.

It goes to voice mail.

I text my mother.

Her response: "I'm in a restaurant with your aunt. Can I call you later?"

I text back. URGENT!!!!!

She calls. I explain. She says, "I'll be there in thirty minutes. Be out front."

The young, bespectacled man who helps me at the Social Security office is named Michael Eagles and he immediately gives me a hard time and I immediately like him.

He looks at my card, looks at me and says, "You don't like the name "XXXX"? "Lisa XXXX?" What's wrong with that?"

I think he may have winked at my mother, who is seated next to me when he says this, but I'm not sure.

I say, "Look, Eagles, my last name gives so many people so many problems, I didn't want to add one more initial or one more name, okay? That would be twenty-four letters or something. You have a great last name, don't talk to me."

He says, "Oh, all right."

The whole process lasts about ten minutes, there is no fee, I sign a paper and that is it. I said, "How long will it take?"

He says, "They say 10-14 days but really it's 4-5 business days."

I stand and say, "Thank you, young Mr. Eagles, it was pleasure dealing with you."

"Pleasure meeting you," he says.

I motion to my mother. As we exit the building, I say, "That was surprisingly painless. Thank Jan for me."

Painless, yes, but the ordeal still isn't over.

Five days later, on Saturday, my new Social Security card comes. Kentucky races me to the SCSB Monday morning, November the 21st, and a different woman helps me: older, grey-haired, methodical, bespectacled. She takes the Social Security card, photocopies it, handing it back to me along with my license. She says, "Your paperwork is complete. You are to come here for your Substitute Orientation on December the 1st at 7:45…"

I say, "7:45…in the morning?"

"Yes," she says, "7:45 in the morning to about 11:15, give or take. After which you will get your badge number and an email to the Sarasota County School System."

December the 1st is two weeks away. No rush down here in Florida. Desperate cries for teachers from members of the Board of Education, particularly substitutes, on the evening news? You'd never know it from the SCSB.

The bespectacled woman says, "I'll send you an email with detailed instructions today, right after I input all of this. I'll send you the email as soon as I'm finished."

Fine.

I subb at SKY the day after, Tuesday, after which I get eighteen pages via email from SKY to fill out, requesting a background check, CPR course, uploading of my passport, W9, next of kin in case one of the children should accidentally hurl a laptop at my head and kill me. I complete it all.

Saturday after Thanksgiving, another alert from SKY which says: YOU HAVE NOT YET COMPLETED PLEASE DO SO ASAP!

Another request for a background check with an electronic signature, which I complete.

Sunday, November 27. I have yet to get an email with these "detailed instructions" and so will be calling tomorrow to find out what the hold up is this time, whether they need a pubic hair sample, a kidney stone, amniotic fluid (the latter of which I actually do not have, but it would have been so much easier to give them my firstborn if I had had a firstborn.)

And on it goes.

Adventures in Subbing

THE 6TH AND 7TH GRADERS AT SKY ACADEMY in Englewood, Florida, a charter school in conjunction with the YMCA, were in uniform: SKY tee shirts or hoodies and chino shorts. I was subbing for the 6th and 7th grade Social Studies and History classes — not that I know much about either one of those subjects. I am certified to teach English, grades 6th and up, but as a sub, I am put in any class, any subject where needed.

The absent teachers at SKY had left the students previous work to complete and then video games, or just video games. I had not brought a book with me, thinking incorrectly I would be occupied, and there was no cell service in the classroom — nothing for me to do. So I moved around the classroom for interaction, and when I was not walking round the room, I rushed back to the desk to take notes.

Teaching and learning are not only applicable to specified subjects, and in the end, my adventures in subbing can be summarized thus: who taught who?

These are my notes from the day, arranged in a series of vignettes.

1. Me: "My name is on the whiteboard — Ms. del Rosso."
Pause from entire class, then looks of confusion. One girl raises her hand. "May we call you Ms. D?"
I am Ms. D for the duration.

2. A 7th grader comes to my desk.
"Sorry to bother you, but were you born in France?"
"In France? No, I was not born in France."
"Oh, I really like your accent so I thought you were born in France."

I explain where I have lived, London for ten years, then in New York City. She seems satisfied with this, and sits back down.

❋

3. Anna is a 7th grader and her father died four years ago. She shows me a YouTube video of him, tattooed, shirtless, handsome. She mixes past and present tense when she speaks of him and tells me she misses him every day. She pulls up his obituary, and shows me that, too.

"He was twenty-five" I say.

"Yes," she says.

"Do you mind my asking how?" I say.

She says," No one knows. He just collapsed one day."

I asked her if she journaled, if she wrote about him, and she said, "All the time."

In the YouTube video, he has a striped towel on his head and is doing a funny dance. And so it will be for Anna — her father immortalized on tape, young and perfect — for her to view repeatedly at a touch. I don't know if this is good or bad, but the way she talks about him, her father was only ever wonderful and she never got to an age when he would become a nuisance or a disappointment — in other words, a real person.

❋

4. At SKY, students are divided into 3 levels:

Advanced, meaning super-smart.

Regular, which is self-explanatory.

Intensive, meaning "Those are the dumb kids, Ms. D."

❋

5. The students were looking up meanings of names, their own given names included. One boy, who insisted on being called, "Mr. Papi," was not finding anything of interest, so went to the Urban Dictionary. I was

walking around the classroom and had almost reached his desk when he burst out laughing and put his hands over his mouth. He covered the screen on the laptop with his hands.

"Show it to me."

"I can't!" said Mr. Papi.

"Show it to me," I said, "I don't care what it is."

He did. The name he had looked up was Dylan. Urban Dictionary for Dylan: "If you are named Dylan, you have a big penis..."

I looked at Mr. Papi's now-red face and said, "That is why you cannot trust the Urban Dictionary — anyone can write in whatever they want. Just like Wikipedia."

✳

6. The female students like videos of puppies, photos of puppies, kittens, cats, videos of kittens and cats, and show me their pets' photos on their phones (which is the only exception I allowed for usage — to show me the pictures of their pets).

The boys, and some of the girls but mostly boys, like video games, and these games consisted of one figure beating the shit out of another figure in a boxing ring-style setting, with one winner and one loser. On the day I subbed, the figures were variations on only one theme: someone vs. Donald Trump. Hillary beating the shit out of Trump, Trump beating the shit out of Hillary, anyone black, male or female (Lebron James, Serena Williams, usually an athlete) beating the shit out of Trump. It was all very bloody and cathartic, but it should be no surprise this is what these children now believe politics to be: a blood sport, Colosseum-style, with two gladiators, resulting in one winner and one dead loser.

✳

7. One 6th grade boy pulled up women in bikinis on his computer screen as I walked by, and I said, "Get rid of it."

He said, "I didn't mean to!"

I said, "What did you mean to do?"

He said, "I typed "Ladders"!

I said, "Well, you must have typed in "ladies" because that's what came up so get rid of it."

He said, "It just popped up!"

I said, "I bet it did."

＊

8. A 7th grade girl said, "May I go next door to help hang Christmas decorations?"

I said fine and so she went.

The rest of the class erupted: "She has homework!" "No fair!"

Then hands shot up in the air. "Can I go next door?" "Can I?" "Can I?" "Can I?"

A serious tactical error on my part.

I go and fetch the student next door. I say, "Sorry, but now everyone wants to come next door and I can't have that."

She follows me back into the class.

She looks at another student and says, "Michael, you ruined it for me!"

Michael says, "I wasn't the only one!

The girl says, "Who else wanted to go?"

The entire class raises their hands.

"All of you suck," she says, sitting down in a huff. She pouts momentarily, stands back up and asks, "Ms. D? May I go to the bathroom?"

I say, "Are you coming back?"

Awkward pause. For her.

"No…" she says slowly.

I roll my eyes. "Then, NO," I say.

She says, "At least I was honest."

＊

9. A 7th grade boy says, "How do you say the word 'swausages'?"

I say, "How do I say the word 'sausages'?"

"Oh," he says, disappointed. "Some people with a heavy New York accent say 'swausages.'"

I say, "I do not have a heavy New York accent. You need New Yorkers from the Bronx, Brooklyn and Long Island."

He still looks disappointed.

✳

10. There is a bathroom adjacent to the classroom which sounds great except there is no lock on the door. There are only minutes between classes so one has about 0.5 seconds to pee before a student comes behind the desk, steps three feet and opens the door. What I write next is indicative of the time in which we live: if a school shooting were to occur, all fourteen students plus myself could fit into that bathroom (the bigger classes, no) which would be fine unless the shooter decided to open the door. But if one walks into the classroom, the bathroom is hidden from the naked eye. Only if the shooter advances behind the desk would he notice an unmarked door. Alternately, there are two low-to-the-ground windows behind the desk that can be opened and screens cut through or raised; unlike Hershorin Day Community, a half-Jewish, half Inter-faith school connected to a synagogue, my last sub job, where all of the windows were sealed shut.

✳

11. SKY elects one class president a week, and I have the campaign managers for Dalton in my class. Dalton is running against MacKenzie. Anthony, one of the campaign managers, had a stack of small posters, one of which said, "Vote for Dalton."

I said to him, "Uninspiring. You have to tell me why — why I should vote for Dalton over MacKenzie?"

He paused, thought for a minute, then said, "Because she's an evil witch."

I burst out laughing. "Oh, so you're going negative? I suppose right now, negative is the thing. But please don't write that on the posters."

They didn't.

❋

12. I had a 7th grader named Richard Shakespeare Lodge, who was the only black student in all of my classes. Coolest name ever. So I called him Shakespeare for the duration of the class. He told me his father had jewelry just like mine — a turquoise watch and a turquoise ring.

I said, "Native American? Navajo?"

"Yes," he said.

I said, "Tell your father he has good taste."

❋

13. I have never seen so many distracted individuals all in one room in my entire life. Video games are evil.

❋

14. The students were writing papers on the Constitution, concentrating on the phrase, "Life, Liberty and the Pursuit of Happiness."

One male student said, "Happiness is the most important thing in the phrase because everyone is entitled to happiness."

I said, "No. That is not what the phrase says. It says, everyone is entitled to the *pursuit* of happiness. That means, everyone is entitled to try and find happiness, but that does not mean everyone gets to be happy. Also, America is the only country that has the word "happiness" written into its Constitution."

He said, "Liberty is important to Americans."

I said, "Yes, but the French have Liberty, Egalite, Fraternity, (Liberty, Equality and Brotherhood, written into their Constitution); Liberty you can find written in other countries, but not happiness."

On a side note: Americans are obsessed with happiness. Europeans do not get this at all.

Another girl asked me to read her paper on the same subject. I read it and said, "No. You equate success with happiness. But that is not always the case. There are plenty of successful people who are unhappy: Steve Jobs — happy? Mark Zuckerberg was not but now probably is — Picasso was a genius but he was also a horrible person (I did not explain to them the nine wives, suicides of wives, wives in madhouses, disownment of children, rivalries with other artists, etc…). Then there are people who have little but are incredibly happy. It depends on how you define happiness, and on how you define success."

She said, "Success means a lot of money."

I said, "A lot of money does not guarantee you will be happy. How do you define happiness?"

She said, "Do I have to answer now?"

I said, "No, but it's something you need to think about."

The same student who thought everyone was entitled to happiness said, "I'd be happy if all I did was go fishing for the rest of my life."

I said, "Fishing?"

He said, "Yeah."

I said, "Fishing's a start."

Instigator

I STUMBLED UPON ANECDOTES BY A YOUNG CASHIER at Detweiler's market that I thought would make great reportage, which were essentially complaints about Venice High School: the new principal who decided to enforce a Draconian dress code and ignored the howls of protests from the female contingent as the code seemed only to apply to them. The application of the code necessitated sending the girl in question home to change, or the tempting alternative of putting on oversized, smelly gym clothes kept in a box for such occasions, to cover the offending garment.

I had already interviewed one student and was set to talk to another when I got a four-day sub assignment beginning December 13th for a reading teacher at the high school. The hours were 7:30 to 2:30, and I could cycle there from my tiny villa on the beach. The timing was excellent, as I also had two of the interviewees in my classes.

The reading class was billed as pre-college. Classes had been in session since August 22nd, and the seniors had read "Lord of the Flies" and "Beowulf." The teacher had left a multiple choice mock-test on "Lord of the Flies," which the students regarded as "busy work," and it was: questions about character and plot they could easily look up if they didn't know, no writing required. They completed it as quickly as possible in order to get back to more important things: namely, their cellphones.

"Lord of the Flies" reading level is grade 9. I was told by one student that when the teacher assigned the first chapter, no one read it, so she read it to them. These are seniors, mind you. In eight months, they will be college students. Additionally, I was also told by a few other students that they had already read the book. That they found the class "too easy because Honors English has been abolished and the choices were AP Literature, which was too hard, or the reading class." That the material "wasn't challenging." That they were "bored." That none of what they read was remotely connected to their daily lives.

You Are All a Part of Me

So I threw out some illustrious and important authors' names, for the heck of it, to see if they had read or heard of any of them.

In no particular order:

James Baldwin

Alice Munro

Sherman Alexie

Ta-nehisi Coates

Jhumpa Lahiri

Toni Morrison

Brian Doyle

David Mamet

Tillie Olsen

Junot Diaz

I was met with "No," "No," and "Who?"

No student in any class, and I had 6 periods of roughly 28 students in each, knew any of these authors.

It was then I began to cry inside.

I asked them if they wanted me to bring in something challenging or controversial, something applicable to their own lives.

"Yes!" they said, nearly in unison. On his way out, one of the young men said, "You're my favorite sub."

I said, "Why? Because I'm bringing you in something challenging?"

"Yes," he said, putting on his cap and exiting the room.

In order to take advantage of their cellphones, I chose a piece easily found on the net. It was short, and I had taught it for years. It was also controversial: "Alma" by Dominican-American writer Junot Diaz, a recipient of the Pulitzer Prize, is written from the perspective of a nineteen- or twenty-year-old young man. In it, he describes his girlfriend, who thrills him because, mostly, what they do is have sex. The explicit language is all Diaz: authentic to the characters, and applicable to people of that generation right now.

The point of assigning this short story is addressing the nature of controversy itself: why do you think the venerable *New Yorker* picked this piece to publish? Is there anything in it you found offensive? If yes, what and why? Do you think the language is authentic to the piece or has the writer done this simply for shock value? Why is the piece written in second person? What do you think would change if the story were written from Alma's point of view? Does this depict a Dominican-male perspective only, or a male perspective? What about that, if anything, is problematic?

That sort of thing.

One student said he "didn't like it so I didn't read it." That is a contradiction, but I did not press the matter.

Another student, who was white, had an issue with the "n" word. He said the piece must have been written by a sixty-year-old man, because the term was racist and "it's not used anymore." The whole class disabused him of this notion. We then discussed context, and the re-appropriation of the word by Blacks in order to de-stigmatize and take back the power of it, and why it is not cool and never will be cool for a white person to use it. Another female student said, "This is the way we talk. In real life. I don't think teachers realize real life is like, fifty yards outside the school door." Another female student said she loved it, and was going to find more of Diaz's books. It was an excellent discussion.

The rest of the students appreciated the fact that I had introduced them to Diaz, and some thanked me personally.

At the end of 3rd period, I got a phone call from the assistant to the assistant principal, who sounded very young, possibly a student. She said, "Did the teacher leave work for the students?"

I said, "Yes, but they completed the work in twenty minutes. I brought in additional work for them, because I don't like bored students, and I also don't like to be bored. They have two more days, and I don't want them to play on their cellphones for the duration."

"Oh, okay," said the AAP.

I hung up, and there was another call immediately.

The woman introduced herself as Ms. Schmidt. And poor Ms. Schmidt was so agitated she could barely formulate her words.

"I'm the assistant principal, and, well, you gave the students a... have you read this?"

Now, that is a silly question.

I said, "Of course. I actually teach that piece at NYU."

"And the "n" word and the "p" word are okay with you?"

"Yes," I said, "In context, that is the language of the piece."

Also, students use this language. People use this language. In the past, the 45th president has used this language, his example of which we have on tape. To pretend differently is to live in Mayberry, and Mayberry was fiction. Diaz gets that, which is another reason I gave the piece to my students.

"We have gotten complaints from students' parents, and you are to pull that piece immediately."

"Okay," I said. I hung up. I already knew what was coming.

I told every single class what happened and that if I was replaced with a 100-year-old teacher the following day, this was why. I have to say, they were not happy with this news at all. One said she couldn't wait to leave Venice. Another Indian student said there was "no diversity in Venice, and it's very white and very conservative." She had written an essay on the unfairness of the dress code, a good one, and she emailed me a copy. She also said it felt like teachers were on a "witch hunt" and sexualized the female students, making them "feel dirty," when "wouldn't it be better to teach the boys how to control themselves?"

Meanwhile, the Diaz story and myself had been "all over Twitter" — and as Kylie, one of my interviewees, said, "You're famous."

I am not a Twitter user and have no plans to be.

The way to sell something is to ban it: this is excellent strategy for books, movies, music, plays, and alcohol.

The way to get every student at Venice High to read the Diaz piece is to tell me to pull it, then for me to tell all of the following classes I am not allowed to teach it to them, and let Twitter do the rest. "Alma," for good or ill, spread like wildfire.

At one point in the afternoon, Ms. Schmidt came in with an extremely tall, black uniformed female security guard (To intimidate me?

To escort me out? Because she feared for her life? To shoot me?) to "make sure all the students were doing their work." I said clearly they were, but one student with impeccable timing had just informed me she was sick and did not know where the nurse's station was, so could they please escort her out? And they left.

The last class I had was long, and the same reading teacher had left them the "The Lord of the Flies" movie to watch, but most were on their phones or on the computers, as the room was split into a half class/half computer lab. A lovely student named Seamus talked to me at the back of the classroom while the movie was playing: his mother was a Civics teacher and a Buddhist; he was also a Buddhist and explained why.

"My mother introduced me to many religions and I chose Buddhism because it's more a philosophy than religion. But [referring to the controversy I caused] if no one gets to know other politics, other people, other religions, then no one will ever understand any side but their own. And that breeds an intolerant people. People who live in a bubble, when reality is right outside the door."

Another student said, "I'm in ROTC and I can't say anything political to criticize Trump, other than he's not American enough for me. My people have been here since like the 1500's, he's only second generation." He laughed. "And that's the only acceptable thing I can say, ya know?"

After Seamus and his friends read "Alma," they came to my desk to tell me their thoughts. I gave Seamus my email address in the event I did not see him the next day, and told him to stay in touch. He said, "I think you're an awesome teacher and I'm going to recommend you to everyone."

As I was packing up my knapsack to depart, a woman who could only be the bumptious Ms. Schmidt came bustling into the classroom. Ms. Schmidt, a woman of about seventy with lank, grey hair, wearing a loose teal tunic over teal stretch-slacks, looked extremely pleased with herself.

She came to my desk and said, "I told Principal Jackson what you gave the students and he doesn't want you to come back tomorrow or Friday."

"Okay," I said, and continued packing up my knapsack.

And because I did expect this, and did not cry, and did not fall over myself apologizing; in fact, did not apologize at all, that seemed to annoy Ms. Schmidt, which pleased me. She continued to stand in front of my desk, her comportment slipping.

She said, "It was inappropriate."

I said, "Well, just so you know, Junot Diaz is a Pulitzer-prize winning author, and the piece was published in The New Yorker."

She said, "What is in The New Yorker is not necessarily appropriate for our students."

I said, "Okay."

To have said anything else would have been a waste of breath.

Ms. Schmidt continued to awkwardly stand there, waiting for I don't know what. I continued to be amused.

She said, "The teacher left work to give out."

I said, "The students completed that work in twenty minutes. And as I said, I don't like bored students."

She kept standing there, and her awkwardness changed to insecurity.

"Well," she said.

"Well!" I said, with a smile.

And then she finally departed.

I exited out the front door, got on my bike and went and had an ice cream with my boyfriend. I told him what had happened. I called my mother and told her, too.

When I finally got my substitute teaching badge number, which took time, many journeys to many offices, and money, I was told I could book myself a job every day of the year if I liked, via a sub hotline. That was where all of the schools under the Sarasota County umbrella called when they had absences to be filled, and the jobs were plentiful.

The day after the Venice High incident, I called the hotline. The automated voice told me my ID was no longer valid. I thought, "Oh, they did that, did they?"

I called the tech people first, to make sure. The man on the other end, I think his name was Doug and I think we had met during orientation, paused and said, "Oh Lisa, I'm sorry. You have to call the school board." We must have met, because he sounded genuinely sorry.

I said, "Don't worry, Doug, not your fault."

So I called the Sarasota County School Board and was met with an officious-sounding female whose voice was on automaton: "YOU HAVE BEEN RESTRICTED. YOU CANNOT USE THE SYSTEM. YOU CANNOT…"

"I understand what 'restricted' means."

"A LETTER HAS BEEN SENT OUT TO YOU. YOU CAN COME IN AND VIEW YOUR FILE AND YOU HAVE TEN DAYS TO APPEAL YOUR CASE. YOU CAN…"

"That will not be necessary."

There was an automaton pause.

"YOU HAVE BEEN RESTRIC -"

I hung up the phone.

My tiny villa on the beach, where I had been living for the past four months, contained a kitchen table, two chairs, a couch, a coffee table, a Murphy bed and enough room for pacing, an activity I was incredibly good at. I paced, and I thought.

The blacklisting had transpired on a Thursday. I had a flight booked back to New York City on Monday, December 18, for a reason — all of the Sarasota schools were on break from the 18th to January 3rd. There was no way I was going to ruin my Christmas over this. I hated subbing. I hated getting up at six in the morning to go into a school, any school, that regarded subbing as glorified babysitting. Nothing whatsoever to do with teaching. I knew I belonged back in a college setting, and that was likely where I was headed. My romance… would survive this. I hoped.

So I did not want to appeal because I did not want to be reinstated. I did not want to sue anyone, and I did not want money. I did not require an apology. I did, however, want a voice in all this, a voice I had been denied. The principal had not bothered to have a conversation with me before making a decision, and all of this could have been handled via Venice High School, rather than tattling to the Sarasota County School

Board. More to the point, I am convinced if I had cried and had a meltdown and begged for forgiveness from Wicked Witch Schmidt of Venice High, it would have been.

That kind of response is not in my persona.

No one from the Sarasota County School Board had bothered to phone or email me. No one had asked to hear my side of the story. I had not disobeyed when told to pull the piece, but no one seemed to care about that, either.

I turned from the kitchen and looked out through the bay window at the palm tress that would soon be a distant memory. I stopped pacing. I said out loud, to an empty room,

"I think the Sarasota Herald Tribune would love this story! I really do. And so would Junot Diaz."

Also, the Trib, which was the largest local paper in the county, would have both the opportunity and resources to investigate the "one strike and you're out" rule governing substitutes that I had not been told about; and the fact that the word "teaching" should not be paired with "substitute." I had had about eight assignments. No teaching required. Shepherding, yes. If my experience had been in tending sheep, I'd have been just as qualified as a college professor who had twelve years of teaching under her belt. More so.

Suddenly elated and with adrenaline rushing, I picked up my cellphone and called the Herald Tribune. The editor was very interested. He sent a journalist (Yadira Lopez, wonderful) down *that day* to interview me. He sent a photographer (Matt Houston, delightful) down the next to take my picture. The story, timed beautifully to coincide with all Sarasota County schools resuming after winter break, landed right on the front page, accompanied by my photograph. I was right above the fold, above Donald Trump's face. I sent the story to Junot Diaz, who responded with "jesus christ" then shared it with 1.4 million of his followers. That story resulted in a torrent of letters to the editor. I read them all, with glee, back in New York City.

Addendum

Ultimatum

The night before I left for Venice, Florida, on March 10, 2020 for spring break, NYU announced that we would be going "remote." Two days into my stay, the entire world changed - including the nature of teaching with the reluctant embrace of Zoom - and my mother said to me, "Please don't go back to New York City unless you absolutely have to." Mid-March was the period NYC had the worst Covid-19 outbreak in the country if not the world, so I stayed in the relative safety of Florida.

Actually, I rode out the pandemic at Kentucky's two-room bungalow.

For twelve weeks we made it work, mainly because he also retained his job, he lives five minutes from the beach, and my mountain bike gave me freedom. But he is on a 10:30-5:00 schedule and I had neither time nor space to write. For the record, I also had a book coming out that required editing.

Qualifier: I also had neither time nor space to myself.

My pre-pandemic life was split very neatly in two: in New York City, because my ex works in the restaurant industry, I get most of my work done in the evenings, including writing until the wee hours of the morning. When I am not doing either of those two things, my nights are my own to read, listen to music, think and hash out new ideas in my head, whatever I choose. Then I'd fly down to Florida every three months or so, and be with Kentucky totally for about two weeks, with no distractions in my head. Space and time in New York City. Love with Kentucky in

You Are All a Part of Me

Florida. Wonderful.

The last time I lived in two rooms with a man was never. Those two rooms in Kentucky's place - a bedroom and a living room (there is also a tiny kitchen and an equally tiny table and two chairs, the latter also in the living room) — were fine for two weeks. Even three. But the longer the months went on, and the longer the editing of my book got away from me, the more unhappy I was.

What Kentucky wanted after 5:00 was all my time and attention. This is not necessarily a bad thing. The routine was: walk the beach, watch the sunset, drink wine, eat dinner (that I made), perhaps watch telly, make love, end of night. This sounds wonderful, and it is wonderful. But not every single night. Because then I don't write, and not writing makes me anxious. There was even less time on weekends. He would say: "I can give you writing time. How long will it take? How long do you need?"

Writing, editing, and revising does not work that way. How could I ask him to leave for three hours or more? How is that fair? He is a normal person with normal expectations about a relationship.

I don't expect a non-writer to understand this. I am not even sure how to express to a non-writer that I need time alone to think, to explore, for ideas to germinate. In order to do that, I need a room of my own. In the NYC apartment, I close a door, sit down, and enter into my imagination. This is how I have lived for over fifteen years. This is exactly how I have completed and published countless essays, articles, one book, produced three plays, with a second book on the way.

I went back to NYC in mid-May. Got back into my writing groove. Well...

Every time we talked, Kentucky said: "Are you teaching remote in fall? Are you? Are you? I miss our routine!"

For the first time in our relationship, what I heard was his neediness and what I felt was pressure, pressure, pressure. Kentucky seemed to forget I was a writer with a book coming out. Or, he did not care.

In August, I taught a six-week summer course for NYU and then fled to Provincetown for regeneration and to finish the edit on my book. By that time, I knew my classes would be remote and I already knew what Kentucky would say. I finally texted him the info, then went to Hatches Harbor, where there is no cell signal.

When I returned, his text was waiting: Wow! That's really great! Do you want to come down here and teach?

Despite question mark, this was not really a question. I texted back: No. I will be staying in NYC. I was down there for 12 weeks due to a pandemic; and as nice as it was, your place is not built for 2 people and I need a room of my own to write and teach in.

Kentucky stopped speaking to me.

This was the man who had texted me every single day for four and a half years with a million heart emojis, a million I LOVE YOU BADS. Every. Single. Day. This was also the man who asked me to marry him the first week we were together; who said he wanted to be with me for the rest of his life; who said, "The last thing I want to see before I die is your face" more than once.

Because there was no conversation, I felt no resolve. I felt like he had ripped off our relationship like a bandaid, and that was it.

What bothered me the most was that it elicited the same feelings in me as when my father cut me off: confusion, abandonment, betrayal, loss. I trusted that Kentucky, knowing my history, would never do that to me.

His silence as ultimatum meant, either you come here and teach remotely for fourteen weeks in my two-room bungalow, or…

I chose "or…" and broke it off with Kentucky.

He did contact me again via text to tell me I had hurt him "real bad."

I replied: Just to be clear: I hurt you "real bad" because I said I wouldn't come down there and teach remotely?

He texted: Yes.

I texted: Got it.

We had one phone conversation after that, confirming our impasse.

You Are All a Part of Me

Kentucky said that when he dropped my things off at my mother's, "…the last thing I did was kiss your mother's hand and said, 'I hope Lisa finds what she is looking for — I said, hell, I hope she falls in love with a prince tonight.'"

I said, "I am not looking for that! I am not looking for a someone! I'm looking for my third book. And taking a break from all…this…"

He said, "Well, I'm looking for love."

I said, "I know you are."

He said, "I have a lot of love to give."

I said, "I know you do."

Kentucky used to worry that I would leave him for someone who was smarter or more educated — someone with a better "resumé." I told him that would never happen, that I would never do that. I told him if I left him, it would probably be for myself. I am not sure what I meant by "for myself" then, but I am now. In order for me to love and be a happy person, I need a room to call my own; and a man who is generous and secure enough to give me that space and time unconditionally. Writing is not my career. Writing is my vocation.

My friend Jimmie, who is a seventy-five-year-old Vietnam Vet living in Provincetown, recently analyzed me from a straight man's point of view. He said, "Lisa, you're difficult to deal with from the start. You're self-sufficient. You don't rely on anybody. You don't need a man; if you want a man, that's something else. Want is different. Then you go get it and the want goes away."

I am still trying to understand what Jimmie meant. But I think the difference between me and Kentucky is, for him, love transcended a two-room bungalow, mainly because all of his needs were being met. For me, love does not transcend a two-room bungalow, because as a creative person, not all of my needs were being met.

I have carved out a life that gives me the time and the space to do what I need to do in order to be a happy woman. Happy to wake up in the morning. Happy to be alive. The irony is, who I am — a woman who is in love with life — is the same woman Kentucky was attracted to the very first time I walked into his ice cream shop.

The life I love is filled with writing and publishing, teaching, students, as well as theater, concerts, museums, music, books, traveling. My world is bigger than just him, and Kentucky became part of it. His world is much smaller — by his design — than the one I want to live in permanently.

Addendum to the Addendum

Almost four months pass. I throw myself into work and date no one; Kentucky throws himself into an older, rich woman and tries to become an alcoholic. Neither of these things work.

In early December, I go to Florida, telling myself I am cleaning out the stuff Kentucky dropped at my mother's condo. This is a lie. I went to get Kentucky. Mission accomplished.

A few things have changed: Kentucky gave his notice at the ice cream shop, so as of January 1st, for him it will be a new beginning. He has reversed course on self-destruction. He acknowledges that he was insensitive to the fact that I had a book coming out; and cutting off someone you love out of anger solves nothing. I acknowledge that my text was abrupt and I should have called him. Also, a text is no way to end a relationship. We both agree texting is a bad way to communicate. And I... oh boy.

If I could choose to go through my life without falling in love, I would. Placid waters are preferable to a constant rollercoaster ride. It would be easier if I did not love him. But I do.

Love is a complete and total mystery.

New Yorkers

On 9/11, 2001, I was in my apartment on West 43rd Street. I watched as the second plane flew into the towers (when I say this in class, my students immediately ask, "In real time?") and then there was panic and then there was quiet. In the panic, I got two phone calls: one from my mother, and one from Derek. Then I called Ruth at her home in Maine, knowing she would be in her garden at that hour of the morning, out of her kitchen, away from her radio but within earshot of the phone. "Turn on your radio," I said. "Why?" she asked, "What's wrong?" "Planes have flown into the World Trade Center and it looks like a terrorist attack," I said. Ruth burst into tears. "I know," I said gently, "Turn on your radio." Ruth hung up and then all of the lines went out.

6/9 9/11

I LOVE SCOTCH WHISKY. I LOVE IT ON THE ROCKS in a heavy crystal glass. I love it when my friend Isobel comes to visit from Edinburgh (or, when I go there, only the role of smuggler changes) and smuggles a fine bottle of the stuff in her suitcase – Royal Lochnagar, The Glenlivet – enough so that in fifteen years, I have never been out of Scotch. She is welcome in my home anytime.

A Scotch is what you will need after visiting the 9/11 Museum (pick your own poison). That is exactly what I needed and how I wound up at Bill's Bar & Burgers afterwards, with a Glenmorangie in my hand, talking with Steven the bartender.

Sidebar: I chose June 9th, my birthday, to visit the 9/11 Museum. If nothing else, this fact encouraged Steven to provide me with free shots.

I don't particularly like that there is a 9/11 museum but accept it has to exist, this after a freshman student said watching footage of the planes flying into the Twin Towers was "like the movies." I would like to change that line of thinking. This museum, sunken below the footprints of the Twin Towers, has the power to change that line of thinking.

Never in my life have I been more grateful for film, for tape, for video, for all manner of recording devices, than I was in this museum. There were thousands of MISSING posters that people walked around with like placards on their chests right after 9/11 and they are replicated (originals are in the downstairs rooms) via projections on walls just down from two enormous color photographs, side by side: one of the Twin Towers in the glorious city skyline around dusk, and the other from the same vantage point, but with grey smoke in place of the towers. They are there, and then gone.

There were firemen and policemen in the museum, and not just on duty. They seemed to walk around with a sense of proprietary anxiousness.

On exhibit is the mangled red corpse of the Ladder Company 3 fire truck. They lost eleven firefighters including their Captain, Patrick "Paddy" Brown. His black fire helmet is displayed, as it was on the day of his funeral, which would have been his 49th birthday.

There is a tall iron beam, covered with flowers, notes and scrawls of graffiti in bright colors. "The ironworkers were the first to descend upon the site after the WTC collapse," and they were responsible for the cleanup. There is a large touchpad where you can read the whole story of this beam, thirteen pages, I think. The ironworkers did the cleanup, with all that debris, metal and concrete, with no deaths or injuries. I try to imagine what they saw. I can't. Or I can, but I can't. "You can't help but look at your life differently" — Larry Keating, Ironworker.

There is a film room called "Reflecting on 9/11" that has talking heads answering a series of questions: "Why do you think it is important to remember 9/11?" "What have you learned from 9/11?" "How significant do you consider the events of 9/11 within the context of history?" "How do you think America has changed since 9/11?" All are opinions, and the best I thought came from Bill Clinton (not a surprise) and Colin Powell (a surprise, at least to me). People are invited to contribute to the conversation, so after listening to all of the questions and answers, which takes about forty-five minutes, I went in and recorded my own and gave permission to use for the archives. Mainly, I addressed why it is important the museum exists; why, for my incoming freshman students, 9/11 becomes something real rather than fictional. Particularly because they will be studying here, I tell them, for as long as you're here, you are New Yorkers. This is your city. You need to know what happened here. And you need to know about the aftermath.

There are about ten thousand items I can describe to you, all on the periphery. In the center of the museum are the rooms that come with a guard and a warning that "what you will see beyond this point may be upsetting…" It's nice they don't assume you will be upset. But these were the rooms where grown men were crying. One of the rooms, darkened so words would also appear on a screen and where people could sit if they chose, played the recently released cell communications from people inside the towers on 9/11. I lasted under a minute, impossible grief, impossible.

There are the items found — id tags, a restaurant receipt from brunch on the day, a teddy bear, high-heeled shoes, a handbag — that break your heart; iron crosses and other symbols from Ground Zero because everyone was grasping for some sort of meaning when there was none; a black and white photograph taken at Ground Zero of a column on which was written, "Paris, France is here to help."

The rooms that were the most congested were the ones that displayed photos of those who died that day, and in those rooms it is possible to touch any name, which brings up a photo and a small biography. There is also a room with larger photos and bios, but it was so full I honestly could not get in.

There is no happiness in this museum, but it is easily the quietest and most respectful I've been to (next to the Holocaust museum in DC).

There is a Circle Line tour that goes around the island of Manhattan by boat; it takes about forty-five minutes to an hour and though it is something I have only done when friends or family have come to town, I've enjoyed it, the nice weather, etc.... They have employed the same tour guide, a typically facetious, funny man, for years.

My cousin Dave came to stay about six months after 9/11 and we took the Circle Line tour. When we got down to Ground Zero, the tour guide said, "And that is the site of the former World Trade Center, where almost three thousand people were murdered on September 11, 2001." A shock ran through me. The tour guide's voice had a tone I'd never heard before: Outraged. Hurt. Angry.

I was glad, because that is how I felt.

I wonder what he'd say now, and what he will think when he visits the museum. The new #1 World Trade Center is up and running; if you stand in the middle of 6th Ave at dusk, the sun reflects fuchsia-silver off the building, which seems to twist upwards into the sky, and it glitters —

a New York City building. But replacements are only ever that: replacements. Not the real thing, what was real to me, to my New York.

As I ascended up the long escalator of the 9/11 Museum, I could hear the faint, faint strains of "Amazing Grace," played on a penny whistle, the simplest, most common instrument associated with Celtic and folk music. Unadorned. A pure sound as I came up into the light.

Published in *Serving House Journal,* 2014
Published in *Gateways*, 2019

In Beautiful Weather

WOMEN IN MANHATTAN HAVE A TENDENCY to fetishize firemen, their trucks and all the apparatus that goes with them, and I am no exception. One beautiful spring day, I decided to walk from 44th Street up to St. John the Divine at 110th and Amsterdam Avenue. On the corner at 66th and Amsterdam is firehouse Ladder Co 40/Engine Co 35. The doors were open and I looked in as I walked by; the red trucks were there, all seemed calm.

I began my cross at 66th and had only taken a few steps when I felt a foreign arm link through my right arm and heard a voice say, "You look like you need help crossing the street, young lady!"

I turned, and it was a fireman. A fireman had linked arms with me and was now escorting me up Amsterdam Avenue.

I laughed and said, "No I don't!"

He said, "Oh yes, yes you do. I think you do."

He was not dressed in fireman garb. He had on jeans, a blue shirt, a white tee shirt, and work boots. The ladder insignia was stitched onto the breast of his shirt, and may have had a title – lieutenant – but I am no longer sure.

What I am sure of is that he was one of the most beautiful men I have ever seen: sandy brown hair, a bit long, unkempt; a mustache, bright blue eyes, tall, about 6′2″, lean with a broad chest and muscular arms, and I know the latter because I felt through his shirt one of the arms he seemed unwilling to detach from mine. If I had to type him, he would be like an urban cowboy crossed with the eagerness of a puppy dog.

So, we walked and talked.

"How long have you been a fireman?"

"All my life. Never done anything else."

209

"Wow."

"What do you do?"

"I'm a singer."

"Really? What kind of a singer?"

"I trained classically so I can sing anything."

"Sing for me!"

"Right now?"

"Now is a good a time as any."

"I don't even know you!"

"But there are all these streets to cross and I think you might need help with all of them."

"Do you do this often?"

"Do what often?"

"Help women across the street."

"Never."

"I don't believe you."

"I mean it; never."

"So why me?"

"I told you; you looked like you needed help."

"I think *you* need help," I said.

"I could have told you that for nothing," he said, "Listen, how far you going?"

He still had not let go of my arm.

"Up to 110th Street."

"Mmmnnn…not sure I can go up that far. I'd miss a call. But tell you what; come find me. You know where I am. You can sing for me."

"Okay."

"Okay?"

"Okay."

"Okay. So…I'll look for you in, say, two days."

"Okay."

"Two days. Okay?"

"In two days."

And then he let go of my arm, turned and walked back the way we had come. He turned again and yelled, "Two days!"

I laughed.

Two days later, I didn't go to find him. I can't tell you why: it could be that in the back of my mind I thought that all fireman were on the make because they could be; or that he was just a flirtatious prankster; or that he frightened me a little. A year and a half went by. I never forgot him.

He died in the Twin Towers on 9/11, along with eleven other men from Ladder Co 40/Engine Co 35. They sent in thirteen, and one came back. It was beautiful weather on that day, too. Because so many firemen were lost, there was all kinds of blame to go round afterwards: if they had had radios, the firemen would have been alerted to get out of the second tower; the communication left a lot to be desired. But I think of firemen rushing into burning buildings the way they rushed into the burning towers, and they don't know when a house or an apartment building is going to collapse; they just do it. And I believe that radios or not, the first tower down or not, they would have done the exact same thing on 9/11 in order to try and save people. It is what they *do*.

In order to humanize the three thousand people who died in the Towers, *The New York Times* ran "Portraits in Grief," which were mini-eulogies written by family members along with a photo; they did this for every single person. I read them every day for weeks and weeks and weeks. That is how I saw my fireman's photo. It was said that he liked to laugh and loved life. I think he had a wife, but no children. Having read them all, I no longer knew which was worse: being left with children to raise alone, or being left entirely alone. Either way, I couldn't imagine what the families were going through. What his widow was going through.

It has been over thirteen years since then.

211

Lisa del Rosso

Sometimes, when I am crossing the street, I think of him. I think of him linking his arm to mine. I think of the look on his face when he spoke to me. I think of him happy. Today, crossing 96th Street, in cold, grey and rainy weather, I thought of him, a man I knew for only a moment. I can't tell you why.

Published in *Razor Edge Literary Magazine*, 2017
Published in *Chillfiltr Literary Review* w/podcast, 2020

Process/In Beautiful Weather

MY AUNT, WHO IS MY MOTHER'S SISTER, usually does not ask too many questions; she usually complains about her children, many grandchildren and great-grandchildren. But she read this essay and asked, "So how did you come to write that story? Did it really happen? It happened a long time ago, right? After so much time passed, why did you decide to write it down? Why then?"

All of which made me very irritated, because she forced me to think.

The day I came to write it all down, finally and in a torrent, it was cold and March and as soon as I left my apartment, it began to piss with rain. New York City looked like a grey slate, the people grey, too, and I was wearing funereal black, feeling grim, the weather infecting me like a virus. I rummaged around in my book bag for the umbrella, which was a gift from a student (a replacement, actually, as I had lent her an umbrella she subsequently destroyed, so a replacement/gift). I got to 96th and Broadway, took it out, opened it and the color of the umbrella was hot pink, and hot pink can't help but make me happy, that color and shape above my head like a hot pink halo made me happy, the pink among all the black and slate grey, and that fireman popped into my head, smiling, putting his arm through mine and "helping" me across the street. That meeting was such an odd event, so short; maybe it was a sort of life-force emanating from him, a sort of heat-seeking happiness missile. The kind of man who would spend a lot of time trying to make a woman laugh. It is true that I never forgot him. It is true I did consider going to the firehouse to see him again. On that morose-feeling day, the hot pink umbrella linked with happiness that linked with him altered my mood, and the feeling gripped me; he had made me feel lighter, better, had made me laugh on what was an ordinary day on an ordinary walk to St. John the Divine. He did it again on the corner of 96th and Broadway. And it mattered so much to me at that time on that day to write him, to (memorialize?) immortalize him, because though he died in such a horrible way and in such a seminal event, he still makes me happy.

I have heard that you are only really dead when there is no one left to remember you; I have heard that it takes about one hundred years. The memory of that beautiful firefighter who helped me across the street on that day continues to lighten the weight of living.

Published in *Razor Edge Literary Magazine*, 2017

Livin' Large at the Times Square

WHEN I LIVED IN MIDTOWN, I acquired a new friend who asked, as friends eventually do, where I lived. "Forty-third Street between 7th and 8th," I said.

"There's no residential building on that street," he replied.

I sighed. "There is one, next to the Ben and Jerry's. Number 255."

My new friend's eyes glazed over, mentally searching for placement, then sharpened. "Oh," he said, "You live in the crazy people's building."

I sighed again.

For four years, I resided in a building called The Times Square. 255 West Forty-third Street is now registered as a historic building, erected in 1922. Like a shady lady, it is a building with a past. In the late nineteen seventies and eighties, it was a welfare hotel that became riddled with drugs. "Crack Corner" was its nickname, a resident told me. The city took over The Times Square in 1991. It was refurbished, cleaned up, cleared out. To illustrate this point, in the foyer stands a glass case displaying before and after photos of the apartments. Before: squalid, spoiled, awful. After: bright, clean, new.

There is an income-based, three-tier rental system at The Times Square. The highest tier affords you the largest apartment, which is a studio measuring roughly 250 square feet (including, absurdly, an enormous bathroom). If you were in the middle tier, your apartment was about 200 square feet (but still with an enormous bathroom.) The lowest tier afforded you a studio the size of an abbreviated corridor, with a shower stall and one sink. Some apartments had an attached kitchen; some did not. Still, there were few complaints. If a repair was needed, maintenance fixed almost anything within twenty-four hours, including installing an air conditioner. All apartments had ceiling fans, and most had a large toaster oven, big enough for a small turkey, and two stovetop rings. Tenants could have pets, which I thought was wonderful in a city that could be, at times, very lonely.

The Times Square is an SRO comprised of four groups: the mentally challenged, the elderly, the people living with HIV/AIDS, and the creative poor types. Housing is subsidized so the rents are incredibly cheap. Some residents believe the tradeoff for inexpensive living in the middle of Manhattan is sharing space (elevator space, foyer space, communal dining room space) with colorful characters. I myself liked this aspect of the building, as any journey was never dull, and like the subway, the elevator in our building was the great equalizer.

A small, fifty-ish Asian woman who wore diaphanous kaftans liked to sit and crochet in the foyer. She would sometimes go on a tirade, spouting off about injustices in the world to the hapless security people, who simply ignored her. Perhaps that is what most people do, perhaps it is easier to compartmentalize her as "crazy" rather than consider how and why she got to where she is. But there was one time when I was on the elevator, she got on and began a conversation by telling me that she liked my necklace, that the colors reminded her of her home in the Philippines. She was perfectly sane and very articulate. Then she wished me a good night, and got off on her floor.

Encounters liked that happened on a daily basis. An elderly woman with the hair of Einstein always carried around at least five plastic bags full of God-knows-what. She refused help; they were her bags, she would carry them herself. I had seen her berate her friends in the building for not attending the tenant meetings I was told she consistently disrupted. I took a dislike to her based on this, but once, we were on the same elevator together and she was looking at my outfit intently. "Did you cut your jeans that way?" she said.

"No," I replied, "Believe it or not, they came that way at the Salvation Army thrift, where I got them."

"They look really nice like that," she said, "and you are wearing them with those pointy boots, very fashionable, because you know, a square-toed boot wouldn't have worked so well. It's just right." And she got off at the mezzanine level, leaving me speechless. She was right about the boots. My building was filled with examples of looks being deceptive, and of preconceived notions. Of humbling moments.

Not all elevator encounters were good ones, however. There was a gentleman of roughly seventy, who had lived in The Times Square since 1972. When he first tried to talk to me in the elevator, he stood uncomfortably close. Later, he tried to touch me. I told him to stop, but did not physically defend myself because I felt it would be tantamount to striking my grandfather. But when he lunged at me, I slapped his face. After that, he maintained a cool distance.

One woman in the building resembled a small white mouse; she never looked happy. Whenever she was in the elevator, she complained about the building: too noisy, the elevators took too long to arrive, security people were idiots… I tried my best to ignore her. But one day, there was a third woman in the elevator, a middle-aged black woman wearing a yellow bandana. So the mouse lady started with her rant, and bandana lady whirled on her. "You listen to *me*, now," she said, hand on her hip, "the next stop after this is the street! You ever been on the street? This place is clean and tidy. I have a place all to myself. Where else do you think you can get that, huh? For this price? So if you cannot be grateful, do *not* fill me up with your complaining, honey — just go on and find another place to be." And bandana lady got off the elevator. I wanted to applaud!

Every Christmas, Thanksgiving and Easter, Common Ground, the organization that runs the building, threw a dinner party. A number of local restaurants, bakeries and grocery stores donated food for a holiday dinner, and it was a feast. The entire building was fed, floor-by-floor in the upstairs dining room, for free. Roughly that amounts to three hundred people. Many people who reside in The Times Square have no kin and would have no celebration whatsoever unless something was done. So, every year Common Ground made magic happen.

There were other events in the building: art exhibitions. A potluck supper once a month. Cost: two dollars. Karaoke and talent nights. The tiny Times Square magazine, produced by the residents. There was even a thrift store in the basement, where all items, even shoes, were a dollar.

I heard about The Times Square from JT, who lived in the building for ten years and then moved to Brooklyn. JT is the friend who denied having a cat as a pet when he really had a cat, and then that cat, Aurora, named after a shredder, adopted me. I asked him to reminisce.

"I had lived in The Manhattan Plaza on 43rd and Tenth for twenty years, so I knew the neighborhood and wanted to stay there after my divorce in 1993. It was convenient for auditions but finding something affordable was tough. I found an ad in one of the trade papers for this place just up the street. I went and saw the apartment; the building was half refurbished, but looked nice. I was interviewed and passed a psychological evaluation, which was basically an eighteen-page questionnaire to find out if I had ever used drugs, been in jail, or been in therapy. That was in April; I moved in July. As small as the apartment was, everything worked; it was clean and well kept. The elevators were maintained, the hallways were swept and mopped daily by Ramoso, the maintenance man. The building was better taken care of than most places I've visited.

"I had seen some of the people from the building in the neighborhood so I was well aware of whom my neighbors would be. I have two strong recollections. There was a big woman named Rosita, I'm sure she was pushing two hundred plus pounds. She wore frilly crinolines and high-heeled open-toe shoes, and gloves that went to her upper arms, and her hair blond and very long. She reminded me of Bette Davis in 'Whatever Happened To Baby Jane?' And she wore enough makeup to do Kabuki. I was leaving the building one night and found karaoke going on in the lobby. There, in all her glory, Rosita was singing 'Over the Rainbow' with two other tenants. Now if that didn't make you want to break down and weep… Anyway, the very same week I happened to be on Central Park South and I saw a big black stretch limo pull up to one of the fancy apartment buildings. The driver, who looked like his name could have been Guido, got out and went around to open the door. A woman got out, about sixty, I'd say. She was wearing a black hat over her long blond hair, black gloves and an outfit that no one would ever mistake for contemporary. And she wore enough makeup to do Kabuki.

Now, it struck me that this woman had no greater grasp on reality than Rosita did. But because her husband probably left her fifty million bucks, the woman on Central Park South is eccentric, while the woman in my building is crazy.

"My other recollection is of a particular Thanksgiving dinner at the Times Square. I was sitting at a table with two other men, about my age, in their fifties. One was a Vietnam vet; the other didn't say. And the entire conversation revolved around which food pantry was open on what day and what one could get if one went to a different part of town. And I thought, there's no out for these guys, this is it. It's just one hand out after another. At the same time I thought, there's no hope here, no future but *this place* is the net that catches these people who have fallen through the cracks. It will be the closest they ever get to independent living in the city. I did worry from time to time that I could wind up in The Times Square forever, alone and lonely. But my attitude was, 'I'm here but I'm not one of them, and I'm going to get out.' It was a place I was grateful to live in, but also, happy to leave."

Now that I no longer reside there, I can examine the unsavory aspects of The Times Square more closely. Whenever there is communal living space with "mixed" residents, on a good day, the results can be interesting. On a bad day, the foyer could resemble one of the more frightening scenes from "One Flew over the Cuckoo's Nest." And I am reminded of this from time to time, in other places.

I was journeying downtown and I had taken along my new Saul Bellow book, *Seize The Day*. Hadn't even opened it yet. The train came and I sat down in a half-empty compartment. It was a Saturday; there were tourists, people going out to films, theatre and dinner. I sat down, and beyond the closing doors to my right was a handsome black woman in a tan coat who looked to be in her forties. There was a couple in front of me, an Asian man and a squeaky-clean blond: an elderly white couple to my left.

So I opened my pristine, sweet-smelling new book, and at that exact moment, the woman to my right began a loud rant, talking to no one but addressing the entire train. I was transfixed, and so on the inner jacket of my new book, I wrote down what she was saying:

"Willard. Willard. Now that's a movie from the seventies. About a rat. I love the rat. The rat loves me. I do what the rat says. I thought people were supposed to dominate animals. Well, the animals are dominating people. I'll tell you about domination; I dominate me. Why on this goddamn earth would I ever want to suck your dick. I'd rather eat pussy. And I do. And it's a good thing. Sick of you!"

Pause

"Most of you guys tried it, you wouldn't be in so much trouble. 'Oh no, I'm not doing that, I'm not going there!' But you expect me to give you a blowjob! Well you better start going downtown more often! Sick of you."

Pause

"Don't even know how to wash under your testicles; there's shit in your pants. If you ate more pussy, you wouldn't be in so much trouble. And that's a good thing."

Pause

"I'm vulgar; I'm vulgar and profane. Cause men don't understand nothing til you put it like that."

The elderly couple muttered, I don't know, we just got on the train, is this normal? At one stop, a young woman got on, sat down, then hurriedly got off. The couple opposite me looked embarrassed, the blond blushing deeply. Now, if I had not had a work obligation, I would have stayed on until the end of the line to listen to this woman. She was shocking and funny and sad. And it could have been an elevator moment in my old building. She easily could have been a resident there because nowadays there seems to be no safe place for the mentally ill.

So there were problems at The Times Square. On the way to Stiles Market, I passed a resident outside of the building. There are grates that run alongside; she was standing over a grate, peeing. This woman was elderly, tiny, and always wore long, colorful gypsy skirts and sandals. When I told a security guard, he said he'd look into it. The same thing happened again, and I brought it to the attention of the caseworker.

In the Times Square, one has a caseworker whether one wants one or not; one is told this with the psychological evaluation. I never met mine. But the caseworkers are not social workers; they place people depending on their needs. They are there if one wants them. They are not equipped to intervene and it is not their job to check up on people. They can, however, relocate a person if necessary.

The caseworker said other people in the building also apprised her of the situation, and they were trying to move the elderly woman to a more suitable place. That conversation took place in September, 2002. Eight months later, in April, I saw this elderly woman again. She was sitting in the foyer staring straight ahead, her eyes not moving.

There was a resident who begged in front of the building. I went to retrieve my mail one night on the ground floor, and she was there, digging through the garbage. I grabbed the security guard, and we both went to talk to her. I told her I'd get her something to eat and she said she didn't want my food. The security guard told her to stop, and she said to leave her alone. Then he said if she didn't stop, he'd have to call someone to make her stop, and the woman moved along. I went up to my apartment feeling helpless.

While I lived there, we had a number of suicides. Jumpers. The last one was a man who had been there for ten years or so, and everyone liked him, though he frequently stank of alcohol. After his death (he jumped from the roof garden, on the fifteenth floor) there was outrage from tenants as well as those who knew him personally. He was a depressive and had gone off his medication, they said. He should have been monitored. No one was watching him. Someone said he shouldn't have been there. He should have been someplace where he could have been looked after. And everyone agreed, shook their heads, and went to his memorial service. They did complain to Common Ground. Then they went back to their apartments, expecting nothing to change.

People could visit and stay over, as with any building, but after September 11th (actually, even before then) security got very tight. If you had a visitor, they had to sign in, the front desk would ring your apartment, and you would come down and get them. After two drug-related incidents in The Times Square, a sign was posted next to the front desk, informing all who entered that they needed a photo ID in order to visit. We all thought this a bit much, as the incidents in question were perpetrated by a couple of residents and their friends, *who were let into the building with the residents' permission*. Another, separate incident hit the *New York Times'* Metro section (and that is exactly how I found out about it). Two men held a tenant hostage for two weeks, forcing him to sign over his social security checks to them. And they were his *friends*. He admitted them into the building, and into his apartment. Tough to weed out criminals unless they are wearing that "I am a CRIMINAL" T-shirt. So JT, incensed, wrote a letter to the head of Common Ground, saying that if he could identify who was visiting him, then why did the building need the friend in question to produce an ID?

A large, orange-colored box was located in the foyer of The Times Square, marked, "For Your Suggestions." The building prided itself on listening to its tenants' complaints. And JT did receive a response. His letter, from the director of Common Ground, can be summarized thus: If you don't like the rules here, please feel free to move. The director mentioned security problems in the building, and said that JT had no idea what had been going on. JT replied that if there were grave security problems, shouldn't the tenants be made aware of them? The reply back was that tenants were not told for their own protection. JT and I then made resolutions not to be at The Times Square any longer than we had to be.

My own story with The Times Square ended after my long-term partner and I decided to combine households. We needed space for three cats, furniture, and far too many books. So now we live in a two-bedroom apartment on the Upper West Side, with trees and a ball field outside of the bedroom window. The new friend who has become an old friend came to visit recently. He said, "I can't believe you had all this squeezed into that tiny room of yours in The Times Square!"

"I know," I replied, "But when I closed the door, it was mine."

Maybe other buildings in the city are not so different from The Times Square; maybe the usual set-up of apartments, with no communal living space, means that residents are just better hidden. Still, after I had lived there for a time, when walking up 43rd Street, I'd look ahead and be able to guess which of the people in front of me were going to enter my building. They looked as if they belonged there; it may have been their gait or demeanor, their speech or their dress sense. Later, I wondered if someone would have guessed the same about me.

Light in Rome, Seminars in Sardinia, Lisbon with a View

ROME WAS NOT WHAT I INITIALLY EXPECTED.

When we drove from the airport to Trastevere, I was surprised by the amount of graffiti covering every single building like brightly colored ivy. Some of it was quite beautiful. Some of it, not so beautiful. And it was on everything — except, notably, the churches. The landscape looked very New York City, albeit with the wrong light, on the wrong buildings. I don't know what I expected, really. To step out of the airplane into the Colosseum? To have history immediately smack me upside the head? That didn't happen coming in from Heathrow to London, where I lived for ten years; and it doesn't happen coming from JFK or LaGuardia into New York City, where I currently live, either. In short, I fell victim to what my NYU students do: the films & television series depicting Rome, in the same way they tell me, mid-term, that New York City is not like Sex in the City or Gossip Girl and this surprises them. The fantasy burst by reality.

But once I acclimated and chose the comparative route, I realized Rome and New York City do have their similarities.

Rome is approximately the same size (496.1 square miles) as New York City (468.9 square miles), but has far less residents — approximately 4.2 million to NYC's 8.5 million. In season, Rome is overrun with tourists: 9 million international tourists visit Rome per year; but that is a drop in the bucket to the 65.2 million tourists that annually visit New York City. No need to wonder why New Yorkers are depicted as short-tempered, cynical and hard-edged: tourism is anathema to those of us who actually reside in the City.

Yet, Rome and New York City cater to tourists. It's big business and they are two of the most visited cities in the world. But I went to Rome in late January, low-tourist time, which was perfect for me. Once I was ensconced in my wonderful Airbnb, it was off to the races. I embraced the graffiti. Stepped into a few local churches. Ate the glorious local artichokes paired with fantastic local, inexpensive red wine. Drank way too much coffee. Stood inside the magnificent Colosseum with the space to contemplate the bloody, horrific history that took place there. I wondered about the renovations, what kind of "sport" would go on, and then hoped, like Gaudi's Sagrada Familia in Barcelona, that they would never be finished. Found one of the oldest thrift shops in town because I brought the wrong wardrobe. Walked the Tiber River with friends. Noticed the tents along said river. Spoke with locals about the migrant and refugee housing crisis, created in part through the current government's efforts to make Italy as inhospitable to them as possible. So a lot in common with the current United States as well as New York City.

My father was born not far from Rome, and there has always been something about being in Italy, about being Italian-American, about locals recognizing my last name and asking, "You're Italian?" and fitting in perfectly that I love. Rome is the capital, and it is unlike anywhere else I have been: Florence, Pisa, Siena/San Gimignano, Tuscany, Umbria, San Remo, Venice. The city is insane in the similar ways that New York City is, with scam artists, pick pockets, hustlers, streets teeming with life. But the feel of Rome, the terra-cotta late afternoon light on the buildings, complete with graffiti, the friendliness of the people, and so much more that I want to explore made me wish I had stayed longer. Next time.

From Rome I flew to Cagliari, and from Cagliari, a three-hour coach ride to Galtelli in Sardinia. Why, you might ask? The New York Writers Workshop offered an "immersion workshop" excursion to Sardinia, Italy, in January for eight days. The cost was over two thousand dollars, well past my price point; however, there were scholarships available and I was lucky enough to receive one of them, after submitting two published pieces and a letter of indigence. There were approximately thirty-two of us, including four other scholarship recipients.

225

A friend said, "Do you have any idea about the food in Sardinia? About the wine in Sardinia? Well, I am very jealous."

And I was very much looking forward to the trip.

Galtelli, according to Sardegna Turismo, is "A medieval village in Baronìa, in the central part of eastern Sardinia, built of stone, authentic, fascinating and extraordinarily religious." Even in the dead of winter, the landscape of Galtelli (population just over 2400) is impressive. It is half valley/half mountain, "sitting on a spectacular high plain at the feet of Tuttavista." A number of us climbed partway up that mountain daily to reach the workshops. In January, Italian valleys get freezing fog. A medieval village in January = stone buildings that are difficult to heat. Italy in the winter is not like winter in New York City. Freezing fog penetrates right to your bones, even when the temps are in the 50's. The damp, the humidity — right to your bones. One friend I made on the course, Maid Marion, left her heat on 24/7. We had lunch daily *outside* in the villas courtyard, right outside her door, so I typically asked to use her restroom. Her room was like walking into a sauna. It was lovely.

Because the sun warms things up considerably in Galtelli, despite the cold it is also green. Lush. Lemon and orange trees are common in back gardens, and though it was tempting to pick and run, we were told it was a felony and we believed it. It is a perfect place to farm and raise sheep; and the cheese. Was. Wonderful. So was the honey — earthy and tangy. There are a number of churches. There are three cafes that also transform into bars. There are a few restaurants. There is one super mercado (supermarket).

I have lived in cities for the better part of my life, and regard my birth in the suburbs as a geographical accident, particularly because my grandmother was born in New York City. So you would think that staying in a medieval village would be a change of pace. It wasn't. We were busy from early morning until night: I was up at 7:00 to get to breakfast by 8-8:30 am, workshops began at 9:00, break for lunch from 1:00-2:00, workshops in the afternoon, yoga practice in there somewhere, communal dinner around 7, lasting till 9 or 10 or so. Lots of time for absorption, not a whole lot of time for writing per se. I actually wrote a lot once I left Sardinia, however, chalking this up to food for thought. But the workshops were worth it, as the instructors that Tim Tomlinson, the president of New York Writers Workshop, brought together for this immersion excursion were outstanding.

Pulitzer-Prize winning poet Forrest Gander came to give workshops, and his walks and talks, exploring burial caves of Galtelli, were peerless. He was an enthralling lecturer as well. Poet Moira Egan and her husband, translator Damiano Abeni, who is also an epidemiologist, gave fantastic workshops on synaesthesia combined with poetry that pushed me totally out of my comfort zone, and I was glad for the experience and expertise they brought to the table. (And on a personal note, you can find them in a Google search in the *NY Times* Vows section in a piece written about their wedding in 2007. It is totally delightful.) Ravi Shankar, also a poet and a charismatic teacher, gave workshops that encouraged — gasp — class participation, and also peer discussion groups, so we had to talk to one another, had to find common ground. The atmosphere, rather than competitive and cutthroat, was casual and collaborative. That worked for me, because under normal circumstances, I would not have elected to take *one* poetry workshop, never mind many.

There were other notable differences for me coming from New York City: like how clean the mountain air was to breath, and the fact that I did not need to take an allergy pill for the duration of my stay. The wine we had nightly to accompany dinner, which was lovely, rich, and potent, as a local said, "Sardinian wine is stronger than typical" — never resulted in a hangover. That someone enticed me to sing, which never happens — but that was the night of wine, grappa, and a myrtle digestive, which did result in pain the next day. Ahem.

The wonderfully funny people from the workshops I met the first night in Galtelli at dinner, those who sat near me — Fritz, Maid Marion, Colbert, Big D — were the people I hung out with for the duration. They were terrific and all simpatico. Fritz is a poet who lives in Beacon, New York. Big D is a published poet who also teaches at NYU Shanghai. Colbert is a teacher and artist masquerading as a poet who also looks like a New Yorker masquerading as a Californian. Maid Marion is working on an incredible book of fiction about the crossing over of the living and the dead, and I say that because we all did readings and in hers, the characters jumped off the page. And, she lives in Brooklyn! They are people I will continue to keep in touch with: smart, serious writers with wit and a sense of humor.

While we were Galtelli, the annual Feast of St. Anthony, who is the Patron Saint of lost things, was celebrated. We were the guests of honor. There was a proper mass, with very fine local male singers, attended by us, women and some delightfully squirmy children. I looked around and asked, *sotto voce*, "Where are all the men?" Afterwards, we traversed from the mass down the main street of Galtelli, with what appeared to be the entire population, to the biggest pagan ritual bonfire I have ever seen. You had to walk around the bonfire three times or bad luck would ensue; I walked round with the children, who had zero fear of heat. Men poured wine out of large glass bottles into small plastic cups — again, delicious — and women threaded through the crowd with baskets full of soft cookies bearing crushed grapes in the center that were so good, one of our instructors, Damiano, an Italian from just outside Milan, collected them for his breakfast the next morning. I needed a rest after all that, so I went back to my digs, did yoga, took a shower, then showed up a couple of hours later for the feast. It looked like only the men were allowed to come to the feast (!), about 200 of them, or perhaps the women didn't want to come and stayed home and ate pizza instead. So I assumed the men had cooked the feast, which was a rustic soup consisting of whole onions, pork, fava beans, potatoes and then there were also small plates of fresh fennel and radishes passed up and down the long tables. To accompany every meal was a gorgeous, paper-thin crisp bread, locally made in (what looked to me like) a pizza oven, where it inflates to pillowy proportions, and then deflates into an addictive accompaniment to cheese, pasta, wine, or simply on its own.

Toward the end of the celebration, a new Prior was elected for the following year. This was a big deal, because the position of Prior is an honor. So the new Prior, who was tickled pink, invited the lot of us back to his quite magnificent home: terra-cotta colored marble tiled floors;

grand entryway; huge kitchen and event room; and that is where we were and that is where the Prior and his male friends were as he passed out cups and poured in his potent homemade wine. A few teenagers came by with delicious slices of cake that the new Prior also told us were home-made by his wife. All I can say about the massive carb count is this: it is a good thing we were walking up and down part of a mountain multiple times a day to get to workshops, taking our own walks, walking with the instructors, and that the weather, though brisk, was bright, clear, and perfect walking weather. I actually lost weight in Sardinia. Brava!

There were a few bumps in the road that I assume NYWW will sort out for the next trip. I understand that Sardinia was their first immersion workshop abroad. For me, it was a great experience surrounded by fan-tastic people in a location I have never been to before. I do wish they had hired a person to teach Creative Nonfiction — like me, for example. The next excursion for the NYWW will be to Katmandu, Nepal.

After Sardinia, I flew to Lisbon, Portugal, for a week. I behaved uncharacteristically in Lisbon. I did in Italy as well. Like collected sugar packets as if they were precious objects. I don't typically put sugar in my coffee, but all I seemed to drink there was espresso (or a dopio espresso) and just as I did at my Nonna's house, my paternal grandmother, I added zucchero.

The Airbnb eco-penthouse was small, Lilliputian, but the view was gorgeous, the bed bliss and the location — Amalfa, the oldest part of the city — perfect. There are swell people in the neighborhood: the Middle-eastern proprietor who made me buy a mango "You come back if it is no good" along with my yogurt and gave me free apples whenever I made a purchase from his shop; the couple from the Bahamas, Natasha and her husband who moved to Lisbon after an earthquake because they lost everything. They now run a cafe with house-made veggie samosas, fresh fish, great house wine, coffee and they also gave me gratis: cod fish fritters and a custard tart, the latter being the official dessert of Portugal. I ate so much fresh fish I should by all rights have gills and sprouted a tail. I loved Lisbon. Like Galtelli, Lisbon was built on a hill (or re-created, with the exception of Amalfa, after the Great Earthquake in 1755). I loved walking up and down those cobbled streets and frequenting the miles-long, open-air Mercado de Santa Clara, haggling with stallholders, that reminded me so much of the sprawling Portobello Road Market in Ladbroke Grove in London. Loved getting around by tram — above ground is Very Fancy. Unlike the subway. Loved the spa I found when a friend came to town, and the price tag lounging for hours after a massage, which I could not have afforded in New York City. I loved the driver arranged by my Airbnb host who collected me at the airport, who was a fountain of information and when she said, upon meeting me, "You look like a Portuguese." The only thing I hated was leaving.

I have been telling people for years that New York City was the only one that would have me. In truth, I was not sure I could live anywhere else. Perhaps that is no longer the case. Perhaps it is just that the other cities I find alluring — Lisbon, Rome — lie beyond the boundaries of the United States. But that harkens back to living in London in my teens, originally for college, then staying and traveling from there. I like change. I like getting out of my comfort zone. Complacency is not possible if you are concentrating on navigating language, location — and in Sardinia, terrain as well. So many places to see and so much to do in the short span of a lifetime. The best thing I can do, really, is get on a plane, and just go.

Published in *The Literary Explorer*, 2020

Difficult Men

…which is pretty much self-explanatory.

Lightning in a Jar

IN 2007, WHILE VACATIONING in Provincetown, Massachusetts, I bought an ornate, sterling ring by two local artisans: Phyllis and Izzy Sklar. Wonderfully eccentric, they appeared to be in their 80's: Izzy spoke out of one side of his mouth, and I couldn't tell whether this was because of a stroke or a lack of teeth. Nevertheless, he was the more talkative one, while Phyllis, who moved slowly and I thought, regally, opened up once she found I lived in New York City, as the Sklars had a shop there in the 1970's. They lived in a dilapidated house on the West End of Commercial Street, half of which appeared to be sinking into the ground, a tilted ship the sand would eventually claim. The interior was overrun with cats and unframed paintings lying on almost every surface.

Alas, the ring was too big. I asked if they could size it, and the reply was no. I asked if they knew anyone in town who could size the ring, and they both hemmed and hawed and finally said, "Jimmie. We only trust Jimmie."

"Okay, tell me where to find him."

I thought that was an easy question but they answered, "It's tricky," gave me an address on a scrap of paper and then, because he was by referral only, "Be sure you say we sent you."

Baffled, I set off. I'd been coming to Ptown since I was two years old, knew every inch of it, every nook and cranny of the three mile long, one mile wide "island." I'd find Jimmie.

After about thirty humiliating minutes of asking for directions, cursing and sweaty, it seemed that Jimmie lived in a tree house, behind and up in the sky from Spiritus Pizza. I finally found a wooden door leading to a dark, mosquito-ridden backyard and a rickety staircase. Holding on for dear life, I climbed. At the top, the door was open, so I stepped in.

It was a hovel. An honest-to-goodness hovel. Made the Sklar's house seem a palatial palace. I was looking at all unfinished wood, including walls, floor, and slanted ceilings. There was a large workbench covered in small tools, gems, gold and silver chains, earrings, watches, and other assorted sundries. Pinned to the wall behind the bench were about fifty watches in small plastic bags, some with bands, some not. Tools of every kind hung from the ceiling. To the left of the workbench was a seat that once belonged in a car. To the left of that, a mangy sofa. There was also a smaller workbench where pink and white playdough-like molds mingled. There was a large, old television set trussed up near the doorway where I walked in, the sound turned low, tuned to the History Channel. There were huge, blown up, faded photographs of a young, bearded man lying down with two tigers; the same man, younger, in fatigues holding a rifle, and a few photographs of a beautiful, blond, young woman and the same man, but older. Lastly, there was a door, that I suppose must have led somewhere, pocked with marks and deep gashes.

I was afraid to step any further, lest I'd go through the floor. Or something would fall on me. Or blow up.

"Hello?"

Maybe I should just get the fuck out of here.

"Hello?"

If I'm held hostage, will anyone ever find me?

The door with the gashes burst open, and an adrenalized man with piercing blue eyes and a Civil War goatee stared at me. He looked about forty-five, average height, in a tight army-green tee shirt and pants. Slim below the waist, all of his weight, in sinew and muscle, seemed to be carried in his upper body. He was very fit, as I learned later, from running the breakwater and keeping up with his military exercises. But it wasn't just his physicality. It was something else, something difficult to define. A man once described me in the following way: Like lightning in a jar. That description is what went through my head when I met Jimmie.

"Who sent you?"

He had a Texan accent.

"Izzy and Phyllis Sklar."

"Oh." He visibly relaxed. "That's okay. What do you need?"

"A ring sized down."

He took the ring, looked at it, looked at me up and down, taking all of me in.

"Why silver? You can wear gold; you've got the skin tones for it."

"No. I gave up on gold, and I'm a silver girl."

"Why?"

"Burgled."

"In Ptown?"

"No. I was at college in London. It was my first New Year's there. My roommate was a DJ and had a party to play at, so he invited me. We got home about four in the morning, and our door had been kicked in, and every piece of gold I owned had been taken. Pieces my grandmother had given me: opal earrings, a thin gold Italian chain. My friend had given me an opal and diamond ring the night before I left the US. It had gotten too big for my finger and I decided to leave it home that night because I was afraid I'd lose it."

"Ah, the sentimental stuff," he said.

"That's right," I said.

"That's why you shouldn't get attached to material things."

"Thanks so much for that," I said.

"It's true," he said, looking at the ring again.

"Aren't you a jewelry maker? That's what the Sklars said."

"Yeah, I am. Jewelry designer."

"Don't you see the irony there?" I said, annoyed.

He said, "Let's see your finger."

He put a ring sizer on the second finger of my left hand, went over and sat on his bench.

He said, " I fucking hate silver. Cheap-ass metal, and it's so fucking hard to work with."

I said, "Can you size it or not?"

He said, "Yessum, have a seat, and I'll do it right now."

Have a seat? Where? Where was I supposed to put my clean ass down and still have it clean when I got up?

"Thanks, I'll stand."

I paused. "I'm Lisa."

"Jimmie," he said, and stuck out a grimy hand to shake. I took it.

Jimmie seemed to have no filter, and said what he thought when he thought it. He was bracing, like a dip in the Atlantic in March. He had a quick mind, a sharp tongue, a foul mouth. I found him intriguing, an eccentric in a tree house.

"So what'd ya do?" Jimmie asked, as I walked around, gingerly, looking at his things.

"I'm a writer and a professor."

"Yeah? Where do you teach?"

"NYU."

Jimmie actually looked impressed. "How'd ya get that gig?"

"I fell into it," I said.

"What?"

"I have a performance background. I trained as a singer and an actor. So, I was working a coat check gig at a terrible but lucrative tourist trap and I had two conversations with the brother of my boss. Two. And he called me a few days later and said that his college was looking for a teacher, he thought I'd be good at it, and he had set up an interview. I just had to call to confirm. I said, What the hell do I know about teaching? I'm a performer for Christ's sake!"

Jimmie said, "Oh, but that's perfect. How'd he get your number?"

"Not from me."

"Hmmnn… somebody helped you out. Or, they wanted to fuck you."

"I… guess," I said, wishing that had stayed a thought rather than a sentence.

"So what happened?"

"I went on the interview. Halfway through, I said to the Chair, do I have this job? He said, do you want this job? I said, sure. When do I start? He said, in a week. He handed me the textbook. And that was that."

"At NYU."

"No, at a business college. Mostly minority students. I absolutely loved it. NYU came later."

"Then you found where you belonged."

"I did. You know, I don't believe you know if you can teach until you get up in front of a class. Because if you can't connect with students, if you can't reach them, you're screwed."

"I've written some."

I said, "You have?"

"Yeah. Mainly for my daughter Rose, so she has some kind of a record, ya know. Wanna read some?"

"Sure."

Jimmie said, "You can help me, maybe."

I said, "What do you need?"

He said, "I think the stories are okay, ya know. But I'm not good with grammar an' spelling. I got an education up to eighth grade then dropped out, lied about my age and went to 'Nam at seventeen. So maybe ya could… edit them."

"Edit them?"

"Well. Yeah. If you could."

"Okay."

I should just say from the outset what a fucking idiot I was to say yes before looking at Jimmie's stories.

A. Fucking. Idiot.

"Come tomorrow and I'll have 'em for you."

I went back the next day for the stories. But Jimmie wasn't quick with letting me in and out of his shop; I had to wait until he actually *gave* me the stories, and that took hours. I thought maybe he was lonely; maybe I was filling a gap. Jimmie was entertaining enough to make me want to stay. He had a million stories, and wanted to tell all of them, it seemed, to me. Me, The Writer. But he also seemed interested in me as a person, which is why we became friends.

Later, I came to see Jimmie's place as a sort of lair, and Jimmie was the spider; everyone else was prey, caught in his web.

"When's yer birthday?" Jimmie said.

"June."

"June what?"

"June 9th.

"Mine's the 10th. I knew you were a Gemini."

"How?" I asked.

"Because Gemini women are dangerous."

I didn't ask why. I didn't really want to know. Jimmie did volunteer that he was over sixty, and I was stunned; the man looked decades younger. Then I asked about the photos.

"Yep, I used to keep tigers. They were beauties, but eventually, they took up too much bed. Ate furniture. I trained 'em right, and it worked for a couple years…."

"So what happened?"

"There was an animal sanctuary I reckoned they'd be happy at."

Good, because I was afraid they had come to a bad end.

"And who's the blonde?"

"My ex-fiancé."

"You keep photos of your ex up on the wall?"

"Yep. I keep 'em up so no one asks questions about my personal life. Assume I'm still with 'er. Ptown's small, ya know? Everyone's in everyone else's shit. I don't want anyone in my shit."

"Okay," I said.

Jimmie sighed. "Renata. We were engaged. She's from the Czech Republic."

"She's very beautiful."

"Yep, and she has no character."

"Um…"

"We were together for eight years. She was gonna move here permanent. She's come here, and I went there, see how she lived. I musta given her half a million dollars in jewelry, most I made myself. Shoulda seen the engagement ring, it was a thirty-thousand dollar rock — it was gorgeous. Well, I get a call from her after we got engaged, after she went back again and she said she fell in love with someone else. I said send the ring back. She said it's mine. I said it's not yours to keep. So she sent it back and ya know what, I was looking at it and I sent it back to her. I didn't want it no more."

I was looking at the photos on the wall and thinking. "Do you mind my asking how old she was when you started seeing each other?"

"Nineteen"

"And you were…"

"Fifty-two."

"MMnnnn."

"What."

"She changed."

"What?"

"You do most of your changing between the ages of twenty and thirty. Your brain changes; you're not the same person at twenty that you will be at thirty."

"No," Jimmie said, "She has no character. No loyalty. Either ya have it or ya don't."

I paused. "It must be hard looking at those photos everyday."

Jimmie said, "To be honest, I don't even see them no more."

Jimmie told me he had been married and divorced three times, and had two daughters who wanted nothing whatsoever to do with him. "Their mothers turned 'em against me," he said. He had lived in Ptown for over twenty years and the daughters and two of the ex-wives were in neighboring towns.

This is how Jimmie described his relationships with women:

"I hung out with my mom and her friends and listened to them talk about men. It wasn't good — men were gone somewhere, or just gone. I listened and learned. They said they didn't want a man who cheated, so I didn't cheat; they said they didn't want a man who beat them so I never raised a hand to a woman; they said they didn't want a man who was disrespectful so I was never disrespectful; they said men never cooked, so I learned how to cook; they said men never cared about the children so I raised my children right; they said they didn't want a man who did drugs, so I didn't do drugs; they said they didn't want a man who drank so I didn't drink; they said men never liked to eat pussy so I learned to eat pussy and love it. I did everything right — and they still all left me!"

I didn't ask if his mother, a German Catholic who had lost most of her family in WW II, had really used the words "eat pussy" because that wasn't the point; it was Jimmie's personal checklist, dictated by women, and it had failed him. Women had failed him, repeatedly.

But for the moment, I was new and of interest.

Jimmy finally went through the gashed door and came back with three, fat folders. Handing them to me, he said, "Here's a few stories."

"A few!"

Jimmie said, "I got more, but they ain't finished. See what ya think."

I said, "Hey, what happened to that door?"

Jimmie said, "Nuthin. I use it for knife practice."

I said, weakly, "Oh."

Jimmie said, "Hey, listen, I have like half a million bucks worth a stones up here at any given time. Never had an alarm system, 'cause people know me. When I first moved here, I had a problem with one of the locals, and he said somethin', I'm gonna come up there and you watch, gonna steal your stuff. I said, when? 'Cause you know what? That'd be like Christmas mornin' to me! That's the law, son: break into my house, I'll shoot you dead. And let me tell you, I have weapons of choice up here. So go ahead! It'd be like Christmas mornin'! Guy never said a word to me after that, not one word."

I thought, I should really be writing this shit down.

Jimmie freely admitted to being "a redneck" but a polite redneck. I knew his politics were Right of Center, but they were not in the forefront of his mind when I first knew him. He once said, "Two things I love: the military and this country, and both are changin' in ways I don't like."

I tried to avoid talking politics with him at all costs.

Jimmie said, "Okey, dokey, sit down, have a look at the stories.

I sat down, causing a cloud of dust to puff out around me, and began reading. After a few pages, I stopped.

"Jimmie?"

"Yeah?"

"Jimmie, there's no… punctuation. At all. And no… paragraphs. At all."

"I know," Jimmie said, sounding almost pleased with himself, so I thought it was time for me to leave. I had been in his shop for hours. I was hungry. Tired. Cranky.

"I should go," I said, standing up and stretching.

Jimmie looked at me, then rummaged around on his workbench. As if by magic, he produced a beautiful black pearl pendant on a glittery chain that he dangled from his fingers and said, "I'll pay you in jewelry!"

I rolled my eyes, and sat back down.

✳

So I became Jimmie's "editor."

The stories drove me nuts. In addition to no punctuation/no paragraphs, the spelling was atrocious, the tenses inconsistent, and the editing (or rewriting) was long, slow and tedious. Plus, he would fight me on spelling words properly, such as "Hay!" I corrected them all, and he said that's how they say it in Texas. I said say it anyway you like, but this is how "Hey!" the greeting is spelled correctly everywhere. It took Jimmie two months to admit I was right.

But.

The man knew how to tell a story. On paper, Jimmie sounded the way he spoke, and had a really strong point of view. He had a couple of beautiful stories about him and his mother: "Crane Dancing" was about his mother teaching him the difference between sex and love; "Banana Pudding" was what he dreamed of during and asked for when he came back from Vietnam and what his mother made him. The other stories were about him and his now-estranged youngest daughter from his last wife, when they were as thick as thieves, and there was an unfinished one about Vietnam.

From a teaching standpoint, what Jimmie did not know could be taught. What he did know was much harder to acquire. However, he did

241

not want a teacher. He wanted someone to transcribe what he said while he said it.

We began with Vietnam.

I pointed to the photograph of Jimmie as a young man in fatigues, holding a rifle.

"That you?"

"Yeah, that's me. In Nam."

"How long were you there?"

"Four years. Would've stayed longer, but they discharged me with crazy papers, ya know? Can't fight crazy papers."

"Crazy papers?"

"That's right. I still say my brain don't work right: it didn't before I went, and Nam kind of… put icing on that cake. Or what was left a' that cake."

"Ever heard of Tim O'Brien?"

"Nope."

" He was in Nam. I can lend you his book, if you want. It's called *The Things They Carried*."

"Nope. Don't want to read nothing I don't already know."

"That's kind of a… shitty attitude, isn't it?"

"Maybe. But that's the truth. I got my own Nam stories; I don't need anyone else's."

"Okay, so no books on Nam."

Jimmie said, "I hate reading, man; it gives me such a headache. I hate email. I told you, my brain don't work right. Too many fights. Pistol whipped a few times. If you shave my head, it looks like the surface of Mars, you know? I have to read something like eight times just to make sense of it. It's like real work for me, like tryin' to make my eyes see straight. I can watch movies and stuff: I like PBS and the History channel and the Discovery Channel. I like learnin' stuff. There's nothing wrong with readin', I can see you love it. I just can't do it myself."

I said, "That makes a lot more sense than saying 'I won't read anything I don't already know.'"

"Well, it's not the kind of thing I'm happy to talk about; no one wants to stand there and say hey, I've got an eighth grade education, it's not like it's somethin' to be proud of. It's like my defense. You're a Gemini, so you know; we're quick. You're real smart, and you've got a lot of learnin'. When I talk to you and this other guy I know, an Irish filmmaker, he does beautiful work, the lighting is just incredible, I think I could have gotten a lot out of college if I'd a went, you know?"

I said, "Yeah, but understand, I didn't do it alone: I was encouraged and had people to push me along the way; even people who didn't know me that well, like the first chairperson I had who said, get the MFA so you can teach anything, and get it as fast as you can. I was just… smart enough to listen to them."

Jimmie said, "I didn't have nobody to push me. No sir. You teach at NYU now; you're a writer. That's good. One feeds the other. See?"

He fiddled with something on his workbench.

"Do you know when he was there? O'Brien?"

"No… but I can find out."

"Know what division? Was he in special divisons?"

"I can find that out, too."

Jimmie said, "The more you can do as a soldier, the more you're paid. You can be making a lot of money in the service, but you got to be real good at specific things. And each thing you can do, the more you special-ize, the more you earn at being a specialist. I went in as a nothin', and was earning nothin', but I knew eventually, I'd find somethin' I was good at."

"What were you good at?"

"Gemini women are dangerous, ya know," Jimmie said.

"Why?" I said.

"Because they can get laid anytime they want to," he said.

"Oh, so you were a specialist at being a mind reader? At dirty talk?"

"It was by accident. The drill sergeant lined up all the men and each one of us had a rifle; we were there for target practice. Drill sergeant said, "Okay, get it up and start shootin' at the cat." Everybody got it up, and started shootin'. Except me. Sergeant came over to me and says,

"Why aren't you shooting at the cat, boy?" I said, "Which one?" He said, "Whaddya mean, which one?" I said, "The grey one or the black one, sir?" Sergeant says, pointing, "You go and stand over there."

I said, "You could tell the difference between a grey cat and a black cat?"

"I could tell the difference between a grey cat and a black cat at night."

"At night?"

"And that's how I became a sniper. I always had real good eyesight. After that, I learned how to be observant. Every person that comes in here, I can tell as much about them in five minutes than most people can in five years. Most people talk a bunch a shit. I'd say in a year, I meet maybe three people that are interesting, worth talkin' to. That's okay. I can get along with most anyone."

Jimmie said that Vietnam was the single most important experience of his life, despite the fact that he was a cancer survivor from Agent Orange and still suffered from PTSD. If he were still allowed to serve, he'd be in Afghanistan right now. For him, it was about loyalty, brotherhood, and he was mistaken to think the kind of loyalty he found in the military could be found when he got back home, back in the real world.

In the Real World

Loyalty. Character.
Either you're born with it, Jimmie said,
Or you're not.

Texan Jimmie.
He's 66 and if they'd take him,
He'd be in Afghanistan right now.

Instead, he tells me stories.

Jimmie said,
I thought it would be the same in the real world
after 'Nam.
I thought people would have my back
like my brothers.
It ain't like that.
But I'm not right in the head.
Too many hits, I reckon.
So it could be me.

Link. Kansas boy.
Was the meanest toughest motherfucker I
ever met.
He killed men with his hands in ten seconds.
I seen it.
He'd been in Nam two terms, came back
for a third.
I said,
Why'd you come back to this shithole?
I was 17.
Link said,

Boy, shut the fuck up and
Learn something.
So I did.
For a long time.

Months go by.
Link warms to me, in a foxhole.
I had a girl back home.
I said, If I find out she's cheatin'
I'll kill her and the guy she's with.
I didn't know shit about love or women.
Link said,
There ain't nuthin' to fuckin'.

I said,
What?

You wanna know why
I came back for a third term,
Link said.
I married my high school sweetheart.
She's a good girl.
When I got drafted, she lived with my parents
to save money for an apartment.
I sent money home every month.
Finished first term, came back.
Second term, a little different.
In-depth, doing crazy shit, still sending
home money leave
can happen anytime.
Finished a mission, sergeant said,
Take a week, boy.
First place I go is my parents' house.
My wife moved to an apartment, couldn't take the parents

You Are All a Part of Me

anymore. I get it.
My Dad handed me the keys
and because he was a military man
his WW II gun. I said okay.
I get to the apartment.
So good to lighten my load.
Heard the television on.
Went into the bedroom.
My wife was fucking
some other guy I startled 'em.
The guy jumps up
grabs a big fuckin' knife
tries to stab me.

Well
two days before that
I was killing guys doing
hand-to-hand combat
in the woods and it was
just reflex:
I took my Dad's gun
out of my waistband
Shot him.
The bullet that killed him
went through my wife
Killed her too.

Police came.
Arrested me.
Looked at my military record.
Looked at my Dad's.
Said it was self-defense.
All charges dropped.

I went back to Nam
signed up for a
third term right after
the second finished.
So boy, there ain't nuthin' to fuckin'.'
But when you kill
your best friend in the world
the one you could talk to
tell anything to—
when you lose that
That's somethin'.'
That's really somethin'.'

Jimmie said,
And I thought about it different
After that
Years later
After each of my marriages ended
Losing my friend
The connection I had to that person
The part I missed most
Gone.

Jimmie said,
Me and Link
became friendly after that.
He wasn't afraid of nuthin'.'
He taught me to be real observant, like.
Eight or nine months later
we were lying in a field of tall grass
on our bellies
and I could hear the bullet comin'
cause it makes a whizzing noise
through all that grass.

You Are All a Part of Me

We both moved back
but it caught Link
right across the throat
a perfect slice
Opening him up.

Now I'm no medic
but I'm good in the field
I was tryin' to stopper the blood
but I couldn't shut
the vein.
If ya have a man down in the field
there's a hospital
15 minutes
from wherever you are.
I got help got him
in the chopper
trying to hold
his neck together
sayin'
C'mon man, hold on
you motherfucker.

We got him there
Doc got him on the table
Link looked at me and
seems like he decided
to give in.
Just give in.

The doc said
You can take your hand
away now I tried
and couldn't

'cause Link's tissue
had grown onto my fingers
from the field
to the hospital
like we was
part of each other.

Tissue grows real
real fast and
the doc had to cut us
apart.
He led me to a sink
and made me wash
real good
with Phisoderm.
I can still remember
the green bottle
with the black lettering.

Jimmie said,
I always thought Link
Wanted a part a him to go with me
I reckon
And it kinda sorta did.
There ain't nuthin' to fuckin'.
There just ain't.

Published in *Vietnam War Poetry*, 2015

Lear & My Father

OUT OF ALL OF SHAKESPEARE'S PLAYS, "King Lear" is my favorite. I first saw Lear when I was eighteen while training at LAMDA, performed by my fellow students. When Cordelia, at the beginning of the play, has her asides to the audience, troubled and trembling, wondering what she will say to her father, it struck a visceral chord in me that still resonates. Since then, I have seen many Lears: Anthony Hopkins at The National Theater in London, Christopher Plummer, Ian McKellen, Antony Sher here in New York City. For me, the best plays are the ones that are so specific they finally become universal. Lear is that specific and that magnificent.

My father is a perfect age for Lear now: eighty-three. Probably too old to carry Cordelia, but that is the trouble with the part. It is said once you are old enough to play Lear, you are too old to carry her onto the stage for the final scene. But I refuse to see any Lear that is fifty or sixty years of age. That is too young for my taste, and if the tradeoff is Christopher Plummer wisely dragging Cordelia's body out on a burlap sack in lieu of carrying her, I'll take it for the stunning performance he gave. It diminished nothing.

I imagine that Cordelia was the apple of her father's eye and had a lovely childhood. That makes his treatment of her and subsequent banishment all the harder for her to take. I was the apple of my father's eye and the first-born. For five years, I was an only child and spoiled rotten. My father, knowing no better, raised me like a boy. I reveled in being a tomboy. He erected a swimming pool and taught me how to swim — no lessons. He rigged spotlights to our house and used to wake me in the middle of the night to go moonlight swimming with him. I do not know what Freud would say about this; however, my mother did not swim, so she watched and waved from the kitchen window. My father taught me how to ride a bike — no training wheels, because he insisted that "training wheels are for pussies" and "then later on, you can say you never needed the training wheels." I have the scars on my knees to prove it. An avid hunter, my father took me to a rifle range and taught me how to shoot. The gun closet was in my room. Again, Freud calling… He showed me all of the big, black, shiny rifles, locked them up and told me never to touch them. I never did, even though I could reach the ledge where the key was kept, because I knew he would beat me within an inch of my life. We went camping as a family, which I liked and my father liked — he was a huge nature person and we watched "Wild Kingdom" together on Sunday nights — and my mother hated, mainly because she had to do most of the work. I have seen a few of those camping photos: my toddler sister outside the camper in her portable playpen and my mother in the camper, sullenly watching her while in the midst of preparing food. I would have been unhappy, too.

Up until I was ten, my father was an enormous presence in my life. All of those things we did together bonded us. I wanted to do well in whatever he taught me, whatever we did together, and do well for him. That made him proud. I knew it. I saw it. I heard it.

And then just like that, he moved his heart away from me.

It would have been so much easier if I had had no memory of him. One cannot miss what one never had. But miss him I did. Even his brutality I excused, because mostly, I knew he loved me. Then like Lear, after the divorce, it was like my father was cast out into the wilderness and literally went mad. The divorce broke him.

In 2006, I began a monologue that branched off into a more fully-formed full-length play. "Clare's Room," my first play, was picked up by the New York City International Fringe Festival, got great reviews, and caused me many headaches, not least because my sister thought it was written about her; while my mother resented the "airing of dirty laundry" and refused to attend — which was fine by me. In truth, "Clare's Room" is an autobiographical play that tries to make sense of the house I grew up in. There are six characters based on me, my two sisters, my mother, my step-father, and my father. The more I re-read and revise, though, the more apparent it becomes that the play is really about my father. This is an excerpt from "Clare's Room" between Joan, the mother, and Giuseppe, the father, after he has cancelled yet another Sunday date

252

with his children:

Joan (*To audience*): I was furious, so many, many times! I never thought I would be left to clean up Giuseppe's mess. My children's: yes. His? No. (*To Giuseppe*) You were a bad father.

Giuseppe: I couldn't come back to that house again.

Joan: Too painful for you, so you said. But your children come first, not you.

Giuseppe: The Church became my family.

Joan: That's the most irresponsible thing I ever heard.

Giuseppe: You wouldn't understand; you have no faith.

Joan: You don't know the first thing about *faith*. You believe in a God that forgives whatever you do here on earth; you have forsaken all that you have in this life for what you think exists in the next. What if you're wrong? What if you've squandered it all for nothing, and dead in a box is all you get?

Giuseppe: Didn't parochial school teach you nuthin'?

Joan: Yes: it taught me that God forgives your sins if you have learned your lesson from the sin. Go forth, and sin no more. There is no weekly pass for the same sin, over and over and over again! You have never repented where your children are concerned; you stopped seeing them, as if they no longer existed. Then, because Clare is the only one who'll still speak to you, you used her to get to me, because you have never forgiven me for divorcing you.

Giuseppe (*Explodes, and in agony*): WHY SHOULD I? YOU RUINED MY LIFE! THIS IS NOT WHAT MY LIFE IS SUPPOSED TO BE! I'M NOT WHAT I SHOULD BE! I'M NOT! I'M NOT!

(*Pause*)

Joan (*Quietly*): We have been divorced for over twenty years now. We have both remarried other people. Don't you think it's time to move on?

Giuseppe: I love you, Joan. And I have tried everything: everything except exorcism to get rid of it. But it's still there. I love you. And I hate myself for it. Until I die, I'll have it with me, every day, like a scar, to remind me. And that I can't forgive you for.

(*Joan says nothing. Giuseppe fingers his rosary beads.*)

That I believe with my whole heart, the reason the divorce broke my father, the reason he never got over it. And never will.

Giuseppe Del Rosso, Italian, immigrated to the US when he was thirteen (or fifteen?) in 1949 from Anversa degli Abruzzi, has five brothers (one of whom, Phil, was my godfather) and sisters, is built like a rugby player, broad, strong, average height, learned a trade, became a butcher, hard-working, traditional, loved his mother, good-looking like a green-eyed Elvis when he was young (according to my mother, but I have some photos and she wasn't far off the mark), a Catholic then an ex-communicated Catholic then a re-born Catholic, a hunter, a trash-mouth, a man who mixes plaid pants with checked shirts and flat caps (I have those photos, too).

My mother said the real problems, apart from his cruelty toward her, which was mental, not physical — he used to humiliate her in public, calling her a "cold fish," ridiculed her looks, asked if she wanted a nose job and he'd pay for it, all in front of friends and family — began over how to discipline children when the children came along. And my mother drew the line at hitting little girls.

Every Sunday after church, we went for dinner at Nana and Grampy's house (Maria Philomena and Achilles), which entailed simply walking through the backyard.

One Sunday, we went round to my grandparents' as usual, and it must have been right after I was able to use the bathroom all by myself like a grown up, old enough to reach the sink and wash my hands.

Daydreaming, I had forgotten to flush the toilet, and my father went into the bathroom right after I did. It could have been to check, or it could have been for himself; he never told me. He came out in a fury, grabbed me by the arms and bent down, yelling into my face, "What are you supposed to do, what are you supposed to do?"

You Are All a Part of Me

I remember the black-dial telephone on the wall above my head and my grandfather's phone number – 335-3706 — and higher up, to my left, my grandmother had hung a large wooden quarter moon with four small shelves built into it, and figures on each: one was a cat & fiddle, one a cow, one a dog, one a dish & spoon. Looking at it always made me happy, because I could sing the nursery rhyme in my head.

My mother was on one side of my father while he screamed, and my grandmother was on the other, and my mother was saying, "Don't hit her, Joe, you'll ruin the day," and my grandmother was saying, "She didn't mean it, she's just a little girl," at the same time and I was standing there like a mute and my father slapped me in the face, and the day was ruined.

My grandfather had been outside in the garden, missing this entire scenario.

That night, after I had taken a bath, my mother came into my room. She seemed not angry but glacial, like she was trailing a cold wind. "Your father has something to say to you. In the bedroom." I went into their bedroom, and my father, who was in his pajamas, got down on his knees and apologized to me. He kept saying, "I'm sorry, I'm sorry, forgive me," put his head into my hands and cried. I felt really bad for him because he didn't stop, so I patted him on the head and said, "It's okay, it's okay." I didn't know what else to do.

It's not that I grew up in a violent household per se; it's that my father wanted to raise his children the way he was raised, which meant corporal punishment, regardless of gender.

So I learned, in order to avoid the belt or his hand or a shoe, to be good or be hit. I became the "good child." I tried to do everything perfectly: to speak when spoken to, to not answer back, and finish all the food on my plate, a pre-requisite of my father's for leaving the kitchen table. Ten years of that kind of indoctrination stuck, even after my father had moved out and they divorced. My mother still maintains that I was the "perfect child" but I suspect that I behaved well out of fear more than anything else.

My parents separated once, for approximately eight months to a year, due to my father's violence, and my mother said she was through. But both of my grandfathers — the elder heads of their respective families — went to her house and told her that my father wanted to come back to try and make the marriage work. She said no, she didn't want to do that. But they wouldn't leave until she gave in. Instead, they said, "You have to reconcile because of the children. You have to reconcile for the families." She told me: "I was sitting in the blue chair in the parlor crying, saying that I didn't want to take him back, and I felt like I was having a nervous breakdown."

She took him back. She said they really gave her no choice.

During the time my mother and father were separated, they had both dated other people.

Once a couple has reconciled, it's best not to talk about what one did with whom when the two people in question were separated, because:

It's irrelevant

It's in the past.

No good can come from this.

My parents had been reconciled for five or six months. Toward the end of that sixth month, in the kitchen, my father brought up a man my mother had dated during their separation. It must have been a Saturday, sunny and bright, early afternoon, because I was not in school. I was in the parlor, sitting in the blue chair reading. On the ground level of our house, there were no doors to the rooms, only archways. So if I had been allowed, I would have ridden my bike from the kitchen to the parlor to the den and round and round again, because it was designed like a big circle. No doors also meant no privacy.

I believe my father wanted to know if my mother had had "feelings" for the man she had been seeing. There was a necklace involved, an ivory rose on a gold chain the man had given her, that my mother had kept. The necklace was a bone of contention. I don't know how she answered him. I don't know if there is any answer that would have pacified my father. But "had" to her meant past. They *had both* seen other people.

The kitchen in the house that I grew up in was not a big room, and most of the space was dominated by a large, ugly brown table and five heavy wooden chairs.

Whatever she did say upset him, he began the yelling, then both voices were raised, then both of them were yelling, and then my father erupted into a screaming, crazed person and picked up one of the heavy wooden chairs, holding it high above his head to throw at her. My mother put her hands up and said, "That's it! This marriage is over! Take your things and get out!"

And he did, hurling suitcases down the stairs of our two-story house, hurling the box with the necklace in it down the stairs, screaming, "He gave her this! He gave her this!" hurtling himself down those stairs after those suitcases and punching the closet at the bottom of those stairs, leaving a splintered indent in the shape of a fist that I looked at multiple times a day for the next eight years.

Throughout this, I sat in the blue chair, hid behind my book, and cried. My mother sat on the parlor couch and cried. She had called my aunt for moral support, and my aunt was on the couch next to her, also crying. At one point, my mother looked at me and said, "I can see you behind your book. I know you're crying."

I don't know why she said that. I wasn't crying because I was sad. I was crying because I was terrified. My father had spun completely out of control, deranged, making way too many trips to his truck, each time slamming the screen door so hard I thought the glass would shatter, screaming all the way out and all the way back in. He finally just drove off without saying goodbye to me, and a long, long time went by before I saw him again.

In "King Lear," Cordelia is betrayed by her sisters out of greed. That did not happen with my sisters, but it did with another woman who ingratiated herself with me not through flattery or fawning. She succeeded because I was a voracious reader.

Right after the divorce, my father moved back in with his mother, my Nonna. Within six months, he began dating, and the three of us met a blonde named Kay, whom he did not marry because she had an unexplained (at least, to us) medical condition, and an Irish beauty who was also divorced and had three children, whom he did marry in a Protestant Church. This was his new wife (who shall be known as NW from here on in).

Early on, NW suckered me with books. She was sweet and kind, and always willing to listen if I wanted to talk. The awkwardness I felt at that age, physically and emotionally, rendered me a near-mute. I always had a book with me when my father picked me up, and she must have noticed. So one day, after I had jumped into the back seat as usual, she turned around, smiled and said, "I have something for you." She pulled out a brown paper bag full of books and handed them to me. "For me?" I said, shocked. We didn't have a lot of books at home, so the only time I had seen that many books together all at once was at my beloved Tufts Library. "Yes," she said, "My girls [whom had elected to live with their father] are older than you, and have outgrown these, so they're yours."

"Wow!" I said, digging my hands into the bag, "Thank you!"

The books kept coming. I kept reading. My eleventh year was filled with the fairy tales of Oscar Wilde, the lives of Helen Keller and Annie Sullivan, the Plains of Laura Ingalls Wilder. The books transported me and were given so often as gifts I thought they meant that she loved me, too. She opened me up a bit, enough so that I could laugh without blushing in her presence. I used to go home and tell my mother how wonderful my father's new wife was, how much I liked her. In retrospect, it must have been hard for my mother to take all my gushing. I was just so happy she liked me because I thought that also made my father happy.

After my parents divorced in the 1970's, the Roman Catholic Church ex-communicated them both. My mother, who had been raised to be a good Catholic and attended parochial school, never forgave the church and never went back. My father, on the other hand, never recovered.

NW and my father moved to a small apartment in Quincy and we (me and my two younger sisters) saw them fairly regularly. During the time they were courting and after they wed the first time, NW seemed genuinely interested in me. That is when she began giving me brown paper bags filled with used books.

Shortly after, my mother was sitting on her bed, looking at a piece of paper. I walked in and asked what she was reading. She said my father had asked her for an annulment, which, once granted, meant that their marriage had never existed. He wanted to marry NW again in a Catholic Church, and only an annulment stood in his way. All my mother had to do was sign a piece of paper. I was confused. If the marriage didn't take place, did that mean we also did not exist? Did it make us bastards? Invisible? I said, "You were married to him for ten years. Don't sign it." But my mother had a different take. She sighed and told me she wouldn't stand in his way. Then she said, "Besides, they'll burn in Hell with the rest of us."

Once NW and my father remarried in the Catholic Church, everything stopped: her presence, the books, all communication from her. In turn, my father became increasingly remote.

Cordelia
[Aside]What shall Cordelia do? Love, and be silent.

For a few years, approximately twelve to fourteen, I didn't say anything to my father about his repeatedly not showing up on the appointed day to see me. About breaking plans at the last minute. About leaving me waiting on my brick front steps — all dressed up in my Sunday best — for Godot.

I was hurt and confused. I also still had misplaced loyalty for respecting my elders. But at fourteen I discovered my voice, literally: I could sing, and it not only propelled me into proper lessons, musicals, theater companies, and contests, it bolstered something in me I hadn't felt before: self-worth. It was a revelation. Though I was a good student, singing was the only thing that made me feel at all confident.

That confidence spilled over into my tenuous relationship with my father: I wanted answers to questions only he could give me. Those conversations always took place in his truck, while he was driving. It didn't give me a lot of time to state my case.

Cordelia
[Aside] Then poor Cordelia!
And yet not so; since, I am sure, my love's
More richer than my tongue.

I became obsessed with the "why" of his not seeing me. Was it because I was a girl? Once, my father said, "If you had been born boys, I never would have left the house." That statement stunned me into silence. Later, when he said the same thing to my youngest sister, she jumped all over him and he qualified, saying he only meant that he "would have known what to do with boys, could relate to boys." He didn't know what to do with girls. So, my gender was a problem that I could not change. But it was more than that, because I churned with emotional whiplash: what happened? There had been such a marked personality change: the voluble, vibrant and granted, violent father had morphed into a spineless jellyfish who now deferred to NW:

"NW was feeling sick, so she didn't want company."

"NW isn't up to seeing anyone right now, so I can't come."

"NW made other plans for Father's Day, so I have to cancel."

What happened to the father who taught me to swim? Who took a million photographs of me when I was two years old, complete with outfit changes and hair all done up? Where did he go? Why had he been abducted and replaced by a man who no longer cared? When I had the rare opportunity, I asked too many questions and my father said, "You have a big mouth, just like your mother."

In retrospect, what I should have asked was, "Why did you stop loving me?"

Letter-writing campaigns were a better arena for me to express myself. I could say what I wanted to say, rather than be cut off once the car ride was over. I addressed them to my father, and sent them via mail. When I learned to drive, impatient for answers, I dropped them personally at his house. Later, he said that NW had read my letters and threw them out. Did this mean he read them as well? Did he read any of them at all? Did he even see them? I never knew. I asked why she opened his mail and he shrugged. I did get one response in the mail: a letter of mine, torn into pieces. I assume that this was NW's handiwork. My father claimed no responsibility.

King Lear
Nothing will come of nothing: speak again.

This is Joan again, the mother in "Clare's Room":
"I just remember feeling anger. Rage. Like I wanted to stab him through the heart. Do you remember that one Father's Day? You were a teenager, about thirteen. You and your sisters had made gifts for your father in school. You were very excited to see him. All three of you were dressed up, waiting downstairs for him to arrive at two o'clock. The phone rang at about quarter to, and I picked it up. I was upstairs in the bedroom. It was your father. He said, 'I have to cancel.' I said, 'Why?' And he said, 'NW doesn't feel like company.' I said, 'Oh really?' He said, 'Tell the kids I'm sorry.' I said, 'No, *you* tell them.' I wanted him to tell you, not me. So I put the phone down and called to you to pick up. When you got off the phone you were crying. And I just wanted to kill him."

My father told me that NW had decided not to see her children because they were a part of her past, and had encouraged him to do the same. He told me he didn't want to go through a second divorce, so he obliged.

They bought a huge, old house two towns over from mine, in Braintree. I thought it was ironic that the house was quite beautiful, Victorian and enormous with many bedrooms, and yet they welcomed no visitors.

My father also told me, on one of his bi-annual visits, that he and NW had found God and they were both very happy to be back in the church. I didn't say anything. I had read enough by then, I think, to know what betrayal was, but thousands of words printed on pages did not prepare me for the gut punch it would feel like.

﹡

When I called my father and told him I was going to London to study singing, he said, "I can't look after you over there." I was so completely perplexed by this response, I muttered an apology and got off the phone. Look after me? Is that what he thought he was doing? He barely saw me at all. By that time, he was living on a mountaintop in Vermont, near his church, becoming increasingly more isolated from his parents, brothers and sisters. He rarely came off the mountain.

Lear went into the wilderness and went mad.

I left for England, Cordelia for France. She married France and I married to stay in London.

My father used to write me letters while I was living in London, in his beautiful, broken English:

3-12-90

Dear Lisa:

Hi, the pool may be gone, the swings may be gone, the dog may be gone, butt our wonderfull memories will <u>never be gone</u>. The years that I spent with you kids will always be in my hearth and mind untill god takes me home. The lait night swims the wonderfull times that we had in the pool shall <u>never</u> be taken away from us. Those memories will last a lifetime. You felt cheated out of a father, and I felt cheated ou of my 3 little girls. I can not tell you how many times I left the hose and came back to try to make the marriage work, not for your mother but for you kids and god only knows what I went true when I finally realied that I would no longer be with my childrem ony god knows the many many times I cried for your love. For me it wass davestetting because I never thoght that it could happen to me. Your mother should never married me because she never loved me. What ever I did it was never enough, she wass never happy. If I took her to the moon she wass never satisfied. I broke my ass working 2 jobs to make more money and still she was not happy. The only reason that we got maried is because of the house that wass being beilt nex door, and your grandfather said, what are our frends goin to say if you 2 don't get marred , its goin to looke bad for all of us.

When it came time to finaly leave the house and you kids, my dear Lisa only I know what I went trhogh. I would wake up in the middle of the knight crying for many months after I left you kids and hask Our Lord why me. Its very difficult to write this letter to you and bring up the pass. Divorces are never easy, for the kids or the parens, butt time heal evrything. I had to leave the house at time when you were small, because your mother and I hated one an other with a passion. And living next door to your grandfather did not help. Dear Lisa please come home, America is the best country in the world no matter where you go. I know your not riligios butt if you please start to say the rosary it will help you a ghreat dile deal in your life. The rosary is the most powerfull weapon that we have to fight the davel on hearth.

Love DAD

PP: Don't ever forget those <u>memories</u>

I responded in kind, until he asked me to stop writing the word "Dad" on the envelope, and to use his full name instead. My banishment felt complete.

In 2004, a week before I was to be married in New York City, my father, who had said he was going to attend, causing much consternation on my mother's side of the family, left a particularly brutal message on my answering machine, ending with, "I'm not coming, I'll send a card." And I just could not work out, again, why the message; why the brutality; why the complete lack of feeling. Everything was tangled in my head, like a cube filled with a jumble of paperclips. So I called an emergency session with my therapist, who was not very pleased to be disturbed when it was not my designated day or time, but she did see me. As I told her the story about my father, her face changed from annoyance to alarm until she stopped me and said, "Wait. You have to know this is not normal."

"Really," I said.

"This is the behavior of a mentally ill person. This is not normal."

For the first time, someone impartial had said something that finally made me believe it wasn't me. It was not my fault. It was just the luck of the draw that this was the father I had gotten.

My mother was a grounding force for me, a rock, for the seventeen years I lived in her house. Though we are very different people and don't always see eye to eye, she has always been a superb mother. Only she knows what she went through with my father, and I know she does not like to revisit the past. But she had choices back then just as my father did, and she chose to be a superb, present mother.

If Cordelia's mother had been living, maybe she would have been okay.

Think about how short the first scene is in "King Lear." His one decision — to disown and banish Cordelia because she did not sufficiently flatter him — sets in motion events that inextricably link them together in tragedy. Lear determines Cordelia's future as well as his own. That is why I have difficulty feeling sorry for him at the end of the play. When he dies, it's not that I think, "Oh, good." It's more that I want to shout at him, "Why? Why were you such a vain idiot fool? Why did you do this? Cordelia is murdered, you realized too late that your actions led to the following terrible consequences, so much pain could have been avoided!"

But Lear, before he dies, does have his moment of self-realization:

King Lear
Be your tears wet? yes, 'faith. I pray, weep not:
If you have poison for me, I will drink it.
I know you do not love me; for your sisters
Have, as I do remember, done me wrong:
You have some cause, they have not.

Cordelia
No cause, no cause.

He briefly reconciles with Cordelia:

King Lear
You must bear with me:
Pray you now, forget and forgive: I am old and foolish."

That scenario, much as I would want it to, will never happen with my father in my lifetime.

I cannot forgive a man who is not sorry, has never apologized, or, when he has apologized and promised to be a better father, almost immediately reneged. So that's out.

It is more coming to terms with what made him who he is, why he has done what he has done, made the choices he made and accepting it.

Easy.

In "Clare's Room," Giuseppe's last monologue comes toward the end of the play. He is in a church pew, attempting to confess why he has done what he has done and continues to do.

Giuseppe's Story Part II

I'm back in the church now. I was away for a long time, after the divorce. Then I met Kimberly, my new wife. (*Gives Lee a look.*) I say new, but we've been together for twenty years. Kimberly was divorced, but had got her marriage annulled. She was anxious to get back to the church, too. So I got an annulment from Joan; she signed the papers, she knew.

But like I said, I'm back now. Back in the fold. I have to go to confession. I had forgotten about confession, and about how much I didn't like it. But it's part of making up for things you're not too proud of. Things that are… embarrassing. Once, I said to Lee that if she'd been born a boy, I never would have left the house. But I didn't mean it the way it sounds. I had no way to relate to girls, no experience, only my own. If I had had a boy, I would have known what to do. With girls... I didn't know. I treated them like boys, especially Lee. I taught her to be independent. Afraid of nuthin'.. It was easier when they were small. But when they became women... I couldn't put it together, my little girls with breasts and waists and hips. I teased Lee on the beach, told her she was getting a big ass. I was thinking, is this my daughter? I snapped the bra straps on their training bras, I was AWFUL! (*Giuseppe puts his head in his hands.*) I was awful. I had to make a joke, because it made me... uncomfortable. God forgive me.

Going to the old house, I felt bad, angry. Kimberly, she didn't like it, so she said, don't see them. She said she didn't see her kids after her divorce and annulment; that was in the past. So I shouldn't see mine. And I agreed. In a way, it was her decision, and I didn't want a problem with her. I couldn't go through another divorce. So Kimberly made my decision for me.

Lee: Don't you see what you've done?

Giuseppe (*Ignores her*): But she was right! It killed me to drive over there. I got it down so I'd see them birthdays and holidays; then I'd really notice how much they'd grown, especially the baby, Jules. But sometimes I'd just drop the presents with Joan, so I didn't have to think about another Christmas gone by.

Jules: Don't you understand what you've done?

Giuseppe (*Ignores her*): When Lee was eighteen she told me she was going to London; she was accepted to some fancy place that gave her some money, on account of her grades. I was so... I couldn't believe she would leave her country! Her own country; when I was forced to leave mine. I said I couldn't give her my blessing. She said she didn't need it. I said I couldn't look after her over there. She said, well, you haven't done a very good job here, have you? I wanted to slap her in the mouth, but we were at the IHOP and I didn't want to make a scene. But, driving home, I could count the times I had seen her from age ten to eighteen. Then I felt sick. I couldn't expect her to listen to me now. Too much time: too much time gone by. Same thing with Jules; one day, she was all grown up and I looked at her like she was a stranger. I never got to know her, so she was a stranger. Too much time. And Clare... Clare I always wanted to take care of because it didn't seem I was able to teach her nuthin'. It always comes out... bad. But I don't know any other way.

Clare: You have always chosen you.

Giuseppe (*Ignores her*): I said that I didn't like confession. That's true. But it's easier telling all this to a priest, or to God. I could never, ever, tell my children. But I can tell God. And God will forgive me.

No matter how many times I see "King Lear," at the end of the play when Lear howls in agony, which is first heard offstage and then grows louder as he makes that long walk to centerstage while carrying the dead body of his beloved daughter Cordelia in his arms, I am broken in two. It is too late, for both of them. For both of us.

Inheritance

TRANSCRIPT OF GROUP THERAPY: 5.12.20

In group: Brody, an Italian ex-cop, 59; Vaş, a Canadian-Greek divorced engineer with 2 kids, approximately 50; Cathy, a journalist and single mother; Dr. Silver, 77.

Dr. Silver, whom everyone calls Joel, begins each session by asking if anyone has any distractions. So I said that my best friend Derek's mother had died, and in a subsequent phone conversation, Derek said, "I'm sorry to ask this, but is your father still alive?"

"Yes," I said, "He turned 84, same age as your mother was."

"When he passes, are you going to the funeral?"

I said no.

He said, "Are you okay with that?"

Yes, I said.

"Are you sure? No regrets?"

I said, "I might have to crack a bottle of champagne and get very drunk, but no, no regrets, because I tried everything I could to have a relationship with that man, and nothing."

Dr. Silver paused and said, "Okay, I think there's some work there to do, but we'll get to that later in the session."

Later, Dr. Silver said, "Okay, Lisa, tell me what it was like growing up with your father, who sounds like a piece of work."

So I told them my father was an immigrant, born just outside of Rome in Abruzzi; that he was a shepherd in the mountains, that he came to America at 14 and became a butcher, that he and my mother's marriage wasn't exactly "arranged" but the families organized a meeting; that he believed in corporal punishment, that I was beaten but not as badly as my sister, and the reason for the divorce was because my mother could not stand by and watch my father "beat little girls."

Dr. Silver said, "That's a good reason."

He also said, "So your father was never socialized, never came into contact with other people."

I said, "With the exception of his family, no."

I told them after the divorce, my father remarried quickly: to a woman in a Protestant church, then he had the marriage to my mother annulled, then married the same woman again in the Catholic Church. After that, his new wife told him as she no longer saw her children (from a previous marriage, also annulled) he should no longer see his, because he found it upsetting. So, he agreed.

I told them he had visitation rights every weekend that mostly he did not take advantage of; but it would have been a lot easier if he had just stopped seeing us cold turkey. Instead, he came back sporadically: on the odd birthday or Christmas Eve or a graduation. Or, on Father's Day, when my mother would get us all dressed up and my father just didn't show up.

Before I went to London, we went to the IHOP (always his choice, and I cannot go into one of those places ever again because I break out in HIVES) and he was very angry: he said that I was "chasing the rainbow," that if he had still been in the house, I would have done a nice secretarial course, gotten married, had his grandchildren, never left the state, never mind the country. And I said, "Then it's good that you don't live in the house." He said, "If we weren't in the IHOP, I'd rap you in the mouth."

So, like other times before, I was glad we were in public.

I told them that when I was 6 or 7, I had done something naughty and my father had chased me out of the house and into the yard, picked up a pitchfork that had been left out for turning soil in the garden and an alarmed neighbor called my grandfather, who came flying out of his house, tackled my father and said, "What did you think you were going to do to her when you caught her? Eh?" And he sent me into his house where he gave me a glass of water, leaving my father in the yard, ashamed.

"Wow," Cathy said, "Your grandfather saved you."

Yes, I said, "He was my savior throughout my childhood, and my one positive male role model."

"Good," said Dr. Silver, "I'm glad there was one, because your father was not." Then he said, "Do you think you got any love from your father?"

I said, "Mmmmmmm.... before the age of ten, yes, but it was sporadic (I should have said it was conditional on my behavior.) After the age of ten, after the divorce, no."

I told them that when I was in London, my father wrote me a series of letters that did not sound like him: they were nostalgic, sentimental, a part of him that I had no context for. They said things like, "Please come back to America; this is the best place on earth; we didn't have shit in the old country."

Brody said, "Well, he must have been listening to someone, someone else, to write those letters."

I paused, and said, "The other part of the corporal punishment was, he learned it from his father (my Nonno). So when his brothers and sisters were living here, and Nonno was too old to beat the youngest son, Michael, he would call my father to come over and beat Michael for him. And my father would go."

Brody said, "Your father would go and beat his youngest brother because his father told him to?"

"Yes," I said. "My mother would beg him not to go. But every time Nonno called, my father went and beat him."

"Wow," Cathy said, "Your father had a lot of rage."

I said, "Yes. My father had an incredible amount of rage." I told them that the only times he had reached out was to Kris, asking to see a photograph of the three of us "before he dies."

Brody said, "That's bait!"

I said, "Yes."

He said, "Did you bite?"

I said, "No."

He said, "Good."

Then Vas asked if I thought my father had regrets and I said, "My father became a Born-Again Christian, and he believes that no matter what he does, God will forgive him. So I find it very hard to believe that he has any regrets. I would say no."

Vas said, "But he wouldn't have asked for a photograph if he didn't care." Then Vas compared my father to his grandfather, who was a "different person at 70 than he was in his 30's."

I said, "Yes, but my father in his 70's was still cruel. He did not mellow. My sister Jen called me when I was visiting London because my grandfather (my Nonno) had died and she was going to go to the funeral. I begged her not to do this. I told her that my father would find a way to ruin it, and she pooh-poohed this, saying she and her husband James were going to drive from Long Island to Boston for the funeral. I wished her godspeed. Well, she went. My father ignored her at the wake. She was told that everyone was meeting at the church the following morning, 9 am. So that is where she and James were, and she couldn't understand why they were the only ones in the church. Until a procession came in, accompanying the casket, and the procession comprised all of the family members — everyone, except Jen and James. Because my father had deliberately excluded her. She called me crying. I said, 'I told you it would be a nightmare.' She said, 'He stood in front of me during the service, and I just stared at the back of his neck, thinking about how much I hated him and wanted to stab him.' That was the last time Jen saw him. Kris was the last to cut off. She kept in touch and he would do things like, ask to come for dinner, and Kris, who is a wonderful cook, would spend all day cooking, set a nice table and then my father would not show up. About 10 pm, she called him and asked where the hell he was. He said, 'I decided to drive back to Vermont to beat the traffic.' And my sister cried, 'Then why didn't you call me and tell me?' So, no. My father did not mellow. He was a punisher."

Vas said, "Why?"

I said, "At first, it was to punish my mother, to get to her. Later, it was to punish us because we reminded him of her."

Dr. Silver said, "What is the worst part for you?"

I said, "The fact that he does not know me. He doesn't know that I have published a book. He doesn't know I'm a professor. He has no idea who I am — and he doesn't care."

Dr. Silver said, "How does it make you physically feel telling us all this?"

I said, "Tense. I feel really tense."

So Dr. Silver took me through a series of breathing exercises. He said, "Sometimes this works, sometimes it doesn't. You all (referring to the others in the group) can try these, too."

After that, Dr. Silver said, "How do you feel?"

I said, "Sad. There is just a prevailing feeling of sadness."

Dr. Silver said, "Where?"

I said, putting my hand to my chest, "Here. My chest."

Dr. Silver said, "If you can, describe the feeling."

I said, "A sadness. A great, big, empty void. Never filled."

Dr. Silver said, "It's a familiar feeling, isn't it?"

I said, "Yes. It never leaves me."

Dr. Silver said, "I can imagine."

Everyone was quiet for a time. Then I said, "'You know, every now and then, someone says, 'Don't you think it's strange that you and your sisters never had children?' And I say, 'No'. And they say, 'But statistically, the fact that the three of you didn't have children, don't you think that's strange?' And I say, 'Well, not if you grew up in the house that I did.'"

Dr. Silver said, "Right, that makes perfect sense."

Then Dr. Silver said, "So Lisa, I'm just going to ask you directly: Why didn't you have children?"

I said, "Because I didn't trust a man to be there; because I thought it would all be me."

Dr. Silver said, "Do you trust yourself around children?"

"No," I said.

"Why?" Dr. Silver said.

"Because I was afraid that the rage that is in my father was also in me," I said.

Dr Silver said, "Bingo."

It was then that I began to cry.

Dr. Silver said, "That is what makes you one of the best professors on the planet."

I laughed through my tears and sputtered, "What? Why? What makes you say that?"

Dr. Silver said, "Because you sublimate any urge to have children and become everybody's favorite parent."

I cried for the rest of the session.

Cathy said, "Lisa, you are such a force, you have such power, don't give it away."

I said, "Oh, I won't. I don't."

She said, "My father was also violent. I became a mother at 45. He wasn't planned."

I said, knowing her son was 9 or 10, "And how has it been? Has it been okay?"

She said, "Yes. It's been fine! I have occasionally raised my voice to him, especially since quarantine has dragged on, but that's about it."

I said, "Cathy, how old are you?"

Brody said, "Whoa, wait wait wait. .."

I said, "I will tell her my age, there is a point, shut up, Brody."

Cathy said, "I'm 53."

I said, "I'm 54."

Brody, Cathy and Vas all began talking at once: "I never would have put you at 54! I thought you were about 40! I thought at most you were 41…"

I said, "Right, it's the guinea skin, it's the olive oil."

Dr. Silver said, "I heard that growing up. It's the olive oil."

I said, "Cathy, the reason I asked is, it's too late for me."

And she didn't say anything, nodded.

Vas said, "I've listened to Lisa and I'm sorry; I'm sorry for what she had to go through."

Dr. Silver said, "Well, she didn't have a father. She didn't have a father." He paused. "Lisa is not the first person I have had who chose not to have children because they thought they would turn into their parent (s)."

The session ended. We all signed off.

It feels like my chest has been cracked open. I did have a large drink afterwards. And I feel very tired right now. But I guess you have to go through the bad and the sad and the revelatory to get to the other side.

Acknowledgments

I would like to thank:

The incredible generosity of Jim Veatch for the writer's retreat at the Commercial Street house by the sea. And the ghost.

Jimmie McGaugh, the "mayor" of Provincetown.

Neil Bradley and Robert Kenefick, readers extraordinaire with astute feedback.

Mark Lawitz, for his support and his beautiful mind.

Priscilla Hallberg, who reconnected so many people with Mrs. Hodges and made her memorial service such a joyous occasion.

Derek Stearns, a rock-solid sounding board who could also have a third career in hilarious voice texts.

Walt Cummins for his editorial brilliance, his infinite patience, his time, and his wisdom.

Steve Finch, for giving me an incredible gift: casting his astonishing mind and eagle eye on my manuscript, making it far, far better than it would have been otherwise.

Lise Olsen for her altruism with regard to her editing and her time.

Lisa del Rosso originally trained as a classical singer and completed a post-graduate program at LAMDA (London Academy of Music and Dramatic Art), living and performing in London before moving to New York City. Her plays "Clare's Room," and "Samaritan," have been performed off-Broadway and had public readings, while "St. John," her third play, was a semi-finalist for the 2011 Eugene O'Neill National Playwrights Conference. Her writing has appeared in *The New York Times*, *Barking Sycamores Neurodivergent Literature*, *Razor's Edge Literary Magazine*, *Sowing Creek Press*, *The Literary Traveler*, *Serving House Journal*, *VietnamWarPoetry*, *Young Minds Magazine* (London/UK), *Time Out New York*, *The Huffington Post*, *The Chillfiltr Review*, *The Neue Rundschau* (Germany), *Jetlag Café* (Germany), and *One Magazine* (London/UK), for whom she writes theater reviews. Her first book, a hybrid memoir, *Confessions of an Accidental Professor*, was published in 2018, and she had the pleasure of being interviewed about the book by Brian Lehrer on his WNYC radio program. She is the recipient of a 2018 NYU College of Arts & Sciences Teaching Award, where she currently teaches writing. In 2019, she was awarded a New York Writers Workshop scholarship to Sardinia.

Made in the USA
Middletown, DE
03 February 2021